GOD, VALUE, AND NATURE

God, Value, and Nature

FIONA ELLIS

OXFORD
UNIVERSITY PRESS

OXFORD
UNIVERSITY PRESS

Great Clarendon Street, Oxford, OX2 6DP,
United Kingdom

Oxford University Press is a department of the University of Oxford.
It furthers the University's objective of excellence in research, scholarship,
and education by publishing worldwide. Oxford is a registered trade mark of
Oxford University Press in the UK and in certain other countries

First Edition published in 2014
Impression: 2

Published in the United States of America by Oxford University Press
198 Madison Avenue, New York, NY 10016, United States of America

British Library Cataloguing in Publication Data
Data available

Library of Congress Control Number: 2014931570

ISBN 978-0-19-871412-5

Printed and bound by
CPI Group (UK) Ltd, Croydon, CR0 4YY

For Anna, Gemma, and Mike

Preface and Acknowledgements

The philosophical framework for this book began to take shape many years ago when I was fortunate enough to be taught by David Wiggins. David inspired the approach I take here, although I have an equal but later debt to the work of John McDowell. David never mentioned God, and it was my other great teacher and friend—Roger Scruton—who circled relentlessly around this issue. Two other figures were influential at this early stage: Paul Snowdon who encouraged me to move in the direction which was gradually opening up, and the late Brian O'Shaughnessy who bombarded me with everything under the philosophical and musical sun, especially Nietzsche, Schopenhauer, and Wagner.

Thus far no theologians or philosophers of religion, but the situation was remedied a few years later when I met Gerry Hughes. Gerry showed an interest in my work, he was doing interesting work of his own, and for these and other reasons became one of my dearest friends. He also told me about Heythrop College, encouraged me to apply for a post there, and convinced them that I was worth employing. Everything changed from that point on. I was surrounded by colleagues for whom the question of God was paramount, they were eager to engage in dialogue, and the theistic dimension of my work began to take shape. Special thanks go to Anna Abram, Michael Barnes, John Cottingham, Peter Gallagher, John McDade, and Gemma Simmonds, all of whom have become good friends. The final significant link came from Mike Inwood. I wrote to him out of the blue with a bizarre question about Heidegger's Being, and he was quick to latch on to what I was trying to do philosophically. He became a regular visitor to Heythrop, the closest reader and critic of my work, and the writer of an ongoing and utterly life-saving campus novel in the post-post-modern tradition.

Other thinkers and friends have helped to bring this book to completion. I thank Douglas Hedley for inviting me to be part of his natural theology reading group, and its members—John Cottingham, Chris Hamilton, Tim Mawson, Mark Wynn, and Bill Wood—for their feedback on chapter 5. I am grateful also to Robin Attfield, Sarah Coakley, Craig French, Anthony O'Hear, and the anonymous referees chosen by OUP, particularly the final reader who provided such incisive comments on the entire draft. My students—who are too numerous to mention individually—have been equally important, as have those of my friends who are not academics. Special thanks go to May Allan, Rhona Cameron, Lesley Chamberlain, Gohar and Jules Goddard, Sue Hall, Eva Jacobs, Judith Lancaster, Harold McMullen, Alison Nolan, Brian Pearce, John C. Ross, Yassi Safinia, Tania Tuft, Zita Zigan, and the Kenwood Ladies' Pond in whose idyllic waters some of these friends can be found. Finally, I must mention my parents, Marjorie and Martin Ellis, my sister, Cathy, and my niece, Angelie. They, along with my wonderful friends, have provided the love, support, and humour which made it possible to bring this project to fruition.

In various places I have drawn from material from the following previously published articles, and my thanks are due to the respective editors and publishers for being able to make use of it here: 'God, Value, and Naturalism', *Ratio*, 2011, vol. 24, issue 2, pp. 138–153; 'God and Other Minds', *Religious Studies*, 2010, vol. 46, issue 3, pp. 331–351.

Contents

Introduction

1 CONTEXT AND AIMS

Many philosophers in the Anglo-American tradition believe that God has been put to rest. Naturalism is the default position, and the naturalist can explain what needs to be explained without this unnecessary and problematic detour. This attitude towards God is part and parcel of contemporary, non-philosophical consciousness, although it has become apparent that some of the proponents of this atheistic movement are working with conceptions which bear little resemblance to the God with whom theologians—and indeed, ordinary believers—have wrestled throughout the ages. We are encouraged to suppose that God is on a level with the various 'supernatural' agents to which the primitive and uneducated remain in thrall, and that such people lack the benefit of a good scientific education. Hence the well-known author of *The God Delusion*:

> I am not attacking any particular version of God or gods. I am attacking God, all gods, anything and everything supernatural, wherever and whenever they have been or will be invented.[1]
>
> God's existence or non-existence is a scientific fact about the universe...the presence or absence of a creative super-intelligence is unequivocally a scientific question.[2]

For Dawkins, the scientific fact about the universe is that God is absent from its domain, and he concludes on this basis that atheism must be embraced. His attitude would be applauded by those naturalists who insist that the limits of nature are to be circumscribed by science, and they express a similar antipathy towards 'anything and everything supernatural'. Nevertheless, they seem in danger of including under this 'supernatural' rubric at least some of the things which, one would hope, demand a rightful place in the ontology of any remotely human being. Like, for example, value. One response to this worry

---

[1] *The God Delusion* (London: Bantam Press, 2006), p. 36.
[2] *The God Delusion*, pp. 50–58.

has been to expand the limits of science to accommodate modes of enquiry which seem better placed to accommodate the relevant phenomena—the so-called human sciences have been significant in this respect. Other philosophers (of whom David Wiggins and John McDowell are the leading representatives) see in this move a residual commitment to scientism, and have defended a conception of nature and naturalism which exceeds such parameters whilst giving due respect to the findings of modern science. They agree, however, that nature thus conceived must be shorn of any reference to gods or God, and we are encouraged to suppose that a move in either of these directions exceeds the limits of intellectual propriety.

Expansive naturalism[3]—as I shall refer to it—offers a defensible form of naturalism and I shall argue that it should be embraced. So I agree with philosophical orthodoxy that we should be naturalists, but I deny that we should be scientific naturalists, and believe that the typical expansive naturalist can go further. I shall spell out the details of his proposal as it applies to the case of value, and make clear the precise force of the term 'naturalism' in this context, as well as the advantages of retaining it. In short, the position—in its original inception—is motivated by sound philosophical presuppositions. It involves acknowledging that we are natural beings in a natural world, and gives expression to the demand that we avoid metaphysical flights of fancy and ensure that our claims remain empirically grounded. These undoubted virtues have been appropriated and monopolized by the scientific naturalist, and this has led to the unsupported and disastrous conclusion that science provides the only means of satisfying the relevant constraints. The expansive naturalist seeks to recuperate these virtues, and he is anxious to avoid 'anything and everything supernatural'. Crucially, however, this avoidance no longer implies that we have sold ourselves and the world short, for 'nature' is not limited to whatever is the object of scientific inquiry, and we have the philosophical resources for lending justice to this expansion.

The expansive naturalist grants at least some of the items which are deemed 'supernatural' by scientific naturalist lights, but he stops short of God. His reluctance to concede in this direction is understandable at one level—after all, God is not a part of the natural world in one clear enough sense. Nevertheless, I shall argue that his position can be expanded to give us a form of theistic naturalism which can accommodate the distinction—and indeed, the relation—between God and nature. This conclusion will be contentious by most lights—including those of the typical expansive naturalist. However, I shall argue that the resources for making this move are internal to the position itself, and that it can be defended provided that we resist the lure of scientific naturalism.

What follows from this conclusion? First, it moves us away from the temptation to suppose that scientific naturalism is the default position, and that

---

[3] I borrow the term from James Griffin's *Value Judgement* (Oxford: Clarendon Press, 1996), p. 51.

we are forced to choose between either science or God. Atheists like Dawkins assume these terms of engagement, but they are neither philosophically nor scientifically supported, although their acceptance by such 'authorities' has helped to sustain the view that believers in God are intellectually challenged. Second, it means that we must reconfigure our understanding of the traditional naturalism versus theism debate. In philosophy of religion today, it is standard to define 'naturalism' in a way that excludes the existence of God or gods,[4] the implication being that naturalism and theism are logically incompatible. According to my position, by contrast, naturalism and theism can both be true.

Why take 'naturalism' in this broad sense? Why not simply accept a scientific interpretation of the position and grant that the question of God exceeds such parameters? Part of the answer goes back to what I have said already. The scientific naturalist does not have the monopoly on the meaning of this term, and recent philosophy testifies to its pliability. So its meaning is hardly fixed, and those who have embraced the term to their own particular ends have done so with an eye to the advantages it procures. In particular, it gives their philosophical endeavours the seal of empirical respectability. This meaning has not been stretched in a theistic direction—at least not by contemporary naturalists—and reservations on this score are therefore understandable.[5] However, this does not rule out such a move, and if I am right then there are naturalistic arguments to this end—on a suitably expanded conception thereof. The virtues of this move should be apparent. For we are in a position to challenge the conclusion—common to most naturalists—that talk of God belongs to the realm of idle metaphysics, that it comprises an esoteric discipline which is irrelevant to what really matters philosophically, and that it has no bearing upon the question of nature and of our natural human being.

A further notable advantage of my approach is that it offers the prospects for defending a theistic framework using philosophical resources which can

---

[4] See, for example, Alvin Plantinga, *Where the Conflict Really Lies: Science, Religion, and Naturalism* (Oxford: Oxford University Press, 2011).

[5] Robert S. Corrington is a contemporary exception, although he comes from a very different perspective from that of the naturalists with which I am concerned. See his *Nature and Spirit: An Essay in Ecstatic Naturalism* (New York: Fordham University Press, 1992). The ecstatic naturalist, we are told, 'has a special kind of openness to what can never be circumscribed. In addition, an ecstatic naturalist recognizes that almost all philosophical theology has taken the wrong tack towards the nature/divine correlation', 'An Introduction to Ecstatic Naturalism: Interview with Robert S. Corrington', *Kinesis*, vol. 36, no. 1 (2009), p. 28. I would be happy to describe myself as an ecstatic naturalist according to the first criterion, but it is no part of my position that almost all philosophical theology has taken the wrong tack in this context. However, we can note a similar theme and approach in John Robinson's *Honest to God*, to which I shall refer in chapter 4. Like Corrington, Robinson takes inspiration from Paul Tillich, applauding his claim that 'the Divine does not inhabit a transcendent world *above nature*; it is found in the "ecstatic" character of *this* world, as its transcendent Depth and Ground', *Honest to God* (London: SCM Press, 1963), p. 34.

genuinely appeal to an atheist—at least, one who has moved beyond the limits of scientific naturalism. This point has been of particular significance to me. I have long been persuaded that there is nothing remotely pernicious or embarrassing about metaphysical enquiry per se, and that reference to Plato's heaven or the Kingdom of God does not spell inevitable philosophical disaster. At the same time, however, I am aware of how strange these claims can sound to contemporary philosophical ears—Chapter 1 gives some illustrations. What better way to vindicate such notions than by reference to a metaphysical framework which demands no more than a resistance to scientism, a spirit of open-mindedness, and a preparedness to go where one's arguments lead? I also find it ironic and amusing that the best philosophical defence of the position towards which I have been gradually moving should come from a camp which, at one level at least, will have nothing to do with God. Of course, this refusal concedes nothing to the vitriolic tendencies of the militant atheist—understandably so given that the philosophers in question have no particular axe to grind, and have seen through the fundamentalist faith which tends to drive such attacks. Rather, and in true phenomenological spirit, they seek to return us to the things themselves, guarding against the imposition of frameworks which preclude the possibility of meeting such an aim. It is in the context of appreciating this methodological stance that we can begin to appreciate the theistic significance of their claims. Or so I shall argue.

2 OVERVIEW

Chapter 1 offers an analysis of the familiar contrast between the 'natural' and the 'supernatural' domains, showing how certain standard philosophical moves concerning this contrast end up consigning the supernatural to the 'philosophical dustbin'. The accompanying tendency to interpret 'natural' in exclusively scientific terms is challenged by those for whom scientism is a philosophical prejudice, and they reject the claim that 'nature' is limited to whatever is the object of scientific inquiry—that it is has become 'the all-inclusive category' in this respect. After all, there is more to nature than what the scientist comprehends, and more to inquiry than science. The further claim is that this move is a requirement upon a satisfactory conception of value. The limits of science are unclear, and Chapter 2 considers a scientific naturalist rejoinder: we can rectify the supposed deficiencies of scientific naturalism by broadening its parameters to accommodate the human sciences. Peter Railton offers the best defence of such a position but there is a question—pressed by Wiggins—of whether its scientific aspirations can be upheld.

The next three chapters examine the idea of a non-scientific expansive naturalism, drawing upon the work of Akeel Bilgrami, Wiggins, and especially

McDowell. Bilgrami and Wiggins are familiar from Chapter 2, and the position has something in common with Railton's preferred alternative. However, it concedes nothing to his avowedly scientific standpoint except in so far as 'science' has become a placeholder for any position that gives due weight to the findings of modern science whilst avoiding unnecessary cosmic excess. The scientific naturalist's notion of a cosmic excess has been challenged, and the question of the limits of nature are now in dispute. The remaining chapters gradually explore the prospects for taking this idea of expanded nature and developing it in a direction that will accommodate theism. Chapter 4 provides the crucial link, and involves a discussion of McDowell's idea of an evaluatively enchanted nature. Nature thus conceived has no room for the gods of pre-scientific superstition, and McDowell distinguishes his own brand of enchantment from that which was operative when the magic-making gods were on the scene. His criticisms are well taken, but they do not rule out the idea of a divinely enchanted nature provided that we take care to distinguish God from the gods. I introduce the theologian's conception of the relation between God and nature, and it is shown to bear structural analogies to McDowell's conception of the relation between value and nature. In particular, we are given a picture which makes our relation to God sound rather like the expansive naturalist's conception of our relation to value. The difference with God, however, is that He remains radically distinct from anything within the world even whilst retaining the most intimate connection with it. The nature of this relation is further analysed in Chapter 5, and a challenge is posed to those who wish to expand the concept of nature in a moral direction: is there any good philosophical reason for resisting a further expansion of the concept so as to accommodate God?

Chapter 6 takes up this challenge by way of a discussion of Levinas's claim that relating to value is both necessary and sufficient for relating to God. This position brings God and value into much closer proximity, and Levinas's conception of our relation to value maps onto the expansive naturalist's conception thereof. We might worry that God has been squeezed out of the picture, but it is equally compelling to suppose that the expansive naturalist's framework is already theistic. Christianity offers the prospects for defending a more robust form of theism, and Chapter 7 spells out the details of the position. Levinas's moral objections are challenged, and some of the boundaries between the two positions begin to deconstruct. The dialectic is familiar from our discussion of the relation between the expansive naturalist and Levinas, and indeed, Railton and the expansive naturalist.

The final chapter spells out the implications of my conclusions for an understanding of the relation between science, philosophy, and theology. I consider the relevance of the notion of myth to theology, taking up some of the themes left hanging from Chapter 4, and return finally to the question of naturalism. The claims with which we began—that philosophers should be naturalists, and that 'nature' is the all-inclusive category—are vindicated, but naturalism

is shorn of its scientistic implications, and shown to be compatible with a theistic interpretation thereof. I describe my route to this conclusion as a form of
natural theology. Natural theology, thus understood, involves approaching the
question of God in philosophical terms, these terms are anti-scientistic, and
they are exploited by the expansive naturalist in the context of defending his
own position against that of the scientific naturalist. It can equally be described
as a brand of natural philosophy, and my hope is that it might persuade the
expansive naturalist that it can be intellectually respectable to believe in God
and that he himself has paved the way to this conclusion.

3 AUDIENCE

My arguments are directed primarily towards two types of people: (A) those
like the typical expansive naturalist who are sensitive to morality, but not to
God; (B) those who are sensitive to God as well as to morality. Type B people
may or may not welcome the move to theistic naturalism. If they do, it's likely
to be because they are already sensitive to God, but they may worry that theistic
naturalism compromises His reality in some way. I hope to show that this worry
is unfounded, and that, in line with the underlying philosophical approach,
there is no concession to reductionism or anti-realism. So I am not a pantheist,
and it will become clear that I agree with Karl Rahner that such a position is just
a further expression of the 'dualism' which places God and nature in permanent
and mutually exclusive opposition. (We have a clue here to the question of how
not to conceive of the distinction between God and nature.)

Type A people pose the real difficulty for me. These people are sensitive to
morality, but they have no antecedent sensitivity to God. I have placed the
typical expansive naturalist into this category, but the scientific naturalist is
also sensitive to morality, and Railton offers a version of the position which
promises to be explanatorily adequate. We might agree with Wiggins, however, that we are left with a form of expansive naturalism in all but name. The
typical expansive naturalist (who may or may not include an atypical scientific
naturalist) is reluctant to concede in a theistic direction, and I seek to motivate
him in this direction by showing that the arguments he uses to take us beyond
scientific naturalism have theistic import, and that his objections to this move
are analogous to the scientific naturalist's objections to expansive naturalism—
objections which he calls into question.

I begin with a fairly minimalist conception of God, culminating in the
rather less minimalist God of Christianity. This will ring further alarm bells for
the typical expansive naturalist, and the move is contested likewise by Levinas.
Levinas's objections to Christianity are misplaced, and its spirit lurks in his
position and that of our expansive naturalist. So the move to Christianity is less

outrageous than it might first appear. However, it is certainly not mandatory, and it remains open that there are other available moves for those who seek to defend a theistic framework. I choose this particular example for two reasons: first, it is the framework with which I am most familiar; second, Levinas's objections to it stand in a significant relation to those which the expansive naturalist would level against any form of theism—Levinas's included—and can be criticized along analogous lines.

4 IMPLICATIONS

It is no part of my argument that the expansive naturalist has to concede in a theistic direction—any more than he is suggesting that the scientific naturalist is compelled to embrace his own preferred alternative. The point is simply that the position does not pose the envisaged threat, and that the contrary supposition involves a conception of God (and nature) which can be challenged on expansive naturalist, and indeed, theological, grounds. So the expansive naturalist is free to take or leave this expanded conception of his position, but my hope is that the arguments I offer in this direction will show that the move is worthy of serious consideration. Of course, there is further philosophical work to be done, and no amount of such work could yield a knock-down argument in favour of the view I am seeking to defend—understandably so given that there are few such arguments in philosophy and that the nature of this particular case must surely preclude such a possibility.

I have always been struck by a comment that was once made by a former colleague of mine. 'The problem with theology', he said, 'is that it has no subject-matter.' A damning criticism indeed, and it calls to mind Nietzsche's (unwittingly self-damning) claim that those who have theologians' blood in their veins see all things in a distorted and dishonest perspective.[6] I have no such problem with theology and theologians, and am reminded of yet another comment from a philosophy colleague, on hearing that I was to be working amongst theologians: 'That's good, theologians are more open-minded than philosophers.' They are certainly more open-minded than some philosophers, but the philosophers with whom I engage in this book have seen through the distortions to which we are so understandably drawn, and have paved the way towards honest and fruitful dialogue. It is my aim to make a contribution to this task, to offer a voice to the theologian, and to show that his subject-matter may be of rather more relevance to philosophy—and to nature—than we have been led to believe.

---

[6] *The Antichrist*, in *The Portable Nietzsche*, trans. Walter Kaufmann (New York: Viking Penguin Inc, 1959), p. 575.

1

Naturalism and Supernaturalism

1.1 INTRODUCING NATURALISM

Should philosophers be naturalists? The answer has tended to be a resounding 'yes' amongst those working within the Anglo-American philosophical tradition. Indeed, some would go so far as to challenge the very posing of the question, doing so on the ground that its terms are, or at least ought to be, synonymous. So, for example, J.G. Brennan, writing in 1954, suggests that the textbook phrase 'contemporary American naturalistic philosophy' is a pleonasm, and that the term 'naturalism' is otiose.[1] His near contemporary John Herman Randall Jr claims that 'naturalistic method is the starting-point of genuine philosophizing',[2] and that 'naturalism' can be defined negatively 'as the refusal to take 'nature' or 'the natural' as a term of distinction.[3] 'Nature', he continues, has become 'the all-inclusive category', and 'naturalism, in becoming all-inclusive, ceases to be a distinctive "ism".'[4]

The idea that naturalism has become all-inclusive—that it is no longer a distinctive 'ism'—suggests that it has taken over or eliminated its possible rivals. It might be thought also to hint in the direction of the kind of grand a priori theorizing which contemporary analytic philosophers prefer to leave to their speculative forbears.[5] Randall's gloss on the all-inclusiveness of naturalism is that 'natural' is to be regarded as 'whatever man encounters in whatever way...Nature...is a collective name for "quite a mess of miscellaneous stuff".'[6] The terms are vague enough to be innocuous, for one could hardly deny that

---

[1] 'On Nagel's Reconsideration of Naturalism', *Journal of Philosophy*, vol. 53, no. 14 (1956), p. 444.

[2] 'Epilogue: The Nature of Naturalism', in *Naturalism and the Human Spirit*, ed. Yervant H. Krikorian (New York: Columbia University Press, 1944), p. 376.

[3] 'Epilogue: The Nature of Naturalism', p. 357.

[4] 'Epilogue: The Nature of Naturalism', pp. 357–358.

[5] See, for example, Robert Rein'l, 'Naturalism and Supernaturalism in East and West', *Philosophy East and West*, vol. 6, no. 1 (April 1956), p. 50.

[6] 'Epilogue: The Nature of Naturalism', p. 358. The quotation comes from Harry Todd Costello's contribution to the same volume—'The Naturalism of Frederick Woodbridge'.

philosophers are and ought to be concerned with nature in this all-inclusive sense, although one may wonder what constraint, if any, is being imposed with the claim that whatever man encounters in whatever way is natural. We may agree also that '(n)aturalism thus merges in the generic activity of philosophy as critical interpretation—the examination of the status of all these varieties of "stuff" in Nature—or in Being, or in Reality—and the discovery of their various relations to each other and their respective functions in man's experience.'[7] But the questions remain: What is critical interpretation? What kind of examination is at issue here? And are we to conclude that naturalism can 'absorb all the philosophic theories of what man encounters and in that sense cease to be a distinct position?'[8]

Randall resists this conclusion, and it is at this point in his argument that 'naturalism' assumes a more contentious and arguably less inclusive definition. First, we are told that 'naturalism can be defined as the continuity of analysis—as the application of what all the contributors call "scientific methods" to the critical interpretation and analysis of every field', and second, that naturalism is:

> (f)undamentally opposed to all those theories and interpretations which assert dualisms and gulfs and, as Mr Dewey's polemic makes clear, remains their active antagonist so long as they are flourishing...there is no room for any Supernatural in naturalism—no supernatural or transcendental God and no personal survival after death...Thus naturalism finds itself in thoroughgoing opposition to all forms of thought which assert the existence of a supernatural or transcendental Realm of Being and make knowledge of that realm of fundamental importance to human living. There is no 'realm' to which the methods for dealing with Nature cannot be extended. This insistence on the universal and unrestricted application of 'scientific method' is a theme pervading every one of these essays.[9]

He sums up the naturalist's creed as 'reliance on an unrestricted scientific method and the consequent rejection of any form of supernaturalism', claims that these were the distinguishing features of nineteenth-century naturalism, and agrees with William R. Dennes—a fellow contributor to the volume in which he is writing—that these positions are:

> (p)rotests against all philosophies which allege that events require, for their occurrence or for their explanation, reference to transcendental grounds, orders, causes, purposes, *Dinge an Sich*, or the like.[10]

---

[7] 'Epilogue: The Nature of Naturalism', p. 358. Compare Ernest Nagel, who claims that naturalism is 'a sound generalized account of the world encountered in practice and in critical reflection, and a just perspective upon the human scene', 'Naturalism Reconsidered', *Proceedings and Addresses of the American Philosophical Association*, vol. 28 (October 1955).

[8] 'Epilogue: The Nature of Naturalism', p. 358.

[9] 'Epilogue: The Nature of Naturalism', p. 358. Compare Brennan who summarizes the negative creed of the naturalist as follows: 'no spirit-gods, no disembodied forces, no immortal souls' ('On Nagel's Reconsideration of Naturalism', p. 443).

[10] 'Epilogue: The Nature of Naturalism', p. 359.

1.2 NATURALISM AND SCIENCE

We have the beginnings of a negative and positive characterization of naturalism. At the negative level, we are told that the naturalist rejects any form of super-naturalism. Supernaturalism involves the postulation of a 'supernatural realm of being' and the claim that knowledge of this realm is of fundamental importance to human living. The kind of importance at issue here is unclear, but it would appear that such a realm is intended to serve a fundamental explanatory role with respect to the nature and existence of things. So it is important from a theoretical point of view, but given the emphasis upon human living, we are to suppose that it also has practical significance. As John Dewey puts it, it is common for the super-naturalist to charge his opponent with the destruction of all 'distinctively human values',[11] the implication being that these values have their origin in a supernatu-ral realm of being, and cannot survive in its absence.

Such a realm finds its prototype in the idea of God; more generally, in any reference to transcendental grounds, orders, causes, or purposes; and more generally still, in the claim that 'there is something besides nature'.[12] All such positions are said to introduce 'dualisms and gulfs' into our ontology, doing so, we are to presume, by postulating a supernatural realm of being in addition to nature. We are left in no doubt that this move is unwarranted, and that we can explain what needs to be explained using purely naturalistic resources. As Randall puts it, 'there is no "realm" to which the methods of dealing with nature cannot be extended'.

Reference to the methods of dealing with nature points towards a more positive characterization of naturalism, for the suggestion now is that the relevant methods are scientific, and that there is nothing which escapes their ambit. So the limits of nature are to be circumscribed by the limits of scientific investigation. This might be thought to sit rather awkwardly with Randall's previous claim that naturalistic philosophy engages with and examines the mess of miscellaneous stuff man encounters 'in whatever way', implying as it does that at least some of these ways are to be elimi-nated in favour of scientific investigation. However, it cannot be ruled out that non-scientific modes of relating to things are philosophically prob-lematic, that science provides the most adequate means of comprehend-ing what there really is, and that, as Randall puts it, there is no 'realm' to which it cannot be extended. Equally, of course, it remains open that an exclusive reliance upon scientific method is itself philosophically problem-atic. Dewey objects that such a conclusion stems from a tendency amongst 'anti-naturalists' to place an unduly 'low estimate' upon science, the upshot

---

[11] 'Antinaturalism in Extremis', in *Naturalism and the Human Spirit*, p. 2.
[12] See Robert Rein'l, 'Naturalism and Supernaturalism in East and West', p. 52.

being that its influence is restricted and deflected.[13] He takes this to be an instance of a common procedure in philosophical controversy: namely, 'representation of the position of an opponent in the terms it would have *if* the critic held it; that is not in its own terms'.[14] The point is well taken, but it raises the question of what an 'unrestricted scientific method' really amounts to, and, assuming that this approach hasn't been shorn of determinate content, whether it can really do justice to the variety of phenomena we seek to comprehend.

Randall insists that it provides the only alternative to supernaturalism, and we are led to suppose that supernaturalism is philosophically disastrous. However, the only reason we have been given for this conclusion is that it courts phenomena which cannot be comprehended in naturalistic terms. This justification may be persuasive on a suitably broad understanding of these terms, but once they are interpreted along the recommended scientific lines, we are left with the claim that supernaturalism is to be rejected because it allows that there is more to reality than what the scientist can comprehend. The implication here is that 'supernatural' means 'non-scientific', and that the postulation of a supernatural realm of being is the postulation of a realm which escapes the ambit of scientific investigation. The rejection of such a realm provides one way of granting naturalism the status of an all-inclusive doctrine, and it cannot be ruled out that an expanded conception of the limits of scientific investigation will make the position more palatable to those who oppose scientism. On the face of it, however, its terms are flagrantly question-begging, the supernaturalist is free to reject them, and he is free also to reject the claim that *his* position is philosophically problematic. It is philosophically problematic, according to this way of thinking, because it grants that there is more to philosophy than science. One begins to wonder whether a version of the common procedure to which Dewey refers is operative in this context, too, and that the 'low estimate' which is being placed on supernaturalism here stems from the imposition of terms which the opponent would instantly challenge.[15]

---

[13] 'Antinaturalism in Extremis', p. 10.

[14] 'Antinaturalism in Extremis', p. 12.

[15] Compare Herbert Spiegelberg, who makes a plea for 'breaking the stalemate between the two battle-locked camps...What is needed in this respect is an unbiased effort and readiness to face and accept without fear or favour the phenomena with all their shades and depths, with their striking and their receding aspects, with their continuities and their discontinuities, with their meaningful and their perplexing characters...neither naturalism nor supernaturalism...have been completely free from certain biases for or against "nature", which stands in the way of an understanding of the problem as well as of mutual understanding' ('*Supernaturalism or Naturalism: A Study in Meaning and Verifiability*', *Philosophy of Science*, vol. 18, no. 4 (October 1951), p. 340.

God, Value, and Nature

1.3 CONTEMPORARY NATURALISM

Brennan, Dewey, and Randall belong to a previous generation of philosophers, but similar sentiments pervade our times. Thus, in a lecture entitled 'Whatever Happened to Naturalism?', Richard Bernstein cites a statement prepared for a workshop on naturalism by Joseph Margolis and Mark Gottlieb in which it is claimed that '(n)aturalism, in the current analytic sense, may well be the dominant programmatic orientation of Anglo-American philosophy', and that it is a 'relatively explicit philosophical movement featuring what many believe to be the strongest and most promising achievements of twentieth-century Anglo-American philosophy'.[16] Elsewhere, we are told that:

> (a)n overwhelming majority of contemporary Anglo-American philosophers claim to be 'naturalists' or to be offering a 'naturalistic' theory of a key philosophical concept (say, knowledge) or domain (for example, ethical discourse). Naturalism has become a slogan in the name of which the vast majority of work in analytic philosophy is pursued.[17]

The implication in all of this is that most philosophers belonging to the analytic tradition are naturalists, that this is what they ought to be, and that if they are not, then they are not philosophers properly so called. But what is this thing that we ought to be? Are we saying anything more than that we should be good philosophers? And what are we to make of Bernstein's claim that these moralizing exhortations will raise the hackles of those who believe that naturalism—or as he puts it, the 'new' naturalism—is nothing short of a philosophical disaster?[18]

As in our previous discussion, we can begin to impose some content upon the naturalist's position by considering the object of his attack. This object is likewise supernaturalism, and the territory is familiar. Witness the following:

> For the few who do take the trouble to explain naturalism, perhaps the most familiar definition is in terms of the rejection of supernatural entities such as gods, demons, souls, and ghosts.[19]
>
> Naturalism on any reading is opposed to supernaturalism...By 'supernaturalism' I mean the invocation of an agent or force that somehow stands outside the familiar natural world and whose doings cannot be understood as part of it. Most metaphysical systems of the past included some such agent. A naturalistic conception of the world would be opposed to all of them...Most philosophers for at least one hundred years have been naturalists in the nonsupernaturalist sense.[20]

---

[16] 'Whatever Happened to Naturalism?', *Proceedings and Addresses of the American Philosophical Association*, vol. 69, no. 2 (November 1995), p. 58.

[17] 'Introduction: The Nature of Naturalism', in *Naturalism in Question*, ed. Mario De Caro and David Macarthur (Cambridge, Mass.: Harvard University Press, 2004), p. 2.

[18] 'Whatever Happened to Naturalism?' p. 58.

[19] 'Introduction: The Nature of Naturalism', p. 2.

[20] Barry Stroud, 'The Charm of Naturalism', in *Naturalism in Question*, p. 23.

[N]o entity or explanation should be accepted whose existence or truth could contradict the laws of nature, in so far as we know them...everybody would agree that this claim implies the denial of intelligent designers, prime movers unmoved, and entelechies. (This though, need not be construed as denial *in principle*, since we can imagine circumstances in which we could get evidence for the existence of some of these entities.)....

[A] philosophical view can be supernaturalist even if it does *not* assume the existence of a personal divinity that preternaturally interferes with the natural course of events. Indeed, what really matters for judging the Supernaturalism of a philosophical view is whether the view is committed to the existence of *any* entity or force that is in principle unaccountable by science, ineliminable from our ontology, and contradictory to scientific knowledge...Unsurprisingly, however, these views appeal to special cognitive powers—which typically include some extreme forms of mystical illumination—in order to account for the human capacity to grasp these noncausal and supernatural entities or forces. For the purpose of our discussion, it is crucial to notice that these cognitive powers are absolutely irreconcilable with anything we could intuitively regard as natural forms of understanding. This is enough to rank the views that appeal to such kinds of entities within Supernaturalism.[21]

Dupré

My own version of the ontological aspect of naturalism might better be described as 'anti-supernaturalism'. That is to say, we should try to understand the world, insofar as we can at all, without appealing to anything that is entirely beyond the reach of empirical knowledge. Excluded by anti-supernaturalism are such things as immaterial minds or souls, vital forces, and divine beings. Should such things prove to be amenable to standard methods of empirical investigation they would, I take it, to that extent cease to be properly supernatural. An obvious topical example of an excluded explanation would be a special creationist account of the universe or the origin of human beings.[22]

We are returned to the claim that the naturalist opposes the postulation of a supernatural realm of being beyond nature. John Dupré calls the position 'anti-supernaturalism', takes this negative constraint to define its ontological aspect, and defends it on epistemological grounds. As he puts it, we should try to understand the world without appealing to anything that is entirely beyond the reach of empirical knowledge. Mario De Caro and Albert Voltolini are motivated likewise by such considerations, claiming that the relevant epistemological difficulties arise not merely for theistic versions of supernaturalism, but, more generally, whenever entities are postulated which require for their discernment 'special' cognitive powers and/or 'extreme' forms of mystical illumination. These cognitive powers are said to be 'irreconcilable' with

[21] Mario De Caro and Alberto Voltolini, 'Is Liberal Naturalism Possible?', in *Naturalism and Normativity*, ed. Mario De Caro and David Macarthur (New York: Columbia University Press, 2010), pp. 71–75.
[22] John Dupré, 'How to be Naturalistic Without Being Simplistic in the Study of Human Nature', in *Naturalism and Normativity*, p. 290.

anything we could 'intuitively regard as natural forms of understanding', and it is implied that no self-respecting philosopher would countenance their possibility. It is unclear what we are to make of the rather odd concession that there are imaginable circumstances in which we could get evidence for the existence of the relevant supernatural entities, but we are to assume perhaps that the point is similar to Dupré's claim that such things may prove amenable to 'standard methods of empirical investigation', in which case they would cease to be 'properly supernatural'.

This suggests that the category of the natural is rather broader than we might have supposed, and one begins to wonder whether there is anything to prevent the realm of the 'properly supernatural' reducing to vanishing point. Our naturalists would no doubt resist this move on the ground that the relevant entities must be amenable to the appropriate methods of investigation, but this response depends for its cogency upon a clearly defined and satisfactory characterization of such methods. The idea that we are concerned with '*natural forms of understanding*' is hopeless as it stands, for it is the question of the limits of such forms which is precisely at issue. Ditto for the suggestion that the relevant methods of investigation must be 'standard' rather than 'special' or 'extreme'.[23]

A more determinate characterization of these methods emerges with the familiar demand that they be scientific. As De Caro and Voltolini put it, the supernaturalist commits to the existence of things which are 'in principle unaccountable by science' and 'contradictory to scientific knowledge'. So the idea is that the cognitive powers to which the supernaturalist appeals are 'special' by virtue of being non-scientific, and that they are 'irreconcilable with anything we could intuitively regard as natural forms of understanding' in the sense that they are irreducible to scientific modes thereof. As noted previously, a proper assessment of such claims awaits an analysis of the limits of science. At this preliminary stage, however, we can make a note of their seemingly scientistic tone, and wonder whether the naturalist's complaint that supernatural entities are 'contradictory to scientific knowledge' expresses a similar reductive bias. If it does, then the supernaturalist's insistence that such entities are ineliminable from our ontology may well demand a second hearing.

The naturalist could respond that the point is not simply that supernatural entities cannot be comprehended scientifically, but that they stand in conflict with the findings of science, doing so, for example, by violating the laws of nature, as De Caro and Voltolini put it. They temper the force of this complaint with the caveat that we are concerned with such laws *as we understand*

---

[23] It is tempting here to respond to Dewey's claim that 'the word "mere" plays a large role in antinaturalistic writings' ('Antinaturalism in Extremis', p. 2, footnote 1)—as in 'the merely natural'—by pointing out that the word 'special'—as in 'special cognitive powers', 'special supernatural entities'—assumes a similar role in naturalistic writings.

them. However, it remains to be seen what it might mean to violate such laws, whether supernatural entities stand accused on this score, and whether it matters if they do.

1.4 DAZZLEMENT BY SCIENCE?

We have a sense of the kind of position against which contemporary naturalism is defined, and some evidence to suggest that its positive characterization involves a bias towards science. This positive strand is made explicit in the Introduction to *Naturalism in Question*, where we are given the following summary of two important and characteristic themes of the position:

1. An *ontological* theme: a commitment to an exclusively scientific conception of nature;
2. A *methodological* theme: a reconception of the traditional relation between philosophy and science according to which philosophical inquiry is conceived as continuous with science.[24]

De Caro and Macarthur refer to this position as scientific naturalism, and illustrate the ontological theme with reference to Wilfrid Sellars's claim that 'science is the measure of all things, of what is that it is, and of what is not that it is not'.[25] The most common justification for this view, they suggest, is some version of the 'Great Success of Modern Science Argument'.[26] According to this argument, we are to conclude from the great successes of modern science in explaining and predicting natural phenomena that the natural scientist's conception of nature is very likely to be true, and, furthermore, that this is our *only* unproblematic conception thereof.

The idea that the natural scientist's conception of nature is very likely to be true can be made to sound contentious if taken to exclude the possibility that his predictions and explanations could misfire. We are to assume, however, that the findings in question have been put to the test, so that the point is simply that, in the absence of countervailing evidence, they are to be accommodated within an account of the workings of nature. To put the point even more generally, we are to respect the achievements of modern natural science. It would be difficult to resist such a recommendation, but as noted already, the further suggestion that the scientist's conception of nature is the *only* unproblematic one is rather more contentious. It is in this context that we find

---

[24] 'Introduction: The Nature of Naturalism', p. 3.
[25] 'Empiricism and the Philosophy of Mind', in *Science Perception and Reality* (London: Routledge, 1963), p. 173.
[26] 'Introduction: The Nature of Naturalism', p. 4.

McDowell complaining that 'scientism is a superstition, not a stance required by a proper respect for the achievements of the natural sciences'. He insists that we 'discourag[e] this dazzlement by science' which leads us to suppose that 'genuine truth is restricted to what can be validated by their methods'.[27]

We have noted already that there is a question about how we are to view the scope of these methods, and that, depending upon how broadly their limits are conceived, the claim that we are to commit to an exclusive scientific conception of nature will appear more or less credible. So, for example, if the notion of scientific method is stretched to accommodate forms of philosophical enquiry which are countenanced by those who refuse to be 'dazzled' by science, then we shall no longer feel the need to discourage this naturalistic stance. We may wonder, however, what exactly it is intended to exclude.

De Caro and Macarthur claim that scientific naturalists have tended to adopt a restrictive conception of what constitutes legitimate natural science— one which includes physics at a minimum, or physics, chemistry, and biology.[28] They point out that there is disagreement amongst scientific naturalists concerning the precise nature of this restriction, but that, in its more extreme guise, it involves a commitment to a form of physicalism according to which the natural world contains nothing but the entities recognized by physics. Dupré argues that this picture—and its accompanying hierarchical conception of the natural sciences—has been more or less abandoned, but that its reductive spirit continues to animate philosophical thought.[29] He claims also that such an approach belies a dogmatism which goes beyond 'any decent empiricist strictures', and that it ends up violating the very principles which define the naturalist's starting-point. Hence:

> The universe-wide microphysical machine, the integrated realm of microscopic particles that forms the substance of reductionist fantasies, is not a product of naturalistic enquiry, but a supernatural construct of the scientific dreamer. Naturalists should reject the image not just because it lacks proper naturalistic credentials, but because it violates the most basic naturalistic commitment to the rejection of the supernatural.[30]

The objection then is that scientific naturalism, when taken to this reductive extreme, turns into a form of supernaturalism. It is said to do so in two different ways. First, the claim that the physicist has the monopoly on the contents of the natural world is scientifically unsupported. In this respect, there is a clear sense in which the position can be said to be 'contradictory to scientific

---

[27] 'Response to Charles Lamore', in *Reading McDowell on Mind and World*, ed. Nicholas H. Smith (London: Routledge, 2002), p. 295.

[28] 'Introduction: The Nature of Naturalism', p. 4.

[29] See Dupré, 'The Miracle of Monism', in *Naturalism in Question*, pp. 46–47.

[30] 'The Miracle of Monism', p. 52.

knowledge'.[31] Second, the idea that we can explain the nature and behaviour of everything purely in terms of physical stuff—even granting that everything is composed of such stuff—suggests 'the attribution of supernatural powers to physical stuff in a way wholly inimical to naturalism'.[32]

Dupré claims that there are good scientific grounds for allowing that there is 'a great diversity of projects that can be directed towards the investigation of the natural world', and that we should resist the temptation of looking for some a priori criterion by means of which to determine which of these projects are to be accepted.[33] Exploiting a version of the 'Great Success of Modern Science Argument', he claims that the explanatory and predictive powers of the relevant projects offer cogent empirical means for determining their acceptability, and that we should be ready to accept a 'pluralistic naturalism' according to which the sciences offer us 'a diverse group of practices with a diverse set of partially overlapping virtues'.[34] These practices will incorporate the natural and human sciences, but room must be made also for the various non-scientific approaches and 'humanistic' disciplines which contribute to the task of understanding the variety of phenomena we encounter in the natural world—Dupré's examples are history, studies of the Arts, and philosophy.

We seem to be returned to a version of Randall's claim that naturalistic philosophy engages with and examines the mess of miscellaneous stuff man encounters 'in whatever way', and an interpretation which suggests that naturalism has, indeed, become 'all-inclusive'. In support of this contention we find Dupré claiming that, for the pluralistic naturalist, the thesis that philosophy is continuous with science faces the obvious question: which science? He suggests that philosophy emphasizes rather different epistemic virtues from most sciences and has different goals:

> Its characteristic epistemic virtues are, perhaps, analytic rigor and clarity of argument, though certainly it is subject to others, such as sensitivity to empirical fact, that are central to most sciences. Its goals are typically more abstract, theoretical, and critical... [t]he view of philosophers as a kind of laboratorially challenged scientist seems to me to have been a total failure. Pluralistic naturalism offers a way out of this backwater, but one that does not consign the philosopher to even more unpromising undertakings in the noumenal world or Plato's heaven.[35]

---

[31] Compare Spiegelberg who claims that '[t]here is such a thing as idolatry even of methods', 'Supernaturalism or Naturalism: A Study in Meaning and Verifiability', p. 362.

[32] 'The Miracle of Monism', p. 55. Compare Spiegelberg: '[b]y crediting matter with the capacity to account for everything else, it ended up by making it all the more enigmatic. For it became now necessary to equip it with the most amazing potentialities, more complex than any other school would have dared before' ('Supernaturalism or Naturalism: A Study in Meaning and Verifiability', p. 360, footnote 15).

[33] 'The Miracle of Monism', p. 55.

[34] 'The Miracle of Monism', p. 56.

[35] 'The Miracle of Monism', p. 58.

1.5 LOOKING AHEAD

We began with a characterization of naturalism which suggests that, from a methodological point of view, it converges with good philosophical practice. Naturalism in this sense ceases to be 'a distinct "ism"' but the question of what kind of constraint, if any, it imposes is left vague. One possible constraint comes with the idea that it stands opposed to supernaturalism. Supernaturalism is said to involve the postulation of a realm beyond the natural world. The idea of a supernatural God is prototypical in this context, but so too is any reference to entities which require for their discernment 'special' or 'extreme' cognitive powers. We are led to suppose that such entities are too weird to be part of our ontology, and that they create insuperable epistemological difficulties.

Questions then arose about the details of this negative constraint, and it became clear that a satisfactory answer demanded a much clearer account of the limits of the natural. One suggestion—seemingly prevalent in our times—is that these limits are to be comprehended in scientific terms, the idea being that the scientist has the monopoly on the contents of the natural world. According to this way of thinking 'supernatural' becomes equivalent to 'non-scientific'. It follows that supernatural entities lie beyond the ambit of scientific investigation, and that supernatural ways of knowing likewise elude its grasp. Such a characterization leads one to wonder whether supernaturalism is really as philosophically disastrous as we have been led to suppose, for the implication now is that it is the position to be endorsed if one wishes to allow that there is more to nature than what the scientist comprehends.

Much hangs on the question of how we are to conceive of the limits of scientific comprehension, and Dupré argues that they must exceed the narrow parameters assumed by the reductive physicalist. He goes so far as to claim that such a position inherits the difficulties of supernaturalism, the implication being that it fails to provide a viable alternative. At this stage then, it looks as if we are forced to choose between two equally problematic approaches, and to those for whom scientism remains an ideological prejudice, it will be tempting to conclude that supernaturalism constitutes the better option. Dupré resists this move on two related grounds. First, he believes that it is a position which consigns philosophy to the 'even more unpromising undertakings in the noumenal world or Plato's heaven'. Second, he is convinced that a much more promising way forward comes with the acceptance of pluralistic naturalism. We are to suppose then that pluralistic naturalism provides the required *via media*. It does so because it grants a rightful place to scientific investigation, rejects the monistic model which fails to do justice to the variety of projects which fall under that umbrella, and allows that there are non-scientific modes of enquiry—philosophy included—which have a rightful and essential place in the task of determining the nature of the natural world. The further crucial claim is that it does all of this without committing the sins of the supernaturalist. That is to say, it does not consign philosophy to 'undertakings in the noumenal world or Plato's heaven'.

The idea that the supernaturalist trades in such undertakings returns us to the claim that he takes us beyond the natural world by postulating *Dinge an Sich*, transcendental orders, and the like. We are to assume now, however, that these entities or realms are supernatural not simply in the sense that they elude scientific investigation as reductively conceived, nor even in the sense that they elude such investigation on a much broader construal thereof, for it has been allowed that there is more to investigation than science, and that philosophy has an autonomous role to play in the task of figuring the nature and contents of the natural world. Philosophy, we are told, must be sensitive to empirical fact, and sensitive therefore to the findings of science. We are told also that 'there are fundamentally important classes of questions for which the methods of philosophy are particularly suited and even essential'.[36] Dupré prefers to make no claim on the controversial matter of what these questions are, but it seems plausible to suppose that one such question centres on the issue we are trying at present to adjudicate, namely, that of determining a sense of 'supernatural' which lends proper justice to the claim that supernaturalism stands to be exorcised by good philosophy.

We shall see that pluralistic naturalism is not uncommon in recent philosophical thought, and that its proponents—who refer to themselves as belonging to the expansive, liberal, or even naturalized platonist variety—are adamant that the supernaturalist remains enemy number one. (Enemy number two is the reductive scientific naturalist, but we are encouraged to think that he represents the lesser of the two evils.) Most of them are unconcerned with theistic versions of supernaturalism, and we are led to suppose that the absurdities of this particular brand of the position have long been exposed and put to rest. Rather, they tend to focus upon issues that arise in the context of comprehending the nature of mind and its contents (including, for example, the status of reason and value), and the implications these issues have for accounts of the limits of the natural world. The naturalized platonism of McDowell will be my primary focus, although I shall trade also upon the related work of Wiggins and Bilgrami. McDowell's brand of naturalism is an important case in point given Dupré's eagerness to banish from our ontology any remnants of Plato's heaven and the like. For McDowell implies that such remnants are in perfect philosophical order provided that they have been suitably sanitized by naturalistic treatment. Quite what this means must await further investigation, but at this preliminary stage it is worth bearing in mind something that Randall

---

[36] 'The Miracle of Monism', p. 58.

says at the close of his article. Naturalism, he claims, 'must combine the wisdom of Plato with the sanity of Aristotle'. He continues as follows:

> Is there any other enterprise in our vexed world today where this combination has been successful save in the practice of scientific enquiry? Assuredly, the anti-naturalists are right: our world is perishing for want of faith. The faith we need, the faith that alone promises salvation, is the faith in intelligence.[37]

The idea that naturalism must combine the wisdom of Plato with the sanity of Aristotle suggests that it is far too quick to impose a blanket a priori ban on all undertakings in Plato's heaven or the noumenal world. It suggests also that there may be philosophically respectable ways of retrieving these notions, and hence, that the realm of the natural may be expanded beyond the limits envisaged by some of the naturalists under consideration. Randall implies that the required combination is to be effected at the level of scientific enquiry, and says enough to suggest that its limits, as he conceives them, outstrip those of the reductive physicalist. He also grants with the supernaturalist that our world is perishing for want of faith, but elucidates this theistically loaded term by reference to the idea of intelligence. As he puts it, the faith we need is the faith in intelligence. He is right about this, but we should hesitate before assuming that this concession amounts to the imposition of a theistic exclusion order. On the contrary, and as I shall endeavour to show in what follows, our naturalists—all of them—have paved the way towards a position in which nature does, indeed, become the 'all-inclusive category' and naturalism ceases to be a distinct 'ism'.[38] Crucially, however, this position is shorn of the reductive implications it has tended to carry, and—more daringly I shall suggest—can deal quite happily and legitimately with some of those ingredients which, from the point of view of all our naturalists, spell inevitable philosophical disaster.

There is no quick route to this conclusion, nor to its precise meaning, and I shall begin by mapping out the first stage of the required journey. This stage remains within the ambit of scientific naturalism, and involves a careful examination of the kind of position which becomes available once we move beyond the limits of natural science to accommodate the resources of the human sciences. The case of value will be my focus, and, more specifically, the question of whether there is any substance to the charge expressed by Dewey's supernaturalist that a naturalist of this ilk ends up destroying all 'distinctively human values'. It is to this task that I now turn.

---

[37] 'Epilogue: The Nature of Naturalism', p. 382.
[38] Compare Barry Stroud: 'We must accept everything we find ourselves committed to in accounting for everything that we agree is so and want to explain', 'The Charm of Naturalism', in *Naturalism in Question*, p. 34.

2

Expansive Naturalism I

2.1 INTRODUCTION

Let us refer to the scientific naturalist under present consideration as an expansive scientific naturalist. He is an expansive scientific naturalist in the sense that he grants that there is more to science than physics, and more to it than natural science. Thus, he is prepared to include within his methodological ambit the human sciences, and in this way to broaden his conception of the natural world. Its contents are no longer to be monopolized by natural science, but can be stretched to accommodate social-psychological phenomena. The question of what this concession amounts to is a matter of some dispute, and it is easy to think that—in some contexts at least—it becomes little more than an idle terminological shift which retains the spirit of physicalist reductionism.[1] By contrast, the position with which I am concerned allows that there are modes of investigation which are to be distinguished from anything to be found at the level of the 'hard' sciences, and which are more appropriate to an understanding of human phenomena. The further claim—and this serves as a response to those who believe that the envisaged methodological expansion is bound to violate the strictures of good scientific practice—is that the relevant modes of investigation have achieved a large measure of success in furthering our understanding of the phenomena to which they are applied, and that the results they have produced are empirically grounded. There are good reasons then for taking seriously the explanatory pretensions of such investigations,

---

[1] See, for example, John Dupré, 'The Miracle of Monism', in *Naturalism in Question*, ed. Mario De Caro and David Macarthur (Cambridge, Mass.: Harvard University Press, 2004), p. 41: 'Much work done in the social sciences, especially work that is quantitative or based on some kind of mathematical modelling, quite explicitly aims to be scientific. On the other hand, other social scientists, or at any rate other people with the same departmental and disciplinary allegiances as the first group, oppose these methods as inappropriate to the study of humans.' Dupré makes this point in the context of questioning the limits of scientific inquiry. He argues that science must be taken to include any projects of inquiry that have provided worthwhile empirical results, and that if it turns out that some empirical inquiry has produced such results, but cannot be unified with the rest of science, then we should take this as a refutation of the conception of scientific unity in question.

and for allowing that their application can enrich our understanding of the natural world and the beings within it.

This raises the issue of how far we are permitted to go in this expansive direction, and whether we can produce a constraint which neither begs the question in favour of a restriction that turns out to be unwarranted nor takes us into territory which proves to be problematic even once such restrictions have been lifted. An adequate answer must await clarification of the precise focus of naturalistic enquiry and the approaches best suited to its accommodation. It should be clear from what has been said that it is no answer to the question of focus to say that we are concerned with what is natural. Likewise, and this takes us to the other extreme, we must be wary of prohibiting certain phenomena until we are quite sure that such a move does not rest upon questionable presuppositions. So, for example, the accusation that the relevant phenomena are supernatural becomes problematic if the details of this complaint are spelled out by reference to a conception of 'natural' which remains philosophically unsupported—when, for example, 'supernatural' is defined in opposition to an unduly restrictive conception of 'natural', and the offending items are deemed problematic on the ground that they fail to conform to this paradigm.

The expansive scientific naturalist holds that we commit to an unduly restricted conception of nature if its limits are measured exclusively by natural science. He draws this conclusion on the ground that there are aspects of the natural world which resist such an approach, and which can be accommodated and comprehended provided that we accept a richer conception of scientific investigation. It remains to be seen whether the envisaged approach does justice to the relevant phenomena, and we have noted already that Dewey's supernaturalist remains sceptical on this score. In particular, he complains that it has the effect of destroying all 'distinctively human values'.

2.2 HUMAN VALUES

The question of what makes a value human or distinctively human is unclear as it stands, but we can begin with the suggestion that human values are those which are valued by human beings. This imposes no particular constraint upon the concept of value, for although we can allow that the values of human beings exceed those of, say, cats and dogs, it seems plausible to suppose that we are capable of valuing all sorts of things, and that not all of these things are valued simply because they satisfy our interests in some way. The notion of an interest is hardly perspicuous, and the claim that there are values which exceed our interests will be more or less compelling depending upon how widely this notion is understood. Nevertheless, its introduction paves the way towards an alternative conception of what it is for a value to be distinctively human, human values being those which satisfy our interests. Given the vagueness surrounding the notion of an interest, it is unclear whether we should con-clude that all values are distinctively human in this sense, but according to one way of thinking we can lend further determinacy to the position by linking the relevant values to some suitable subclass of human response or attitude—one familiar contender being the notion of desire.

The idea that there are values which require reference to human responses leaves open the question of how widely the notion of response or, indeed, of desire, is to be comprehended,[2] and need not imply that the relevant values are to be generated from such responses without remainder—as they would be if it were claimed, say, that the value of things is simply a function of whether they happen to be desired. One could allow, for example, that there are values which are not so generated, and that the relevant responses are introduced into the picture for epistemological reasons. This is what Wiggins is getting at when he grants that there are cases where we desire x because we think x good but where we can say also that x is good because x is such that we desire x. The second claim is not intended to imply that x is good simply because we desire it. Rather, the point is that 'such desiring by human beings directed in this way is one part of what is required for there to be such a thing as the perspec-tive from which the non-instrumental goodness of x is there to be perceived'.[3] On such a position the confinement imagery loses its bite, for, in focusing our attention upon values which require reference to human responses, we are

[2] John McDowell suggests that the term 'desire' be used as a placeholder for all the ele-ments which comprise an agent's 'subjective motivational set', claiming that these sets are not restricted to what would ordinarily be called 'desires', 'Might There be External Reasons?' in *Mind, Value, and Reality* (Cambridge, Mass.: Harvard University Press, 1998), p. 96. He cites Bernard Williams who tells us that they 'can contain such things as dispositions of evaluation, patterns of emotional reaction, personal loyalties, and various projects, as they may be abstractly called, embodying commitments of the agent', 'Internal and External Reasons', in *Moral Luck* (Cambridge: Cambridge University Press, 1981), p. 105. David Wiggins makes a similar point in his 'Moral Cognitivism, Moral Relativism, and Motivating Moral Beliefs', *Proceedings of the Aristotelian Society*, New Series, vol. 91 (1990–91), p. 83. See also Philippa Foot, 'Morality as a System of Hypothetical Imperatives', *The Philosophical Review*, vol. 81, no. 3 (July 1972), p. 307.

[3] 'Truth, Invention, and the Meaning of Life', in *Needs, Values, Truth* (Oxford: Oxford University Press, 1991), p. 106. We can assume that 'non-instrumental' in this context means 'intrinsic', and hence that Wiggins is referring to the value a thing has in itself, where this involves denying that its value stems simply from the fact that it is desired or satisfies some need. The use of the term 'non-instrumental' suggests that the contrast at issue here is that between intrinsic and instrumental value, instrumental value being the value a thing has as a means or instru-ment to something else—its satisfying some desire, for example. Christine Korsgaard has argued that 'intrinsic' should be contrasted with 'extrinsic' rather than 'instrumental', an object having extrinsic value if the source of its value is something other than the object, *Creating the Kingdom of Ends* (Cambridge: Cambridge University Press, 1996), pp. 249–273). Korsgaard alerts us to some important distinctions, but they are not conflated by Wiggins, and the dilemma she goes on to pose does not affect his position. In any case, we can allow that at least some extrinsic goods function as means or instruments, when, for example, they are valued for their desired effects.

excluding only those values to which we could never respond, and allowing that not all of the values to which we *can* respond depend for their existence upon those responses. In effect, then, we are returned to a version of the claim that human values are those which are valued by human beings. By contrast, the confinement imagery seems to lose its point if we insist that *all* values are generated out of human responses—after all, there are no values which are not so generated. It remains possible that this generative vocabulary admits of an epistemological reading, and hence that the values which are so generated are irreducible to their psychological origins. The alternative is to suppose that they *are* so reducible, and that all values are distinctively human in this sense.

The position is familiar from the tradition in which Hume was working, and finds its prototype in the following words of Thomas Hobbes:

> But whatsoever is the object of any mans Appetite or Desire; that is it, which he for his part calleth *Good*: And the Object of his Hate, and Aversion *Evill*; And of his Contempt, *Vile* and *Inconsiderable*. For these words of Good, Evill, and Contemptible, are ever used with relation to the person that useth them: There being nothing simply and absolutely so; nor any common Rule of Good and Evill, to be taken from the nature of the objects themselves.[4]

According to this way of thinking, there is no goodness fixed in the nature of things to which we are drawn by virtue of our practical reason. Rather, it is desire which motivates our evaluations, the relevant desires being satisfied by objects which, by virtue of their capacity to satisfy, are called good. It is in this sense that our evaluative vocabulary is 'used with relation to the person that useth them'. Heidegger accepts a version of this interpretation of what it is for values to be distinctively human, and holds that all values count as such.[5]

---

[4] *Leviathan* (1651), book 1, ch. 6 (London: Dent, 1914), p. 24. Hume often expresses himself in a similar manner. For example: 'There is just so much vice or virtue in any character as every one places in it, and 'tis impossible in this particular we can ever be mistaken', *Treatise of Human Nature*, *(1739–1740)*, III.ii.8 (Oxford: Oxford University Press, 1978). However, he objects to the view that moral distinctions are to be founded purely in our subjective preferences, takes himself to be advancing a position which vindicates the reality of moral distinctions, and makes it clear that the disputes of moral sceptics—of which he counts Hobbes—are unworthy of serious consideration. For further discussion of Hume's position see David Wiggins, *Ethics: Twelve Lectures on the Philosophy of Morality* (London: Penguin, 2006), ch. 2, ch. 11, pp. 370–377; 'Categorical Requirements: Kant and Hume on the Idea of Duty', in *Virtues and Reasons: Philippa Foot and Moral Theory*, ed. Rosalind Hursthouse, Gavin Lawrence, and Warren Quinn (Oxford: Clarendon Press, 1995), pp. 297–330; David Fate Norton, 'Hume and the Foundations of Morality', *Cambridge Companion to Hume* (Cambridge: Cambridge University Press, 1993), pp. 148–181. For a fair and helpful discussion of Hobbes's considered position see Jean Hampton, 'Hobbes and Ethical Naturalism', *Philosophical Perspectives*, vol. 6, Ethics (1992), pp. 333–353.

[5] Hence: 'Every valuing, even where it values positively, is a subjectivizing. It does not let beings: be. Rather, valuing lets beings: be valid—solely as the objects of its doing', 'Letter on Humanism', trans. F.A. Capuzzi, in *Basic Writings*, ed. D.F. Krell, (London: Routledge Press, 1978), p. 251.

Nevertheless, he grants that there is more to the worth of things than what is captured at this level, and concludes that we must 'think against values' if we are to appreciate this something more.[6] As he puts it: 'precisely through the characterization of something as "a value", what is so valued is robbed of its worth', and 'thinking in values involves the greatest blasphemy imaginable against Being'.[7]

Heidegger's line of thought stands in a rather interesting relation to that of Dewey's supernaturalist. Like Heidegger, he is concerned to identify and to reject a way of thinking which is said to destroy something of significance—something which, we are to suppose, merits inclusion in our ontology. The offending position is naturalism, and the naturalist, we are told, destroys all distinctively human values. We are to suppose then that distinctively human values require to be preserved, but that they are not preserved if we remain within the ambit of naturalism. Heidegger, by contrast, takes the offending position to be one which *confines* us to the level of distinctively human values, doing so on the ground that this level is concerned simply with the extrinsic value of things and fails to accommodate their intrinsic value. Thus, he agrees with the supernaturalist that there are two levels of thinking to be distinguished, but locates the class of distinctively human values at the first level, and opposes this level to one which can accommodate the possibility of there being values which are not distinctively human in the relevant sense.

Here then are the questions to structure our discussion. First, we must consider what kind of addition is at issue when values are introduced into our ontology, and whether they can be accommodated in naturalistic terms. In particular, we must consider what it means to say that our focus should be upon distinctively human values, and whether this claim is true. Is Dewey's supernaturalist right to say that such values elude a naturalistic framework? And what are we to make of Heidegger's complaint that a focus of this kind is itself subject to serious limitations? Is the disagreement merely terminological? And where is the expansive scientific naturalist to be located in the debate? Does he accept that the values with which he is concerned are distinctively

---

[6] It is difficult to make the point here in Heidegger's terms given his tendency to restrict all talk of value and evaluation to the terms he wishes to reject. His resistance to such terminology is most likely traced back to his view that words are important and coercive, and not easily cleansed from accretions they have acquired from other philosophers. As far as the word 'value' is concerned the relevant accretions come from such figures as Hermann Lotze and Nietzsche. Lotze's claim that 'what we mean by value in the world lies wholly in the feeling of satisfaction or of pleasure which we experience from it' would help to explain why Heidegger wishes to 'think against values', and this negative view would be further substantiated by Nietzsche's seeming commitment to the idea that we are the source of value in the world. In spite of these terminological reservations, however, Heidegger does insist that 'thinking against values' is not a matter of maintaining that things are valueless, or as he puts it a bit later, it is not a way of 'beat[ing] the drum for the valuelessness and nullity of beings'.

[7] 'Letter on Humanism', p. 251. I shall return to this latter claim in chapter 5.

human in Heidegger's and Hobbes's sense? And if so, does he have a response to Heidegger's complaint that we need to go further than this? Finally, if we do need to go further than this, then are we to accept with Dewey's supernaturalist that this move must exceed the limits of naturalism? Or is it, rather, that it must exceed the limits of the particular brand of naturalism at issue here? If this final conclusion seems compelling, then we must take seriously the possibility of taking the expansive exercise a stage further, assuming that there are no good counterarguments in the offing.

2.3 VALUE, NORMATIVITY, AND HUMAN SCIENCE

'Values, being the sort of thing they are, are not primarily the objects of detached observation.'[8] Akeel Bilgrami makes this claim in the context of distinguishing between the perspective of detached observation which is adopted when we seek to comprehend the world, and that which is at issue when we are practically engaged with it. So we have a distinction between two possible perspectives upon the world, and the first is said to be operative when we are in the business of studying, reflecting, and comprehending. This stance is 'detached' in one obvious sense, for it involves a stepping back—the kind of stepping back which is required if we are to reflect upon the things we are seeking to comprehend. It can also be described as 'engaged', for we are engaged in reflection and study, and we might even be said to be *practically* engaged in this respect, for we are doing things with things and adapting them to our explanatory purposes. We are to suppose, however, that there is a way of being practically engaged with things which is not detached in this sense. That is to say that it does not involve a reflective stepping back on our part, and is not therefore motivated by the desire to comprehend. The further claim is that there is something about values which rules out the possibility of treating them primarily in this detached manner, although it is not ruled out that they could be so treated at a secondary level. The implication here is that the aforementioned second perspective offers a more appropriate way of relating to values—that we relate to them primarily at a pre-reflective, practical level.

One thing this could mean is that our everyday engagement with value is of a different order from what goes on when we reflect upon such engagement—that reflection comes after the fact as it were. But that's just the difference between living and studying, the point is not peculiar to value, and it does

---

[8] 'The Wider Significance of Naturalism: A Genealogical Essay', in *Naturalism and Normativity*, ed. Mario De Caro and David Macarthur (New York: Columbia University Press, 2010), p. 26.

not rule out the possibility of studying value or, indeed, of studying it scientifically. This latter idea is ruled out if science is taken to be equivalent to natural science, but we have moved beyond this particular paradigm to accommodate the human sciences. It remains open then that we can reflect upon value at this level of enquiry, doing so by examining the relevant practically engaged responses. If this is so, then values could be objects of detached observation in this sense.

Akeel Bilgrami considers this possibility, taking as his focus the social and behavioural sciences. One of their overarching goals, we are told, is to study and to explain:

> [i]ndividual (possibly even social) behaviour as a kind of desire-satisfaction in human subjects in the light of their (probabilistic) apprehension of desire-satisfying properties in the world, that is, *opportunities* that the world provides to satisfy our wants and preferences.[9]

The study of such behaviour can surely cast some light upon the question of value. In particular, it can tell us about those values which, from Heidegger's perspective, are distinctively human, and which, as Hobbes puts it, are not 'to be taken from the nature of the objects themselves'. They are not to be taken from the objects themselves because the relevant objects are valued only to the extent that they have the power to satisfy our desires. I have noted already that there are those who generalize this model to value as a whole and conclude that all values are distinctively human in this sense. But there are others—Heidegger, for example—who object to such a position on the ground that there is more to value than what can be captured at this level. Wiggins can be understood to be making a similar point when he refers to the non-instrumental goodness of things and insists that we are capable of appreciating it.

These objections do not suffice to refute the scientific position at hand, for there may be good reasons for rejecting a conception of value which exceeds these particular limits. Alternatively, and assuming that these limits capture only a part of the truth about value, it remains open that the position is rather more versatile than this initial characterization suggests, and that it can be modified in a manner which retains its scientific spirit. Bilgrami takes issue with the position on the ground that there is a normative element to value which it fails to accommodate, and we are encouraged to suppose that this problem cannot be rectified from within scientific parameters. More specifically, he complains that the required normative element is constructed 'out of a normative void':

> It emerges only from within human causal and motivational tendencies and *dispositions*—our desires plus our beliefs about opportunities in the world that will

---

[9] 'The Wider Significance of Naturalism', p. 30.

be likely to gratify them. There are two aspects to the normative element, according to this view. The aspect of *value*, which is restricted to some sophisticated and constrained understanding of the desires, and the aspect of rationality, which is exhausted by the idea of acting so as to satisfy those desires on the basis of these beliefs regarding the likelihood of the opportunities in the world contributing to the satisfaction of the desires. No more intrinsic normative element is acknowledged, and that is the reason to think of this picture as rightly describable by the term 'scientistic'.[10]

The approach is familiar from Hobbes who was likewise eager to put morality on a more scientific footing.[11] It involves a rejection of the idea that value is 'to be taken from the nature of the objects themselves' and that we are rationally responsive to value thus conceived. According to the preferred alternative, practical reason is an instrument for determining effective means to desired ends—ends which are fixed by our desires, albeit a 'sophisticated and constrained understanding' thereof.[12] The precise force of this latter constraint remains unclear, but it is implied that practical reason is reducible to this instrumental component—understandably so, if anything more would involve reverting to the rejected conception of value, and if a reversion of this kind is philosophically and scientifically unsupported. We can note that this latter complaint has not yet been vindicated, and Bilgrami seems to be suggesting that the forbidden move is precisely what is needed if the picture is to be rendered remotely plausible. At least, this is so if we allow that the missing 'intrinsic normative element' has something in common with the values excluded by the position at hand.

The notion of normativity is hardly perspicuous, and, in a moral context, has tended to go hand in hand with talk of the special authority or 'binding force'[13] of morality—it is said to be ' "inescapable" in some special way'.[14] We cannot assume the authority of such talk, nor that it poses an intractable difficulty for the scientist. However, it certainly seems amenable to the idea that there is a source of value that comes to us from without, and it seems plausible to suppose that this source grants just the kind of *intrinsic* normative element which is said to be problematic by the lights of our current social scientist. We must consider then what it could mean to grant such an element, doing so

---

[10] 'The Wider Significance of Naturalism', p. 31.

[11] Hampton tells us that Hobbes sought to attack what he called 'the filth and fraud' in Greek philosophy, 'dismissed the existence of any Summum Bonum, the prescriptive entity that his academic contemporaries were most likely to embrace, and constructed what he called a "science" of moral philosophy that he viewed as the equal of scientific theories in the physical sciences advanced by Galileo, Kepler, and Harvey' ('Hobbes and Ethical Naturalism', p. 333).

[12] See Hampton, *'Rethinking Reason', American Philosophical Quarterly*, vol. 29, no. 3 (July 1992), pp. 219–220.

[13] See Philippa Foot, 'Morality as a System of Hypothetical Imperatives', p. 310. Foot claims that 'it is not clear what this means if not that we *feel* ourselves unable to escape'.

[14] 'Morality as a System of Hypothetical Imperatives', p. 312.

with a view to determining whether this move is a requirement upon a satisfactory conception of value.

One important idea—implicit in the above quotation—is that values impose constraints upon our desires. It is for this reason that we can allow that there are desires which are not desirable to have and which ought not to be pursued. The relevant values need not be exclusively moral, for, as I shall spell out in more detail below, we are constrained also by prudential values. Bilgrami is concerned with the constraints which are imposed in a moral context, and claims that this normative component can be accommodated only by allowing that there is a 'source of value from the outside and not merely from within our own causal tendencies and dispositions'.[15] This is said to involve our being responsive to 'normative demands coming from the evaluative properties of the perceptible world we inhabit'.[16] So we have a conception of value which 'is to be taken from the nature of the objects themselves', and Bilgrami runs a version of G.E. Moore's 'open question' argument to lend justice to this position. Human beings, we are told, can ask of any desire, inclination, or tendency: 'Is it good to have it?' The question is intelligible, and if we grant this much, we must allow that the use of 'good' it involves is irreducible to such dispositions.

This particular application of the 'open question' argument cuts across the moral and the non-moral case, and in order to introduce a more explicitly moral dimension to the debate it will be helpful to consider a related Moorean strategy which was used by J.G. Brennan to undermine Ernst Nagel's definition of a moral ideal.[17] Nagel defines a moral ideal as 'the imagined satisfaction of some complex of impulses, desires, and needs'.[18] Brennan comments that 'it seems a little odd to define a moral ideal in such a way that the extension of the term seems so broad as to include the thoughts of a gangster who is planning a robbery the proceeds of which he wants to use to entertain a

---

[15] 'The Wider Significance of Naturalism', p. 33.

[16] 'The Wider Significance of Naturalism', p. 32.

[17] It could be objected that the aim of providing analytic definitions of moral concepts is misguided, and that, once we relinquish such an aim, the force of the 'open question' argument is lost. I agree that there is something problematic about analytic definitions of this kind, although I do not think that this is sufficient to compromise the very idea of conceptual analysis. In any case, it is doubtful that Bilgrami's social scientist would claim to be in the business of advancing analytic truths, but Bilgrami's objections suggest that there is still scope for applying a version of Moore's argument to similar undermining effect. Compare Peter Railton: 'Even if Moore's "Open question" argument cannot be deployed directly against an interpretation of discourse about a person's good that does not purport to express analytic truths, a significant critical function may still be served by pressing Moorean charges against such interpretations. For it would be a challenge to any theoretical identification or reforming definition of P in terms of Q to argue that there is something central to the notion of P that does not appear to be captured by Q; this would make the question "I can see that this is Q, but is it P?" genuinely compelling, not just barely possible', 'Naturalism and Prescriptivity', *Social Philosophy and Policy*, vol. 7, no. 1 (1989), p. 158. I shall be returning to Railton's particular proposal in due course.

[18] 'Naturalism Reconsidered', *Proceedings and Addresses of the American Philosophical Association*, vol. 28 (October 1955).

girlfriend at Las Vegas for a week'.[19] He notes that Nagel's definition involves the important caveat that the relevant ideals be 'handled responsibly', and objects that although this supplement is inserted to remedy the proposed definition, it does so at the cost of undermining the irrefutability of the principle of non-contradiction: 'A thing cannot be and not be.'

We can summarize Brennan's objection as follows. Moral ideals cannot be defined in terms of the imagined satisfaction of some complex of impulses, desires, and needs because these psychological items can be directed towards immoral ends. So we need a way of restricting the terms of the definition, and Nagel imposes this restriction by insisting that the relevant ideals be 'handled responsibly'. This move rules out the desires of the immoral gangster, and it suggests a similar restriction to that imposed by Bilgrami's social scientist when he insists upon a sophisticated and constrained understanding of the relevant desires. Brennan objects, however, that we have now undermined the proposed definition. For what we are really saying is that moral ideals *cannot* be defined purely in terms of the imagined satisfaction of some complex of impulses, desires, and needs. On the contrary, we require reference to some normative element—an element which, we are to suppose, goes missing so long as we remain at the level of the ingredients which figure in Nagel's official definition.

2.4 INTERLUDE

Bilgrami and Brennan claim that moral value cannot be constructed from the psychological materials which figure in the naturalistic accounts at issue. That is to say that it cannot be constructed out of the relevant causal tendencies and dispositions. These accounts promise to deliver an approach which is scientifically respectable, for the materials with which they operate fall within the province of social-scientific investigation.[20] However, they are said to provide

---

[19] 'On Nagel's Reconsideration of Naturalism', *Journal of Philosophy*, vol. 53, no. 14 (1956), p. 445.

[20] Hampton makes a similar point in the context of considering the scientific appeal of the instrumental conception of rationality: 'first, it presupposes only a subjectivist conception of value and thereby eschews the idea that there are value-objects or properties in the world; second, it claims that the hypothetical imperative (which is the hallmark of instrumental reasoning) is reducible to (a scientifically respectable) statement of a causal connection between an action and an object or state of affairs, linked to an appeal to what is taken to be the actually existing preference for the effect in the agent; and third, it assumes what seems to be the unremarkable psychological thesis that people want to satisfy as many of their preferences as possible—or to put it succinctly—to maximize their satisfaction. Together these three features would appear to allow the theory to *generate normative prescriptions even while not presupposing anything fundamentally normative in its foundations*', 'Rethinking Reason', pp. 229–230.

an inadequate source for the normativity of value. The nature of this normative element has not been spelled out in any detail, but it seems clear at the least that it is something by reference to which we can discriminate between our desires and which serves to constrain them. In particular, it allows us to make sense of the idea that some desires are more desirable than others, and that others—like those of the gangster—should not be pursued at all. According to Bilgrami, the source of normativity must lie beyond such psychological items, and he claims that we can accommodate the required 'external' source only by allowing that the relevant psychological items are 'responsive to norma- tive demands made by evaluative properties *in the world*.'[21] These evaluative properties are said to grant us the 'intrinsic normative element' which eludes the naturalistic picture at issue, although if Brennan is to be believed, it lurks implicitly in at least some versions thereof. Either way, we are to suppose that this picture is undermined.

2.5 AN EXPANSIVE SCIENTIFIC NATURALIST REJOINDER

Peter Railton agrees that the ethical naturalist has struggled to define a satis- factory conception of normativity. He sees the task at hand as that of provid- ing a plausible synthesis of the empirical and the normative, and complains that the task of retaining a properly normative component has usually come at the cost of losing any firm connection with descriptive social or psychological theory.[22] It is his aim to rectify this deficiency, and to make a case for claiming that 'moral inquiry is of a piece with empirical inquiry'.[23] The implication here is that the connection with descriptive social or psychological theory must be maintained, and that this provides the only way of guaranteeing that the approach remains empirically grounded. It is unclear whether an inquiry into morals could exceed the scope of social or psychological theory whilst remain- ing empirically grounded. We are to suppose, however, that an approach which was not 'of a piece with empirical enquiry' would return us to the problematic dualisms and gulfs which our naturalist is so anxious to avoid. That is to say that the envisaged synthesis of the empirical and the normative would have been lost.

Railton accepts that there is an intrinsic connection between valuing some- thing and having some sort of positive attitude towards it that provides one with an instrumental reason for action, acknowledges the distinction between 'moral

---

[21] 'The Wider Significance of Naturalism', p. 31.
[22] 'Moral Realism', *The Philosophical Review*, XCV, no. 2 (Apr. 1986), p. 163.
[23] 'Moral Realism', p. 165.

value and other sorts of desirability,[24] and claims that morality can retain its prescriptive force from within an instrumental framework. So the picture has something in common with the framework which, from Bilgrami's point of view, involves constructing the normative element of value from a 'normative void', although Railton's aspirations suggest that the criticism is misplaced. These aspirations become less obviously futile once it is made clear that the envisaged position is a form of value realism, for this suggests that he is precisely not seeking to construct value from some complex of causal tendencies or dispositions. On the contrary, he wishes to make room for the idea that values exist independently of whether we think that they do, that our conceptions thereof may be flawed, but that we are capable nonetheless of causally interacting with them.[25] He insists, however, that it would be 'intolerably odd' to suppose that we could do this if evaluative facts were *sui generis*, and that we must claim, on the contrary, that they are 'constituted by natural facts'.[26] It is unclear how we are to interpret the force of this requirement, but the pejorative terms which are used to characterize the opposing non-naturalist standpoint suggest that *sui generis* evaluative facts are on a level with transcendental grounds, orders, and *Dinge an Sich*.[27] Assuming that this is so, then we have a sense of what it could mean to deny that morality is empirically grounded, although it remains to be seen whether Railton has offered a satisfactory—and indeed the only satisfactory—way of making good this empirical aim.

He begins with an account of intrinsic, non-moral value, taking this to be equivalent to the idea of something being desirable or good for an individual and which could matter to her for its own sake. He denies that desirability is reducible to what an individual actually desires, for these are merely *subjective* interests which, to the extent that they often reflect 'ignorance, confusion, or lack of consideration', have insufficient normative force to capture the idea of desirableness.[28]

---

[24] 'Moral Realism', p. 170.

[25] 'Moral Realism', p. 172.

[26] 'Moral Realism', p. 171.

[27] Compare Railton: 'Surely, for example, the decline of non-subjectivist value-based ethical non-naturalism in this century has had much to do with the difficulty of making sense of *sui generis* value properties, or of the means by which we obtain purported knowledge of, or reference to, objective value…However, cognitivists who are ethical naturalists need not experience this embarrassment. If, for example, moral facts are identified with—or otherwise reducible to—natural facts, then there is no special mystery about what sort of thing they are, or how we come to have knowledge of them, refer to them, and so on…If moral facts are identical with—or otherwise reducible to—natural facts, then cognitivism may be possible without worrisome ontological expansion', 'What the Non-Cognitivist Helps Us to See the Naturalist Must Help Us to Explain', in *Reality, Representation, and Projection*, ed. John Haldane and Crispin Wright (Oxford: Oxford University Press, 1993), p. 280.

[28] 'Moral Realism', p. 173. In making this point Railton can be understood to be acknowledging a version of the distinction with which Charles Taylor operates in the context of distinguishing between qualitative and non-qualitative reflection. Qualitative reflection involves a use of 'good'—or some other evaluative term—for which 'being desired' is not sufficient, and which permits the classification of desires as more or less fulfilling, superficial, unworthy, worth desiring, and so forth. By contrast, reflection is 'non-qualitative' when being desired is sufficient for

The notion of desirableness is pitched at the level of *objective* interests, and objective interests are those whose pursuit contributes to one's non-moral good: X is *non-morally good for A* if and only if X would satisfy an objective interest of A.[29] A person's non-moral good consists in 'what he would want himself to seek if he knew what he were doing'.[30] Railton takes it to be a consequence of this account that things can be non-morally good for an individual even whilst being morally bad, and claims that we can explain our aversion to certain desires—for example, those involving cruelty—by saying that they are not *morally* good. He takes this to be preferable to supposing that such ends could never be part of a person's non-moral good on the ground that there are people who are constituted in such a way that 'some not-very-appetizing things [are] essential to their flourishing'.[31]

It is notable that Railton takes himself to be discussing *human* value. It is human in the sense that it exists only because humans do:

> In the sense of old-fashioned theory of value, this is a relational rather than an absolute notion of goodness. Although relational, the relevant facts about humans and their world are objective in the same sense that such non-relational entities as stones are: they do not depend for their existence or nature merely upon our conception of them.[32]

So the values with which Railton is concerned are human in the sense that they pertain to our non-moral good, and, as such, involve essential reference to our interests. We are returned then to our second conception of what it is for a value to be human—namely, that it pertains to our interests, but the notion of an interest has been suitably disambiguated, albeit in a manner which accommodates the idea that we care about these values and ought to care about them. First, we have moved beyond merely subjective interests, and, thereby, any suggestion that the relevant values can be constructed without remainder from our desires. Second, however, it is granted that these values are both desirable and capable of being desired—after all, we tend to want the things which are good for us, or at least, to want to want them, and are capable of adjusting our desires accordingly yet not invariably.[33] Third, objective interests are grounded in facts about an individual's constitution and circumstances, and this explains

---

something to count as good, and evaluation is simply a matter of weighing the relevant desired outcomes in a manner which makes no reference to the evaluative contrasts just described, 'Responsibility for Self', in *The Identities of Persons*, ed. Amélie Oksenberg Rorty (Berkeley and Los Angeles, California: University of California Press, 1976), pp. 281–300. It is a further question whether the non-moral level at which Railton is operating is sufficient to capture the normative force of these evaluative contrasts as it is understood by Taylor, but we shall see that there are good grounds for concluding that it is not, and that we must ascend to the level of morality to accommodate the missing element.

[29] 'Moral Realism', p. 176.
[30] 'Moral Realism', p. 177.
[31] 'Moral Realism', p. 177, footnote 20.
[32] 'Moral Realism', p. 183.
[33] See 'Moral Realism', pp. 177–178.

why what is good for one person may not be good for another and why at least
some of these goods are common.

It follows from all of this that there are desires which ought not to be pursued,
namely, those which do not contribute to one's non-moral good. However, this
does not rule out the desires of Brennan's gangster, for the pursuit of immoral
ends can be good in this non-moral sense. That is to say that it can be in one's
non-moral interest to be cruel. At one level this seems perfectly reasonable.
After all, considerations pertaining to the moral worth of a person's interests
are surely irrelevant if we are concerned simply with their non-moral good.
On the other hand, one may wonder whether talk of an individual's well-being
or *flourishing* is really appropriate in such a context, and whether these notions
do not already involve a moral dimension which is missing from the picture
thus far developed. This remains to be seen, as does the question of whether
it is philosophically appropriate to draw upon such intuitions. We can note,
however, that it is an implication of the position thus far defined that things—
including other people—are opportunities or means in the sense presupposed
by Bilgrami's social scientist. *If* this is so, then we can give a point to Heidegger's
complaint that 'thinking in values' in this sense amounts to the greatest blasphemy imaginable against being. It counts as such because it leaves no room
for the idea that things—including other people—could be more than opportunities for furthering our individual objective interests.

2.6 RAILTON'S MORAL REALISM

Railton grants that there is a moral dimension missing from the position so
far described, but believes that the deficiency can be rectified from within a
framework which is naturalistic in the expansive scientific sense at issue. His
starting-point is that there has to be some sort of intrinsic connection between
moral norms and their effects on human interests. It is in this sense, we are
told, that morality must be 'humanized'.[34] The notion of an interest is familiar
from what has been said already, and Railton notes that, in the case of moral
evaluation, the interests of more than one individual are at stake. This leads
him to claim that moral norms reflect a rationality which is conducted from
a social rather than an individual point of view,[35] and that we are concerned
with what is rational from a social point of view with regard to the realization
of non-moral goodness. The focus upon a social point of view is not intended
to imply that morality is restricted to the interests of any particular group or
society, and Railton makes it clear that a genuinely moral point of view, to the

---

[34] 'Moral Realism', p. 197.   [35] 'Moral Realism', pp. 189–190.

extent that it is 'impartial with respect to the interests of all potentially affected', is not itself a socially bounded notion. Indeed, he stresses that one of the patterns visible in the evolution of moral norms is a trend away from social specificity.

The notion of non-moral goodness is used interchangeably with that of well-being, and we are told that an act or practice is better from a moral point of view to the extent that it contributes to 'aggregate well-being impartially considered'.[36] Railton concedes that 'contribution to well-being does not encompass everything that people have found significant in moral assessment', but suggests that 'a standard based upon such contribution does capture something that has been widely held to be a significant part of morality'.[37] The consequentialist commitment is explicit, but Railton's version is flexible enough to accommodate familiar non-consequentialist intuitions, and it is to be distinguished from classical utilitarian conceptions thereof. So, for example, we are told that the idea is 'to *be* and to *do* good, not necessarily to *pursue* goodness',[38] and it is denied that the good in question is reducible to a single measure such as happiness or pleasure.[39] On the contrary, we have 'a pluralistic approach in which several goods are viewed as intrinsically, non-morally valuable—such as happiness, knowledge, purposeful activity, autonomy, solidarity, respect, and beauty'.[40] It is beginning to look as if contribution to well-being is rather well placed to encompass the things that people have found significant in moral assessment, although the force of the term 'non-moral' to describe such goods as solidarity, respect, and even happiness remains unclear.[41]

---

[36] 'What the Non-Cognitivist Helps Us to See', p. 291.

[37] 'What the Non-Cognitivist Helps Us to See', p. 291.

[38] 'Alienation, Consequentialism, and the Demands of Morality', in *Philosophy and Public Affairs*, vol. 13, no. 2 (Spring 1984), p. 170, footnote 42. One of his points here is to capture the idea that it matters to us 'what we actually *do* and *are*', and to avoid any suggestion that all goals are to be reduced to that of happiness or pleasure, anything else being a mere means to this further end.

[39] 'Moral Realism', p. 200.

[40] 'Alienation, Consequentialism, and the Demands of Morality', p. 149. Railton coins the expression 'valoric consequentialism' to capture 'the broad, value-oriented approach to normative ethics I would urge as a replacement for act and rule utilitarianism. The advantage of a value-orientation is nowhere more apparent than in moral dilemmas. I argue that many dilemmas gain their poignancy not from an irresolvable clash of duties—one choice may be clearly right, or either choice is clearly permitted—but from our inability to affirm or express all the values we hold dear, so that, whatever we do, something that matters very much must be lost', 'Précis of Facts, Values, and Norms', *Philosophical Studies*, vol. 126 (2005), p. 431.

[41] I find it difficult to determine where Railton stands on the question of whether the relevant goods are moral or non-moral. At one point he considers whether one could challenge his account on the ground that it does not as yet contain a theory of *moral value*, moral value being attributed only to such things as motives or traits of character. He replies that this (ordinary) usage is not decisive about the term's scope, and claims that his own account involves an equally legitimate use of the term 'moral value', 'What the Non-Cognitivist Helps Us to See', footnote 14. In the same paper, however, he insists that the notion of well-being which figures in his account must be understood naturalistically (p. 291), and that well-being is a *non*-moral good (pp. 291–292).

Having told us that the moral point of view is not a socially bounded notion, Railton insists that it *is* limited in a different sense, for it is essentially tied to 'an impartial yet human one'.[42] This limitation does not imply that it is 'thanks to my attitudes or theories' that human well-being matters.[43] Furthermore, it is made perfectly clear that adopting the required impartial stance is not a matter of rejecting the particular commitments that are part and parcel of a meaningful human life for a 'set of external demands' which are not 'rooted in our lives or accommodating to our perspectives'.[44] On the contrary—and it is for this reason that we can care and ought to care about morality—it involves acknowledging something which is central to our proper humanity, making it possible to 'feel part of a larger world in a way that is itself of great value'.[45] Hence: 'our identities exist in relational, not absolute space, and except as they are fixed in reference points in others, in society, in culture, or in some larger constellation still, they are not fixed at all'.[46]

The constellation has limits, and Railton rejects the idea that morality has a further non-human significance, doing so in the context of considering the claim—attractive to some moral realists he concedes—that the universe itself cares what we do.[47] He objects that if moral realism amounted to *this*, then it would stand to be rejected 'with relief rather than sorrow'. By contrast, his position allows us to see how:

> [m]oral values or imperatives might be objective without being cosmic. They need be grounded in nothing more transcendental than facts about man and his environment, facts about what sorts of things matter to us, and how the ways we live affect these things.[48]

We are to suppose then that this focus upon our humanity is precisely what is required if moral realism is to be a defensible position, that the 'transcendental facts' of the aforementioned 'cosmic' alternative secure objectivity at the cost of illusion, and that this criticism applies equally to the idea that moral principles are 'commandments of supernatural origin, grounded in the will or character of a deity'.[49] Morality, we are told, is ideology that has faced the facts,

---

[42] 'Moral Realism', p. 200.

[43] Hence: '[w]ell being, and the alleviation of suffering, are important...It is not thanks to my attitudes or theories that it matters significantly to a person whether her well-being is enhanced or suffering decreased', 'What the Non-Cognitivist Helps Us to See', p. 292.

[44] 'Alienation, Consequentialism, and the Demands of Morality', p. 164.

[45] 'Alienation, Consequentialism, and the Demands of Morality', p. 164. Railton continues: 'I do want to challenge the simple story often told in which there is a personal point of view from which we glimpse meanings which then vanish into insignificance when we adopt a more general perspective.' There is therefore no 'integrity objection' for Railton's version of consequentialism.

[46] 'Alienation, Consequentialism, and the Demands of Morality', p. 167.

[47] 'Moral Realism', p. 200.

[48] 'Moral Realism', p. 201.

[49] 'Moral Realism', pp. 197–198.

and it is made abundantly clear that they are not to be found by turning our gaze heavenwards.

Railton then considers what appears to be a more troubling limitation to his position, namely, that it involves a rejection of the idea that moral requirements are categorical, a categorical requirement being one which is 'rationally compelling no matter what one's ends'.[50] The rejection is predictable given his commitment to an instrumental conception of rationality and the assumption that it excludes categorical requirements. But how is this commitment to be understood? Hampton tells us that 'if reason can only be instrumental, then it seems that reason itself cannot direct a person to behave morally unless, as it happens, doing so is the means to satisfying one's preferences'.[51] One could purport to accommodate morality by insisting that it pays to care for others, but Hampton objects that this gives the 'wrong kind of defence of the rationality of other-regarding behaviour' by concentrating exclusively upon its instrumental value. More specifically, it makes 'not only cooperative action but also the human beings with whom one will cooperate merely of *instrumental value*'.[52]

We are returned to the framework of Bilgrami's social scientist. Yet it is no part of Railton's position that moral reasoning is instrumental in *this* sense, for he makes a point of rejecting a Hobbesian conception of morality on the ground that it is central to morality that others' interests sometimes be given weight unrelated to one's advantage.[53] His further worry is that the position—like the aforementioned 'cosmic' alternative—suggests that the requirements of morality constitute an 'external' or 'alien' set of demands, for they are hardly accommodating to the perspective of this 'entrepreneurial' self, and can have no motivating force for such a being. Crucially, however, he rejects the Kantian conception of morality on similar 'alienating' grounds, the complaint in this instance being that the fit is skewed in the opposite direction. For instead of being faced with the task of explaining how the demands of morality could motivate a purely self-interested being, we must now make sense of how an ordinary human being who is not purely self-interested could be motivated by a set of imperatives which are 'rationally compelling no matter what one's ends'—even those ends which concern the good of others, we are to assume.[54]

---

[50] 'Moral Realism', p. 204.

[51] 'Rethinking Reason', p. 224.

[52] 'Rethinking Reason', p. 227.

[53] 'Alienation, Consequentialism, and the Demands of Morality', p. 166. Compare Foot: 'No one is counted as charitable if he gives alms "for the praise of men", and one who is honest only because it pays him to be honest does not have the virtue of honesty', 'Morality as a System of Hypothetical Imperatives', p. 313.

[54] 'Moral Realism', p. 204. Kant seems to be forced into this position given his commitment to the claim that ends are all 'self-seeking'. This leads him to conclude that ethics 'cannot begin with the ends that a human being may set for himself', *Metaphysics of Morals*, trans. Mary Gregor (Cambridge: Cambridge University Press, 1996), part II, Introduction, s. II, p. 147. On the other hand, he is prepared to allow that there are (non self-seeking) ends which we *ought* to set

Railton is quite right to deny that reason in this sense could motivate. After all, it has been divorced from anything that could genuinely *matter* to us.[55] We are reminded of Wiggins's point that an adequate conception of value must give due weight to our motivational make-up. But what follows from this? Railton holds that we must deny that moral requirements are categorical.[56] Yet he is equally anxious to distinguish moral reason from the instrumental conception which, by his own lights, is just the other side of the offending Kantian coin. He concedes that the instrumental conception of rationality requires development, but claims that, for all its faults, it provides the clearest notion we have of what it is for an agent to have reason to act. It does so because 'we can see the commending force for an agent of the claim that a given act would advance his ends.'[57] Talk of advancing one's ends suggests a retreat to the Hobbesian account, but given that Railton has rejected this picture, we are to suppose that he is simply lending emphasis to the idea—seemingly missing from the Kantian framework—that practical reason must connect with an agent's ends on pain of failing to count as reasons he could acknowledge as his own.[58] It is in this context that we are told that Kant's categorical requirements presuppose 'the coercive power of an absolute judge', and that moral reasons, thus conceived, are 'both independent of inclination and able to exert a necessary effect upon the will'. Railton concludes that if the normative force of morality depended upon such notions, 'we would be on a short road to scepticism'.[59] Elsewhere, and in similar vein, he objects to the idea that moral requirements are irresistible, doing so on the ground that this would make them into coercive forces rather than authorities which can be both acknowledged and resisted.[60]

---

ourselves, for example, the happiness of others (p. 151), and claims that these ends are duties. Foot objects that we must surely allow that 'quite apart from thoughts of duty a man may care about the suffering of others, having a sense of identification with them, and wanting to help them if he can. Of course, he must want not the reputation of charity, nor even a gratifying role helping others, but, quite simply, their good. If this is what he does care about, then he will be attached to the end proper to the virtue of charity and a comparison with someone acting from an ulterior motive (even a respectable ulterior motive) is out of place' ('Morality as a System of Hypothetical Imperatives', p. 313).

[55] Compare McDowell who complains of the tendency to 'postulate a kind of reasoning that is practical but not shaped by the motivations of those who engage in it; this then looks like a supposed exercise of that bloodless or dispassionate Reason that stands opposed to Passion in a familiar and unprepossessing genre of moral psychology, one that Hume made it difficult to take seriously', 'Might There Be External Reasons?', p. 111.

[56] Foot draws a similar conclusion in her 'Morality as a System of Hypothetical Imperatives'.

[57] 'Moral Realism', p. 166. He adds: 'how many among us can convince ourselves that reason is other than hypothetical?' (p. 203).

[58] Compare: 'Both when we explain the reasons for people's choices and the causes of their behaviour and when we appeal to their intuitions about what it would be rational to decide or to do...we make what use we can of facts about what does-in-fact or can-in-principle motivate agents', 'Moral Realism', p. 189.

[59] 'Reply to David Wiggins', in *Reality, Representation, and Projection*', p. 323.

[60] 'What the Non-Cognitivist Helps Us to See', p. 294.

We can agree that the offending conception of a categorical requirement is to be rejected, but what follows? Railton concludes that we must deny that moral requirements are categorical. However, he is not suggesting that we can escape them by having contrary or 'knavish' desires, and insists that 'variations in personal desires cannot licence exemption from moral obligation'.[61] He claims also that there is an objective reason for, say, not lying 'that does not much depend upon the agent's particular inclinations or interests', and which 'ultimately resides in the various sorts of harm that lying typically effects'.[62] He then argues that a defender of the idea that moral requirements are categorical will find this account insufficient, 'for he wishes to find something like the connection Kant had in mind when he spoke of objective necessity'. He concludes that this is to exaggerate the force of moral judgement, and that it suggests wrongly that they can be ignored only on pain of irrationality. By contrast, Railton wishes to claim that such an individual lacks 'fellow-feeling' rather than 'reasoning or deliberating capacities'.[63] That is to say, he fails to be motivated by the relevant objective reasons—they are not reasons for him—but this is not a rational deficiency on his part. It is made clear, however, that this does nothing to undermine the authority of morals, and could do so only on the misguided assumption that 'moral imperatives cannot exist for someone who would not have a reason to obey them'.[64]

Railton concedes that most of the people for most of the time are not wholly unmoved by the suffering of others, and claims that this fact is 'central to the explanation of why morality has emerged as a persistent and important phenomenon in human societies'.[65] This latter point is fundamental to Railton's account, for it is his aim to treat moral obligation as a 'social creature', a notion which 'does not sensibly apply apart from developed patterns of behaviour'.[66] Hence: '(i)n order that agents be under obligations to one another…there must be a backdrop of social institutions, expectations, and sanctions', and if

---

[61] 'Moral Realism', p. 203.

[62] 'Reply to David Wiggins', p. 322. Railton concedes that this does not apply to lies which are 'typically harmless'.

[63] 'Reply to David Wiggins', p. 322. Compare Foot who claims that 'the man who rejects morality because he sees no reason to obey its rules can be convicted of villainy but not of inconsistency', 'Morality as a System of Hypothetical Imperatives', p. 310.

[64] 'Moral Realism', p. 203. Compare: 'On the one hand, morality has non-hypothetical authority, so that moral judgments can apply even to those who lack any contingent motivation to follow them; on the other hand, no-one has succeeded in explaining this authority by showing that failure to be responsive to moral considerations is necessarily a form of practical irrationality. Progress in treating the normative authority of moral discourse depends, in my view, not on establishing an inescapable conceptual or rational necessity, but on understanding the free *aspiration* of our moral practices. Stevenson's identification of the "magnetism" of moral discourse is quite apt—we should be looking for an attractive pull rather than an unavoidable push', 'Précis of Facts, Values, and Norms', p. 321.

[65] 'Reply to David Wiggins', p. 322.

[66] 'What the Non-Cognitivist Helps Us to See', p. 295.

we accept this, then 'we can see also how it could almost always be the case that when an individual genuinely is under an obligation, he will have a reason—based upon both external sanctions and internalized motives and sanctions—for carrying it out'.[67] Railton concedes that there is no guarantee that moral evaluation will always be accompanied by appropriate motivation, and that this will strike the Kantian as problematic. He suggests, however, that we should be wary of 'establish[ing] in moral theory a connection with motivation stronger than anything we encounter in actual moral experience', and allow for the fact that 'people we rather uncontroversially call rational do not always appear to find in moral evaluation regulative reasons'.[68]

2.7 WIGGINS ON RAILTON

Railton seeks 'an a posteriori account of the origin, nature, and function of moral discourse and practice',[69] and believes that we can best address these issues by working at the level of social science. His methodological stance rules out the possibility of settling the relevant issues by a priori means, but his investigations lead him in the direction of a form of moral realism which promises to accommodate moral facts 'without worrisome ontological expansion', and to solve the epistemological problem of how we gain access to those facts.[70] The result is a form of expansive scientific naturalism in the sense that moral properties are shown to be reducible to properties which pull their weight within some empirical science,[71] the social and psychological sciences being the acknowledged and appropriate prototype. So, moral facts are reduced to 'complex social-psychological phenomena', and the aim is to show how the relevant phenomena 'may bring into being in individuals a notion of obligatoriness that will present itself to them as objective and independent of their personal inclinations'. This reduction is intended to *vindicate* our moral practices rather than to expose them as a sham. For they have developed in response to 'the enhancement of human well-being in a social setting'. It is the connection between morality and human well-being which is said to give us a reason for taking morality seriously,[72] although Railton concedes that it is a possible objection to this brand of moral realism that it 'may not make morality serious enough'.[73]

---

[67] 'What the Non-Cognitivist Helps Us to See', p. 295.
[68] 'What the Non-Cognitivist Helps Us to See', p. 297.
[69] 'Reply to David Wiggins', p. 316.
[70] 'What the Non-Cognitivist Helps Us to See', p. 280.
[71] 'Reply to David Wiggins', p. 315.   [72] 'Reply to David Wiggins', p. 325.
[73] 'Moral Realism', p. 164.

Bilgrami would say that we fail to make morality serious enough if we deny that there are evaluative properties in the world which make normative demands on us, and he implies that the expansive scientific naturalist lacks the resources for defending such a position. Railton is happy to allow that there are evaluative properties in the world which make normative demands on us, and he believes that his own position provides the best way forward for one who seeks to accommodate the required normative element whilst avoiding the metaphysical and epistemological difficulties which arise if that element is located beyond the limits of empirical enquiry. So we must avoid any reference to the cosmic, the transcendental, or the theistic, and bring morality back down to earth.

Wiggins agrees that morality must be brought back down to earth in *this* sense. Furthermore, he concedes that we should be wary of settling the relevant matters by purely a priori means. As he puts it, it is simply a prejudice to suppose that 'any properly philosophical position is, if true, true *a priori*', and grants that we are required to make reference to 'the contingencies of human nature and responses'.[74] He accepts likewise that we must reject the offending conception of a categorical moral requirement, although he denies that this is sufficient to undermine its categorical force.[75] More generally, he has real doubts about whether Railton's approach can yield a morality worthy of its name, and returns us to a version of the 'open question' argument to illustrate the difficulty at hand. His aim here is to capture what he takes to be the real point of this argument, namely, that there is a fundamental difference between 'conceptualizing our experience in a manner that is conditioned by the ethical as such and conceptualizing it in a scientific manner'.[76] More specifically, he tells us that however smooth the transition appears to be between these two modes of understanding, 'it carries us from one sort of thing to a qualitatively different sort of thing', and that it is this qualitative difference 'that is drawn to our attention by the open question argument and stands in the way of the substantive naturalist's succeeding in his programme'. [77] We are reminded of

[74] 'Moral Cognitivism, Moral Relativism, and Motivating Beliefs', p. 79.
[75] See 'Cognitivism, Naturalism, and Normativity: A Reply to Peter Railton', in *Reality, Representation, and Projection*, pp. 306–307. See also McDowell, 'Are Moral Requirements Hypothetical Imperatives?', p. 89. It will be a task of the following chapter to look in more detail at the positive position which arises in the wake of such criticisms.
[76] 'Cognitivism, Naturalism, and Normativity', p. 304.
[77] 'A Neglected Position?', p. 330. A substantive naturalist is someone who 'proposes a semantic interpretation of the concepts in some area of practice or discourse in terms of properties of relations that would "pull their weight" within empirical science', 'Reply to David Wiggins', p. 315. A methodological naturalist 'is someone who adopts an a posteriori, explanatory approach to an area of human practice or discourse, such as epistemology, semantics or ethics' (p. 315). Railton claims to defend substantive naturalism on methodologically naturalistic grounds 'as part of an explanatory theory of what is going on in an area of discourse or practice under study rather than as a piece of "philosophical analysis". The result of such an explanatory theory in ethics might be,

Bilgrami's complaint that the ingredients which figure in the expansive scientific naturalist's account are insufficient to explain what needs to be explained, although we can pre-empt the response that unnecessary dualisms and gulfs are being introduced.

Wiggins begins by considering the kind of synthetic identity claim to which Railton is committed, namely, that such and such a value property V is the same as natural property X. He takes this to amount to the claim that the property V is to be a property discernible by an interest in the ethical as such and the property X is to be a property which pulls its weight within some empirical science.[78] This leads to a discussion of what more can be said about the difference between an interest in the ethical and an interest in what is natural in the defined sense, and we are told that the only way to characterize an ethical interest is by reference to the proper response to the value in question. This will be a response of engagement, and '[t]his will not be the response of merely believing item x to have value V but the response of *finding V in x*'. Wiggins continues:

> If a value has *qua* moral or aesthetic to have some connection with feeling (the particular feeling depending on the particular value), then, in the cases where feeling connects with will, finding the value in x must have some however indirect connection with the will. On the other hand, none of this, neither the point about the response being one of engagement nor any point about the however indirect connection with the will, has to hold of the purely empirical interest that descries this or that natural property. [79]

For Wiggins then, an interest in the ethical is an interest in the values to which we respond in a moral context. As he puts it elsewhere, it is an interest 'that gives us the property V'.[80] The claim seems indisputable and Railton would accept it. Second, we are told that our response to value is engaged. It is engaged in the sense that it involves finding value in things and being motivated accordingly. The idea that our response to value is engaged in this sense is familiar from Bilgrami, and Railton says enough to suggest that he would likewise agree. All three of our protagonists would grant that our practical interactions with value are to be distinguished from what goes on when we reflect upon these interactions. That is to say, they allow that we can think about what is at issue when we are engaged in this manner. Wiggins captures this point by distinguishing between engagement in first-order ethical thinking and issues *about* such thinking.[81]

for example, a synthetic identity claim identifying a moral property with some complex natural property' (p. 316).

[78] 'A Neglected Position?', p. 331.
[79] 'A Neglected Position?', pp. 331–332.
[80] 'A Neglected Position?', p. 333.
[81] *Ethics: Twelve Lectures on the Philosophy of Morality*, p. 322. It is in the context of making this distinction that we can appreciate Railton's response to the objection that it is wrong-headed to treat moral inquiry as continuous in method with empirical science: 'Whatever morality is,

So the idea that we can reflect upon the question of value is not in dispute. However, Wiggins wishes to question the possibility of taking an exclusively scientific approach in this context. We have been told already that the thinking we are reflecting upon is engaged in the sense that it involves finding value in things and being motivated accordingly. The claim now is that our reflection upon these responses must likewise be engaged and 'participative'. It must be so in the sense that it 'leaves intact all the resources and all the commitments' of the first-order thinking it seeks to interpret,[82] and concerns itself with the 'full gamut of valuational considerations that actually weigh with real life moral agents'.[83] There are two ideas here. First, our thinking about what is at issue when we engage with value at a first-order level requires that we operate with the concepts and commitments which are presupposed at this level of interaction. Second, we must operate with *all* of the relevant concepts and commitments. The first idea seems to amount to the claim that we can reflect upon our subject-matter only by utilizing the concepts and commitments which define it—or to make it sound even more indisputable, that we can talk about our responses to value only by talking about our responses to value. We are to suppose, however, that this second-order thinking will involve a critical appraisal of the relevant concepts and commitments, and it is not ruled out that some of them will be undermined in the process. This latter point would be emphasized by someone like Railton given his wish to identify and to eradicate the errors which can befall us in this context—errors he takes to be inevitable if we move beyond his own preferred naturalistic parameters.

Wiggins has similar critical aspirations, and finds one such error in the assumption that the question of value is to be tackled in exclusively scientific terms—an assumption which is said to preclude us from satisfying the required theoretical aim.[84] Railton's social scientific approach is a target in this context, although we shall see that Wiggins has reservations about whether this particular proposal is undermined. We are told that the scientist operates with a very different ideal of understanding from that which is—and ought to be—operative when we tackle the question of value. This scientific ideal is said to be 'clinical',[85] 'neutral',[86] and reductive, and we are to suppose that it

---

they argue, it is *not* an empirical theory of anything—morality's character and methods belong to practical rather than theoretical reason. I believe that such criticisms run together things we *do* with moral language—express commitment, claim authority, guide action, exert sanctions—with what moral claims literally *say* such that moral discourse could sustain such uses', 'Précis of Facts, Values, and Norms', p. 429.

[82] *Ethics*, pp. 323–324.
[83] 'A Neglected Position?', p. 333.
[84] 'A Neglected Position?', p. 333.
[85] 'A Neglected Position?', p. 333.
[86] *Ethics*, p. 318.

is perfectly in order as far as the proper objects of scientific investigation are concerned. The worry, however, is that it is not appropriate for all modes of enquiry, and Wiggins objects that its application to the question of value has the effect of severing us from the very practices and responses we are seeking to comprehend—practices and responses which 'give us the value V'. It is in this sense that an interest in the ethical 'carries us to a qualitatively different sort of thing'.

All of this helps us to explain what it could mean to treat values as objects of detached observation in a problematic sense. For the point is not simply that we must achieve the critical distance required if we are to be in a position to reflect upon the question of value, but, rather, that we must do something which frustrates the possibility of satisfying this theoretical aim. That is to say that we must detach from *value*. So treating values as objects of detached observation in this sense involves treating them scientifically, and such treatment has the effect of removing them from the picture. Should we accept this implication? We can surely allow that part of the explanatory ground can be covered in social scientific terms. Take, for example, Bilgrami's social scientist. He can study at least some of the valuational considerations that actually weigh with real life agents, albeit agents who remain unconcerned with specifically moral matters. Does his approach count as detached? And does it involve a detachment from value? Bilgrami grants that there is a sense in which such an approach is less detached than that of the natural scientist. As he puts it, 'one looks at the world with more practical engagement when one sees something not merely as H_2O but as an opportunity'. We are to suppose then that the social scientist's approach precisely *is* engaged in the required sense, for he is operating with the concepts and commitments which are appropriate to the level of response he is seeking to comprehend. Bilgrami insists, however, that there is no properly normative element in this picture. As he puts it, it is constructed out of a normative void.

The point is well taken as far as this particular brand of social-scientific investigation is concerned, but what of Railton's social scientist? Is he not concerned with even more of the valuational considerations that actually weigh with real life agents, moral agents to boot? And does this not grant him the right to be able to accommodate just the kind of normative element which is said to be missing from the aforementioned social-scientific picture of the practical domain? There are two important questions here and they are related. First, is it not odd to suppose that a social scientist should be barred from studying a mode of practical engagement that is central to human existence? Second, is there any justification for supposing that his approach precludes the possibility of meeting this aim? The limitation is inevitable on the assumption that moral value eludes the perspective of the social scientist, but there is a clear enough sense in which Railton is offering an account thereof, and Wiggins is prepared to grant that the 'open question' argument 'appears empty or captious when it is directed against such a proposal'.[87] We shall see, however, that this concession goes hand in hand with a reluctance to describe the proposal as genuinely social scientific.

So there is a question about how Railton's proposal is to be understood, and, in particular, how we are to interpret the force of the claim that moral properties are reducible to 'complex social-psychological phenomena'.[88] Wiggins worries that the envisaged reduction has the effect of squeezing moral properties out of the picture, hence: 'When the naturalist reconstructs moral predicates, I suspect that he loses hold of moral properties altogether.'[89] Railton retorts that the reconstruction offers the best way of vindicating their reality, and that anything more—like, for example, a claim to the effect that they are *sui generis* or 'qualitatively different'—serves simply to reintroduce the problematic dualisms and gulfs this proposal is intended to avoid. Nevertheless they share common aims, and, terminology notwithstanding, arrive at very similar positions. Witness Railton:

> Where Wiggins and I do seem to disagree, in a way that puzzles me and makes me fear I am simply missing something, is that, while I believe an appropriate naturalistic reduction can furnish essential ingredients for this sort of vindicative account of morality, Wiggins appears to think that reduction stands in the way of vindication and that treating moral properties as *sui generis* somehow helps. In particular, he concludes his discussion by remarking that treating moral properties as *sui generis* helps to explain the notion of obligation and to promote movement along the road to 'objective vindication'.
>
> Yet a reductionist of my sort can say everything Wiggins says about how obligation is realized in social practices through the internalization of norms. And a reductionist of my sort can say everything Wiggins says about the ways individuals draw meaning and significance from the social practices with which they indentify, in such a way that they may have grounds for action in accord with internalized norms but contrary to personal inclination. Of course, my sort of reductionist cannot capture Kant's or Wittgenstein's idea of obligation without some deflation. But Wiggins, too, is deflationary in this regard—as I think any sensible account must be.[90]

---

[87] 'Cognitivism, Naturalism, and Normativity', footnote 6. He adds the following important caveat: 'But, if that is how things appear, it will be salutary to notice how breezily that proposal overlooks the claim of a more deontological or normative conception of goodness and badness in acts. The proposal simply ignores the powerful idea that there are some acts one must have no part in, unless somehow forced to do so.'

[88] 'Reply to David Wiggins', p. 325.

[89] 'Cognitivism, Naturalism, and Normativity', p. 311.

[90] 'Reply to David Wiggins', p. 325.

Wiggins is open to the possibility of a reconciliatory move and suggests that the scientific interest could 'try to *join forces* somehow with the interest that gives us the property *V*'. Crucially, however, he tells us that:

> Where the two ways of thinking are *combined*, what we should really anticipate is the humanization of social science, the abandonment of all ideals of reduction, and then the consequential replacement of a clinical or scientific ideal of understanding by a different, more participative (however coolly participative) one.[91]

He continues:

> When the social scientist embraces *this* ideal in his study of morality...the inquiry that results will be interestingly dissimilar to any modern social science. In honour of Hume, we might call it a *moral* science. The first task of such a science must be to anatomize the unreconstructed character of what we have got in morality and how that evolved. There will be a presumption, as there is in Hume, against consequentialism. This new inquiry may supplement morality with speculations that will organize our practices and sentiments and enable us to understand them better. It can interest us in the question whether there are alternatives to our actual practices. But always it begins from the inside; and when it redescribes, it does not reduce. If this inquiry is to be continuous with moral philosophy, then, where it departs from the phenomenology of our practices, well, the presumption is that it will have failed. For the link with interpretation will have been severed.[92]

Railton believes that the social scientist can tackle the question of value, and that we exceed his parameters at the cost of courting unnecessary and problematic cosmic excesses—values become 'intolerably odd'. Wiggins and Bilgrami object that the programme fails and that we can tackle this question aright only by transcending such an approach. Wiggins takes issue with its reductive constraints—constraints which, from Railton's point of view, must be in place if we are to avoid succumbing to the aforementioned excesses. As Railton sees it then, his own preferred picture can be described as impoverished and reductive only in the innocuous sense that it leads us away from unnecessary metaphysical inflation. The implication here is that he precisely *can* lend justice to the phenomenology of our practices and do exactly what is required if we are to be moral scientists/philosophers in Wiggins's preferred sense. Wiggins remains doubtful on these scores and it is in this context that he identifies two related senses in which Railton is committed to a picture which is impoverished and reductive in a more problematic sense. First, there is a presumption in favour of consequentialism. Second, although the notion of well-being in terms of which it is defined 'promises to pull its weight in a social theory', it is doubtful that it can get us all the way to the idea of moral obligation. This is what he says:

[91] 'A Neglected Position?', p. 333.   [92] 'A Neglected Position?', p. 333.

To do *A* may promote well-being as naturalistically specified. But it is an open question—indeed doubly open—whether it is indeed obligatory. First doubt: is the naturalistic version of well-being something we fully recognize as the proper object of all our striving? Secondly, can one here get from statements about it to statements of right and wrong? Contrast Hume's way: one goes directly from the object as it affects one's moral judgement—and *sometimes* there is no room (in Hume's view, at least) for any other judgement about that object.[93]

We can agree that Railton's position carries a presumption in favour of consequentialism, albeit a version which promises to be acceptable to both Hume and to Wiggins. It is tempered by a preparedness to grant the 'internalized motives' which spring up once the relevant social patterns of behaviour have developed, and Railton makes it quite clear that he is happy to exploit the valuational considerations which are presupposed in 'Hume's way'.[94] We know also that his notion of well-being is to be distinguished from traditional utilitarian conceptions thereof, and that he endorses a pluralistic approach in which several goods—happiness, autonomy, solidarity, respect, and so forth—are accorded intrinsic, albeit non-moral, value. On the face of it then, this naturalistic version of well-being is a plausible contender for something we could fully recognize as the proper object of all our striving, and, notwithstanding Railton's use of the term 'non-moral' in this context, we can see how we might get from statements about it to statements about right and wrong.

2.8 CONCLUSION

Where does this leave the expansive scientific naturalist? We have considered some proposals which fall within the ambit of scientific investigation, and which fail to accommodate a properly moral conception of value. Bilgrami's social scientist can be criticized on this score, as can any position which operates from within the aforementioned Hobbesian constraints. Railton's position promises to rectify the relevant deficiencies, it is motivated by a desire to avoid 'worrisome ontological expansion', and we are encouraged to suppose that this constraint can

[93] 'A Neglected Position?, pp. 335–336, 'Cognitivism, Naturalism, and Normativity', p. 312.

[94] Railton exploits Hume to his own explanatory purposes in 'Précis of Facts, Values, and Norms', and ends the paper with words that could have been written by Wiggins: 'In a final essay, I argue that we can make a case against dismissing our aspirations as so much self-serving ideology, but only if we philosophers roll up our sleeves and develop an empirically respectable vindicatory explanation of our moral thought and practice. Hume, I believe, thought he had done this in the *Treatise* when he wrote somewhat hyperbolically in its Conclusion: "It requires but very little knowledge of human affairs to perceive, that a sense of morals is a principle inherent in the soul, and one of the most powerful that enters into the composition. But this sense must certainly acquire new force, when reflecting on itself, it approves those principles from whence it is deriv'd, and finds nothing but what is great and good in its rise and origin" (III.3.vi)', p. 432.

be met only by working from within scientific parameters. Wiggins worries that these parameters preclude the possibility of satisfying the required aim, although he is prepared to allow that Railton has exceeded them in all but name. It is in this context that he talks approvingly of the 'humanization' of social science, the implication being that such an approach can accommodate the very values which, from the perspective of Dewey's supernaturalist, are fated to be 'destroyed'. Nevertheless, Wiggins identifies aspects of the position which tell against such an interpretation, and which suggest that the offending deficiencies remain.

Railton's wish to avoid 'worrisome ontological expansion' is to be applauded, but it can generate proposals which end up destroying what needs to be explained. This suggests that reduction is no less worrisome than expansion, and that expansion may be precisely what is needed if the required explanatory work is to be completed. It remains open that Railton has conceded this point, and that his reductive terminology admits of a perfectly innocuous interpretation—one which implies not that moral properties must be reduced to *something else*,[95] but, rather, that they must be comprehended in a manner which avoids the dualisms and gulfs which arise when we are tempted to 'assert the existence of a supernatural or transcendental Realm of Being'.[96] It is this latter temptation, we can imagine Railton saying, that brings in its wake a problematic *something else*, and the point of reduction is simply to fend off these illegitimate forays into speculative metaphysics. Talk of a transcendental Realm of Being, pejorative capitalizations notwithstanding, should not mislead us into thinking that this move is bound to be philosophically disastrous, nor indeed, that we know exactly what it means. After all, Wiggins has committed the offending sin if the boundaries of nature are to be monopolized by science, and Railton is similarly implicated if he has transcended these boundaries in all but name. This latter claim seems outrageous as it stands, although it is less obviously so than the suggestion that Wiggins is a closet expansive scientific naturalist. The alternative is to suppose that Railton's position is more properly scientific, in which case we must conclude either that it fails to do justice to the relevant phenomena or that Wiggins has succumbed to unnecessary and problematic cosmic excess. This latter conclusion is vindicated if there are good reasons for insisting upon the truth of scientism. If there are not, then we must take seriously the possibility of moving in a non-scientific direction, leaving it open that the resultant position remains consonant with Railton's implicit if not professed aims. It is the task of the following chapter to defend such a move, and to spell out the details of the form of naturalism which emerges in its wake.

---

[95] Compare Wiggins: 'In place of vindication by reduction or vindication by identification with natural properties, what I suppose value properties or putative value properties might stand in need of is simply vindication', 'A Neglected Position?', p. 335.

[96] John Herman Randall, 'Epilogue: The Nature of Naturalism', in *Naturalism and the Human Spirit*, ed. Yervant H. Krikorian (New York: Columbia University Press, 1944), p. 358.

3

Expansive Naturalism II

3.1 INTRODUCTION

Railton brings some important insights to the philosophy of value. He is right to look for a plausible synthesis of the empirical and the normative, and to object that we fail on this score if values remain 'intolerably odd'. We fail likewise by remaining insensitive to empirical fact, and we do this when we ignore the connection between moral norms and their effects on human interests. So morality must be 'humanized' to this degree at least, and we must acknowledge also that the moral point of view is a human point of view. He is right also to encourage us to take seriously a form of value realism, albeit one which promises to sidestep the difficulties which have led so many philosophers to view such a position as a non-starter.

The question of what counts as a non-starter is both fundamental and unclear, but we can agree with Railton that a position would stand accused on this score if the values it postulated turned out to be intolerably odd. It is familiar from chapter 1 that this response is unhelpful as it stands, for what counts as intolerably odd—or 'supernatural' and 'spooky' to use the more common terms of abuse—is determined by one's philosophical commitments, and these commitments may themselves be open to question. Railton holds that it would be intolerably odd to suppose that moral values are 'cosmic', and that they fall into this category when, for example, they are grounded in the will or character of a deity. He objects that such a position leads to 'worrisome ontological expansion' and we are led to suppose that the human connection is lost.

These worries are not obviously motivated by a commitment to scientism. The point is, rather, that a move in a cosmic direction threatens to do no more than to saddle us with a further realm of being which has no obvious relevance to the issues at hand. We are asserting 'dualisms and gulfs', failing to face the facts, and losing the human connection to boot. The objections are familiar, and we shall see that they are taken seriously by those naturalists who take issue with scientism. Railton's position *can* be interpreted in a manner which takes him to be engaged in a similar enterprise to that of Wiggins. Thus understood, the point is to 'humanize' morality in the aforementioned ways, albeit without any implication that moral properties are to be squeezed out of the picture in favour of something more properly scientific and respectable—as if they are too intolerably odd as they stand. The alternative—equally compelling in the light of some of Railton's professed aims and terminology—is to conclude on his behalf that this is precisely what we must do, in which case we are left with Wiggins's worry that the required synthesis of the normative and the empirical has been lost—moral properties have been reduced to something else. We must therefore look more closely at the kind of non-scientific naturalism towards which Wiggins is gesturing, doing so with a preparedness to allow that it is not so far removed from Railton's considered viewpoint. I shall refer to the position as expansive naturalism.

The expansive naturalist seeks a middle way between reductive naturalism and supernaturalism. Reductive naturalism incorporates scientific naturalism and the expanded varieties discussed in chapter 2; supernaturalism stands as a placeholder for the kind of position which involves ontological expansion of a 'worrisome' kind. We are to suppose then that the expansion under current consideration is not worrisome, and hence, that the entities which are being introduced into our ontology are not intolerably odd. The further claim is that they could appear to be so only to one who continues to insist that reductive naturalism and supernaturalism constitute the only available options. The expansive naturalist seeks to expose this assumption as an ideological prejudice, for he believes that there are no good reasons for insisting that the scientist has the monopoly on the contents of the natural world, and that anything which cannot be comprehended in this manner must be banished from our ontology or located in a further realm which is supernatural in the aforementioned pejorative sense. The question of what he takes himself to have shown is unclear. There need be no implication that expansive scientific naturalism has been decisively refuted—understandably so, given that the limits of this position are so unclear. Rather, the point is to show that a concession to irreducibility—for some phenomena at least—does not pose the threat envisaged by the expansive scientific naturalist, that it could appear to do so only on scientistic assumptions, and that these assumptions are not mandatory. It is likewise unclear where this leaves the question of supernaturalism, but the general consensus—familiar from what has been said already—is that the position stands to be rejected. This may well be so on a suitably narrow and needlessly problematic understanding of what it amounts to. I shall suggest, however, that the situation is rather more complex, and that the expansive naturalist's approach offers a possible vindication of such a position. It is my eventual aim to extend the strategy to positions which take us in a theistic direction, but this is to pre-empt the move that stands to be exploited by Railton's cosmic foe, and there is work to be done before we consider such a possibility.

3.2 WIGGINS, MCDOWELL, AND EXPANSIVE NATURALISM

The expansive naturalist seeks to defend the idea that moral properties are *sui generis*, and to dispose of any difficulty which might be thought to accompany such a position. The difficulty is clear enough to Railton, and he insists that irreducible moral properties are intolerably odd. He expresses serious doubts about whether they could be taken seriously in the conduct of our lives, describes the offending approach as 'anti-reductionist' and 'non-naturalist', and implies that it is an idle substitute for genuine enquiry.[1] We are to suppose then that it is on the same level as those which have undertakings in the noumenal world or Plato's heaven. So there are two related senses in which the offending approach can be described as 'non-naturalist', both of which suggest that this is an unambiguous term of abuse: first, it stands opposed to naturalistic enquiry, which latter has a proper title to be genuine; second, it is focused upon (non-natural) properties which exceed the limits of such enquiry. It follows that irreducible moral properties exceed the limits of naturalistic enquiry, they are the products of idle speculation, and are not to be taken seriously in the conduct of our lives. Ergo, the properties with which we engage at the level of ordinary moral thought and talk are neither irreducible nor non-natural, and we can comprehend them only by adopting an approach which is neither anti-reductionist nor non-naturalist.

The expansive naturalist is happy to describe his own approach as anti-reductionist and non-naturalist in one sense of these terms. As he sees it, however, such an approach, rather than taking us *beyond* the properties with which we engage at the level of ordinary moral thought and talk, is that which guarantees proper contact with them and thereby the resources for meeting the required explanatory demands. The further claim is that the reductive treatment offered by the expansive scientific naturalist cannot guarantee such contact, and that his explanatory pretensions are therefore compromised. His worry then is that the expansive scientific naturalist has failed to make a genuine advance upon the ('intolerably odd') position under attack, and that the criticisms he directs towards approaches of the non-naturalist and anti-reductionist variety apply equally if not more appropriately to his own. So the expansive naturalist's approach counts as anti-reductionist and non-naturalist in the sense that he denies that moral properties can be reduced in the manner demanded by the expansive scientific naturalist. However, he denies that they are cosmic or intolerably odd. Rather, they are part of the natural world—albeit a world whose limits exceed scientific parameters—and can be comprehended as such provided that we grant the possibility of

---

[1] See Peter Railton, 'Reply to David Wiggins', in *Reality, Representation, and Projection*, ed. John Haldane and Crispin Wright (Oxford: Oxford University Press, 1993), p. 325.

non-scientific modes of comprehension. The position is familiar from Wiggins, and it is spelled out further by McDowell.

McDowell's starting-point is the question of whether there is sense to be made of the idea that values are objective, his aim being to undermine the 'metaphysically disparaging attitude to values'[2] which is to be found in the work of J.L. Mackie. His focus in this particular paper is the case of aesthetic value, but the relevant points can be generalized. According to the offending line of thought, a property is objective if it is 'part of the fabric of the world'. Such properties can be understood 'without essential reference to their effects on sentient beings',[3] and they provide the focus of scientific enquiry, scientific enquiry being 'a pure mode of investigation of the world, uncontaminated in itself by relativity to anything local or parochial'.[4] There would be something very weird, McDowell claims:

> [a]bout the idea of a property that, while retaining the 'phenomenal' character of experienced value, was conceived to be part of the world as objectively character-ized. It would be as if we tried to construct a conception of amusingness that was fully intelligible otherwise than in terms of the characteristic human responses to what is amusing, but nevertheless contrived somehow to retain the 'phenomenal' aspect of amusingness as we experience it in those responses. But the phenom-enology of value experience sets up this strain only if we insist on interpreting it in terms of a conception of the world as objective in the sense I have sketched.[5]

The issue then is whether, and in what sense, values are objective. Railton is anxious to defend such a conception, and seeks to do so in a manner that avoids the accusation that they are intolerably odd. The charge of intolerable oddness lies at the heart of McDowell's concerns, and he wishes likewise to undermine the idea that objective values stand accused on this score. But whereas Railton thinks that we can meet this aim only by viewing them in scientific terms, McDowell holds that it is the imposition of such terms which generates the difficulty. It does so, he argues, because an exclusively scientific conception of objectivity fails to accommodate those properties in the world an understanding of which requires 'essential reference to their effects on sen-tient beings', and evaluative properties fall into this category.

Let it be said immediately that Railton is not confined to properties which are 'objective' in Mackie's sense if this is intended to imply that he is working

---

[2] 'Aesthetic Value, Objectivity, and the Fabric of the World', in *Mind, Value, and Reality* (Cambridge, Mass.: Harvard University Press, 1998), p. 117. Mackie's attitude finds expression in his *Ethics: Inventing Right and Wrong* (Harmondsworth: Penguin, 1977) culminating in the familiar Argument from Queerness.

[3] 'Aesthetic Value, Objectivity, and the Fabric of the World', p. 114. McDowell is discussing Mackie's conception of objectivity, and the phrase 'part of the fabric of the world' comes from Mackie.

[4] 'Aesthetic Value, Objectivity, and the Fabric of the World', p. 119.

[5] 'Aesthetic Value, Objectivity, and the Fabric of the World', pp. 115–116.

at the level of natural science. Furthermore, there is a clear enough sense in which he concedes that an understanding of values as properties in the world requires essential reference to their effects on sentient beings. At least, this is so if one of the points of such a concession is to allow that values are things we care about and which motivate us to act, and we have seen that Railton is adamant that this point be accommodated lest we retreat in a problematic cosmic direction. We know also, however, that Wiggins is sceptical about whether he succeeds on this score.

The idea that our understanding of values as properties in the world requires essential reference to their effects on sentient beings suggests that values are a distinctive kind of property, and hence, that not all properties in the world are to be understood in this way. We are to suppose also that their distinctiveness in this respect has something to do with the role played by the subject who is apprehending them as such—the subject who cares about these values and is motivated to act accordingly. Wiggins and McDowell exploit an analogy with secondary qualities in this context. Wiggins reminds us rightly that it is an *analogy*, and that there is no suggestion that values and secondary qualities and our respective responses to them are exactly similar.[6] He claims, however, that:

> [t]here resides in the combined objectivity and anthropocentricity of colour a striking analogy to illuminate not only the externality that human beings attribute to the properties by whose ascription they evaluate things, people, and actions, but also the way in which the quality *by* which the thing qualifies as good and the desire *for* the thing are equals—are 'made for one another' so to speak. Compare the way in which the quality by which a thing counts as funny and the mental set that is presupposed to being amused by it are made for one another.[7]

Wiggins says all of this after having made the point that it can be true both that we desire *x* because we think *x* good, and that *x* is good because *x* is such that we desire *x*, and it is familiar from the previous chapter that his explanation of the second 'because' is that 'such desiring by human beings directed in this way is one part of what is required for there to be such a thing as the perspective from which the non-instrumental goodness of *x* is there to be perceived. So the analogy allows us to make sense of the idea that values exist independently of our responses (compare: we may see a pillar-box as red because it is red). But things *count* as valuable only because there actually exists a perspective from which the value of things can be appreciated ('pillar-boxes *count* as red only because there actually exists a perceptual apparatus [e.g. our own] that discriminates, and learns on the direct basis of experience to group together, all and only the actually red things'[8]).

---

[6] McDowell concedes this point in his 'Values and Secondary Qualities', in *Mind, Value, and Reality*, p. 146.

[7] 'Truth, Invention, and the Meaning of Life', in *Needs, Values, Truth: Essays in the Philosophy of Value* (Oxford: Oxford University Press, 1991), pp. 107–108.

[8] 'Truth, Invention, and the Meaning of Life', p. 107.

Why isn't there an analogous combination of objectivity and anthropocentricity in the properties which count as objective in Mackie's sense? After all, it is true of any property that it *counts* as such only because there are beings capable of responding to it, and even a 'pure mode of investigation of the world' is an investigation nonetheless. Wiggins and McDowell are not simply making the trivial point that the apprehension of properties requires apprehension. Rather, they are seeking to capture a more significant sense in which the categories of colour and value are anthropocentric—one which sets them apart from the properties with are 'objective' in Mackie's sense and which lends justice to the idea that our understanding of them as properties in the world requires essential reference to their effects on sentient beings. Thus, Wiggins tells us that the category of colour is anthropocentric in the sense that it 'corresponds to an interest that can only take root in creatures with something approaching our own sensory apparatus',[9] and that the category of value counts as such by corresponding to an interest that can only take root in creatures with something approaching our own moral sensibility. So Bilgrami:

> Value is more like 'red' than 'square'. If one feels that a congenitally blind subject misses more of the redness of the tablecloth (in knowing merely the wavelength and other such specifications) than the squareness of the table (in knowing merely the geometrical properties of a square), then there is an important sense in which the human subject and its specific kind of visual sensibility is more relevant to the property of being red than it is to the property of being square. Value, too makes an essential reference to the subject, though, obviously, the relevant sensibility here is a moral not a visual one.[10]

A moral sensibility is not a visual one, but it does not follow that the visual (or something akin to it) has no part to play in a characterization thereof. On the contrary, it is fundamental to both Wiggins and McDowell that we are capable of *finding* value in things.[11] So a moral sensibility is 'visual' to this degree at least, but there will be cases where careful deliberative thinking is required before we can respond in the required terms. Furthermore, such responses, whether or not they are the product of such thinking, operate from within a framework which presupposes a variety of background conditions which do not require to be met in the case of colour. Bilgrami concludes on this basis that the anthropocentricity of value may be thought to go much deeper:

---

[9] 'Truth, Invention, and the Meaning of Life', p. 107.

[10] 'The Wider Significance of Naturalism: A Genealogical Essay', in *Naturalism and Normativity*, ed. Mario De Caro and David Macarthur (New York: Columbia University Press, 2010), p. 33.

[11] Mackie is happy to accept this phenomenological claim, but concludes that the appearance is illusory on the ground that values are not part of the (fabric of) the world. See McDowell, 'Aesthetic Value, Objectivity, and the Fabric of the World', p. 112.

The perception of value properties may not be something that we *can* wholly aspire to have speak to us, independent of the context of social and other background factors that shape our perceptions, in a way that we might aspire to with secondary qualities such as red…The relationships between the human subject and the world (including nature) he inhabits have a history and tradition within which his perceptions of the value properties in the world and nature at any given time speak to him and make normative demands. They will necessarily speak therefore in terms that are *contaminated* (I use a strong term such as that here to mark how much the point is supposed to exceed the acknowledgement of the mere theory-*ladenness* of observation in general) by a much richer set of background assumptions, and they may well therefore speak differently to subjects in different social and cultural contexts.[12]

So evaluative properties are not conceivable independently of our sentient responses to them, and these responses will involve certain background conditions which set them apart from our responses to secondary properties. Railton grants the significance of these background conditions,[13] allows also that evaluative properties exist independently of our responses, but continues to insist that they become intolerably odd if divorced from an interest which is social scientific. I have noted already that the expansive naturalist seeks to turn this claim on its head by arguing, to the contrary, that the charge of intolerable oddness is a product of such a focus. We are in a position now to clarify the remaining details of his case.

Let us remind ourselves of how McDowell sees the difficulty. He says:

> It would be as if we tried to construct a conception of amusingness that was fully intelligible otherwise than in terms of the characteristic human responses to

---

[12] 'The Wider Significance of Naturalism', pp. 33–34. See also David MacArthur who proposes that we adopt a 'weak perceptual model' to accommodate our receptivity to normative phenomena. According to this model, there is an element of receptivity in our responsiveness to such phenomena—we find ourselves 'struck by, or subject to, a range of values (e.g. the obvious wrongness of certain acts)'. We also come to see that normative phenomena are '*always already there* whether one knows it or not. Even if normative items are only authoritative for us in so far as we acknowledge them as such, they are not brought into being by fiat'. Finally, 'there is a distinctive form of *objectivity* appropriate to normative facts…The objectivity of normative facts *involves* subjectivity in the sense that such facts are only intelligible from within our practices of evaluating, understanding and reasoning' ('*Naturalizing the Human or Humanizing Nature: Science, Nature and the Supernatural*', *Erkenntnis*, vol. 61, no. 1 (July 2004), pp. 42–43).

[13] The following remarks are telling: 'A further difference, which I will not explore here, is that Wiggins wishes to view moral properties as akin to secondary qualities. In this instance, too, I find myself puzzled at the claim that such treatment helps towards the development of an account of morality that would vindicate its cognitivity. One reason for puzzlement: moral assessments in many areas—perhaps most obviously, in social and political matters—must, if they are to have any title to be taken seriously as claims of objective knowledge, take into account a large number of factors. In such cases (amongst others), it seems to be problematic to view the moral properties as involving a distinctive, judgement-guiding phenomenology' ('Reply to David Wiggins', footnote 20).

what is amusing, but nevertheless contrived somehow to retain the 'phenomenal' aspect of amusingness as we experience it in those responses.[14]

The claim then is that we are trying to construct a conception of value which is fully intelligible otherwise than in terms of the characteristic human responses to what is valuable. McDowell then raises the question of where the phenomenology of value experience fits into this account—a phenomenology which suggests that we experience value in things, that we *find* value in them. If there can be no reference to the way in which we *engage* with value—a move which, from the expansive naturalist's point of view, is necessary if we are to be responding to *value*—then there is going to be a difficulty making sense of this experience. Now the scientific naturalist has at least two responses to this worry.[15] First—and this is Railton's response—he can grant that we find value in things, but insist that it is reducible to properties that pull their weight in some empirical science. Second—and this is Mackie's response—he can say that the phenomenology is misleading. The expansive naturalist objects that, on Railton's approach—assuming that it is not simply a terminological variant upon his own preferred position—we lose our grip upon value. The upshot is that the phenomenology is unaccounted for, and value remains intolerably odd. The details and potential merits of Mackie's position need not concern us here. The important point is that, as the expansive naturalist sees it, it is likewise motivated by a commitment to a conception of objectivity we have no good reason to accept. The further claim is that if we reject this conception, then it becomes possible to take the phenomenology of value experience at face value, and to do so without inviting the relevant metaphysical difficulties. Values are no longer intolerably odd.

3.3 PLATO'S HEAVEN ON EARTH?

Values are no longer intolerably odd because they have been rescued from the framework which forces such a conclusion. They are neither free-floating entities in an inaccessible Platonic heaven, nor are they reducible to properties which pull their weight in some empirical science. Rather, they are part of the natural world—a world whose boundaries are no longer circumscribed by science—and we are capable of appreciating them as such. Are we to conclude that the expansive naturalist has succeeded in combining the wisdom of Plato with the sanity of Aristotle? In order to answer this question, we need to think more carefully about what such a combination could really mean. Our

---

[14] 'Aesthetic Value, Objectivity, and the Fabric of the World', pp. 115–116.

[15] In what follows I shall use the term 'scientific naturalist' to refer also to the expansive scientific naturalist unless this distinction is relevant to the argument at hand.

examination of this issue will allow us to fill in further details of the envisaged position, and to address some of the doubts which may continue to haunt the expansive scientific naturalist.

Let us begin with the wisdom of Plato. Plato's name is a term of abuse for many naturalists, for he is associated with supernaturalism—the kind of position that involves 'unpromising undertakings in the noumenal world or Plato's heaven'.[16] The realm in question is said to be intolerably odd, and the position to be rejected with relief rather than sorrow. It involves a failure to face the facts. The charges are familiar from Railton, and they find expression in Mackie's Argument from Queerness. The target of the argument is moral realism, and we are told that, on such a position, we are committed to postulating 'value-entities and value-features of quite a different order from anything with which we are acquainted', and a special faculty of moral intuition in order to gain access to such entities—a faculty which is 'utterly different from our ordinary ways of knowing about anything else'.[17] So the entities in question are intolerably odd because they are different from anything else with which we are acquainted, and we are forced to postulate an equally odd faculty by means of which to gain access to them.

Railton's expansive scientific naturalist responds to all of this by bringing the relevant entities back down to earth. They are no longer to be situated in a supernatural realm which stands opposed to the natural world. Rather, they are to be naturalized, and they are to be naturalized in social scientific terms. So the wisdom of Plato is called into question by the sanity of the social scientist. Values don't float free in Plato's heaven, they are reducible to natural properties, and natural properties are those which pull their weight within some empirical science. Thus, there is no need to postulate entities of a different order from anything with which we are acquainted, and no need for special faculties of moral intuition.

The expansive naturalist has more time for the wisdom of Plato, and remains unconvinced by the sanity of this naturalistic move. He grants that the sanity of the naturalist is required to give adequate expression to such wisdom, and is happy to borrow Aristotle's name in this context. He believes, however, that the expansive scientific naturalist loses his grip upon value, and hence, that he ends up committing a similar error to that of his platonist rival. He insists also that the Argument from Queerness is not fatal to his own brand of naturalism. The argument suggests that it is problematic to postulate value-entities of quite a different order from anything else with which we are acquainted, and to solve the epistemological problem they bring by introducing a special faculty of intuition which is 'utterly different from our ordinary ways of

[16] John Dupré, 'The Miracle of Monism', in *Naturalism in Question*, ed. Mario De Caro and David Macarthur (Cambridge, Mass.: Harvard University Press, 2004), p. 58.
[17] *Ethics: Inventing Right and Wrong* (Harmondsworth: Penguin, 1977), p. 38.

knowing about anything else'. The expansive naturalist agrees that these moves are problematic if values are situated in a realm beyond the world in which we live and move and have our being, and if our link to this realm is effected by some mysterious faculty of intuition for which there is no defensible epistemology. He insists, however, that values are part of the natural world, and that they *are* different from other things with which we are acquainted. They are different in the sense that they are irreducible to properties which form the focus of scientific interest. So they count as supernatural if 'natural' is taken to be equivalent to 'scientific'. However, they are not supernatural if 'natural' is understood in the expanded sense at issue here—a sense which allows that the boundaries of nature can be expanded beyond scientific parameters to accommodate value. The further claim is that we are capable of engaging with value and gaining knowledge of what is good, bad, right and wrong, and so forth. This way of knowing is different from our other ways of knowing, for it cannot be comprehended in purely scientific terms. However, it is not spookily different. All that it requires is that we have the kind of sensibility which allows us to form an interest in value. This interest will remain irreducibly mysterious to one who insists that there can be no understanding which does not conform to a scientific paradigm. But the expansive naturalist challenges this restriction, and questions the assumption that the contents of the natural world are to be dictated by this paradigm. Thus, he has no need to claim that a moral way of knowing puts us in touch with something out of this world, and that this faculty of intuition—if we insist on describing it as such—is some strange organ which facilitates such contact and which is utterly divorced from our other ways of knowing about things. It puts us in touch with something beyond the world according to science—so its objects are out of the world in this sense. But they are part of the world we inhabit, and the capacity we have to engage with them is continuous with our natural being. It is continuous with our natural being because we are *human* beings, and human beings, unlike, say, cats and dogs, have a moral sensibility.

3.4 ARISTOTLE'S NATURALISM

McDowell spells out this latter thought with the help of Aristotle, albeit an Aristotle who has been rescued from the reading which makes him into an expansive scientific naturalist.[18] On Aristotle's position:

> The thought that the demands of ethics are real is not a projection from, or construction out of, facts that could be in view independently of the viewer's participation in

---

[18] On such a reading, Aristotle is aiming 'to construct the requirements of ethics out of independent facts about human nature. This is to attribute to Aristotle a scheme for a naturalistic

ethical life and thought, so that they would be available to a sideways-on investigation of how ethical life and thought are related to the natural context in which they take place.

The fact that the demands bear on us is just, irreducibly, itself. It is something that comes into view only within the kind of thinking that conceives practical thinking in terms of such demands.[19]

So McDowell's Aristotle grants Wiggins's participative and non-reductive ideal of understanding, and allows that moral demands and thoughts about them have a 'self-standing character'. This might lead one to suppose that we are moving in the direction of platonism,[20] and McDowell is happy to concede as much. He stresses, however, that the relevant form of platonism is perfectly innocuous, and distinguishes it from a more problematic 'rampant' variety. According to rampant platonism, moral requirements involve a 'space of reasons' which is 'autonomous' in the sense that:

[i]t is constituted independently of anything specifically human, since what is specifically human is surely natural (the idea of the human is the idea of what pertains to a certain species of animals), and we are refusing to naturalize the requirements of reason. But human beings must be able to latch on to this inhuman structure. So it looks as if we are picturing human beings as partly in nature and partly outside it.[21]

foundation for ethics, with nature playing an archaic version of the role played by disenchanted nature in modern naturalistic ethics' (*Mind and World* (Cambridge, Mass.: Harvard University Press, 1994), p. 79). So this Aristotle is a naturalist in Railton's sense, assuming that Railton's naturalism is interpreted in the relevant scientific terms. McDowell finds this reading in Bernard Williams's *Ethics and the Limits of Philosophy* (Cambridge, Mass.: Harvard University Press, 1985) and Alistair MacIntyre's *After Virtue* (London: Duckworth, 1981), and claims that it is a 'historical monstrosity'.

[19] *Mind and World*, p. 83.

[20] McDowell uses the lower case to stress that there is no connection with what Plato himself actually said. The point is important when 'platonism' is used in the pejorative terms he is about to set forth, but we are encouraged to think that the sanitized version provides less of an interpretative travesty. Hence: 'I believe it is quite unfair to Plato to represent him as a supernaturalist about reason in this way. Plato is a naturalist of the Aristotelian sort, with a penchant for vividly realized pictorial presentations of his thought' ('Two Sorts of Naturalism' in *Mind, Value, and Reality* (Cambridge, Mass.: Harvard University Press, 1998), p. 177, footnote 19). This point will be fundamental when we move on to the case of God.

[21] *Mind and World*, p. 77. It is important to note that McDowell's criticisms of rampant platonism are not confined to the problems it generates for ethics. Rather, his concern with the idea of responsiveness to reasons has more general application. As he puts it: 'When I resist a restrictive conception of the natural, the point is not to vindicate the idea that we take in more through the senses than the facts accommodated by a scientistic world-view. The point is that the restrictive conception of the natural would prevent us from making sense of the idea of taking in *anything* through the senses—including facts that scientism has no problem with. When I appeal to the Aristotelian conception according to which virtue—a specific responsiveness to reasons—is second nature, the point is to remind ourselves that there is really no tension between the idea of responsiveness to reasons, in general, and the idea of a natural capacity. This recovers a conception that makes it intelligible how experience takes in facts in general—not ethical facts in particular' ('Response to Axel Honneth', in *Reading McDowell on Mind and World*, ed.

We are reminded of Railton's attack upon the idea that moral requirements are cosmic, and McDowell seeks likewise to replace such a picture with one which can allow that the relevant requirements have a bearing upon our moral practices, and can be shown to do so without our having to introduce ingredients which invite the Argument from Queerness. The rampant platonist fails to meet this latter condition, for he insists that our responsiveness to moral requirements is non-natural. It is non-natural not just in the sense that it cannot be comprehended in scientific terms—McDowell stresses above all that it must exceed these parameters. Rather, it is non-natural in the sense that it requires in the subject a mode of intuition which situates him 'partly outside' of nature. McDowell uses the term 'supernatural' in this context,[22] so the claim is that, on the disputed position, our capacity to acknowledge moral requirements requires that we ourselves are partly supernatural. We have a 'foothold in the animal kingdom and a mysterious separate involvement in an extra-natural world',[23] 'our lives are mysteriously split, somehow taking place both in nature and in some alien realm in which reason operates'—'in "Plato's Heaven", perhaps'.[24]

The rampant platonist is applauded for taking issue with the terms assumed by the scientific naturalist, but McDowell contends that he remains within the offending framework. He does so by assuming that the scientist has the monopoly on nature. The upshot is that anything which cannot be comprehended scientifically is pushed beyond the boundaries of the natural world, and there is no prospect for allowing that *qua* natural beings we have the capacity to respond to it. As Mackie puts it, we are saddled with entities of quite a different order from anything with which we are acquainted, and a special faculty of intuition in order to gain access to such entities—a faculty which is utterly different from our ordinary ways of knowing about anything else. We are partly in nature and partly outside of it.

We are returned to the idea that a commitment to an exclusively scientific conception of nature is responsible for generating the conclusion that

---

Nicholas H. Smith (London: Routledge, 2002), p. 301). Compare: 'Moulding ethical character, which includes imposing a specific shape on the practical intellect, is a particular case of a general phenomenon: initiation into conceptual capacities, which include responsiveness to other rational demands besides those of ethics. Such initiation is a normal part of what it is for a human being to come to maturity, and that is why, although the structure of the space of reasons is alien to the layout of nature conceived as the realm of law, it does not take on the remoteness from the human that rampant platonism envisages. If we generalize the way Aristotle conceives the moulding of ethical character, we arrive at the notion of having one's eyes opened to reasons at large by acquiring a second nature. I cannot think of a good short English expression for this, but it is what figures in German philosophy as *Bildung*' (*Mind and World*, p. 84).

[22] *Mind and World*, p. 78.
[23] *Mind and World*, p. 78.
[24] 'Two Sorts of Naturalism', p. 177. We can recall that Railton uses similar vocabulary to describe the Kantian position he seeks to reject.

values—and the requirements they impose upon us—are intolerably odd. In this case, however, the difficulty arises not because we are trying to squeeze these phenomena into a scientific model, but, rather, because we are squeezing nature into such a model and concluding on this basis that we can relate to them only by virtue of possessing a faculty which bears no relation to our natural human being. Now McDowell is happy to allow that we are partly in nature and partly outside of it in one sense, namely, when 'nature' is understood in the narrow sense he is concerned to expand. So he has no issue with this aspect of the rampant platonist's claim. What he takes issue with is the suggestion that the relevant 'non-natural' aspect is utterly divorced from our human being (and our ordinary ways of knowing), and that it provides access to a world which lies beyond the ordinary natural world we inhabit. His aim then is to show that our moral responses are continuous with our natural human being, and to expel any difficulties which might be thought to accompany the idea that values form an irreducible part of the natural world.

The model of human being which McDowell proposes removes any need to see ourselves as 'peculiarly bifurcated'. It is borrowed from Aristotle, and it involves the following conception of the ethical and our relation to it:

> The ethical is a domain of rational requirements, which are there in any case, whether or not we are responsive to them. We are alerted to these demands by acquiring appropriate conceptual capacities. When a decent upbringing initiates us into the relevant way of thinking, our eyes are opened to the very existence of this tract of the space of reasons. Thereafter our appreciation of its detailed layout is indefinitely subject to refinement, in reflective scrutiny of our ethical thinking. We can so much as understand, let alone seek to justify, the thought that reason makes these demands on us only at a standpoint within a system of concepts and conceptions that enables us to think about such demands, that is, only at a standpoint from which demands of this kind seem to be in view.[25]

On this picture, then, the relevant requirements are *sui generis* with respect to scientific naturalist explanation,[26] and we remain blind to them if we adopt the perspective which is characteristic of such an approach. So they have an autonomous status in the sense that 'we are not to feel compelled to validate them from outside an already ethical way of thinking'. However, they are not supernatural, and our capacity to respond to them does not demand 'an occult power, something extra to our being the kind of animals we are'. Rather,

---

[25] *Mind and World*, p. 82.

[26] McDowell claims that, according to the reading he is disputing, Aristotle seeks to validate the relevant requirements by reference to facts about what it would be for a human life to be fulfilling, where the notion of fulfilment can be understood in non-moral terms. Railton's approach comes readily to mind, and McDowell objects that Aristotle's conception of a fulfilling life already involves an irreducibly moral component. Some of my worries about the precise scope of Railton's position suggest that he may be more properly aligned with McDowell's Aristotle, although his terminology suggests otherwise.

this capacity is fundamental to our human nature, and 'ordinary upbringing can shape the actions and thoughts of human beings in a way that brings these demands into view'.[27] This is all spelled out by reference to the idea of second nature,[28]—an idea which is 'all but explicit in Aristotle's account of how ethical character is formed'.[29] Second nature is that by virtue of which we become responsive to reasons, and it is intended to fit:

> any propensities of animals that are not already possessed at birth, and not acquired in merely biological maturation (like, for instance, the propensity to grow facial hair on the part of male human beings), but imparted by education, habituation, or training.[30]

So the propensities we possess at birth or acquire through a process of biological maturation belong to our first nature, and those which are imparted by education, habituation, or training belong to our second nature. Trained dogs have a second nature in this sense, but its manifestations, for example, obedience to an owner's commands, do not place them in the space of reasons. By contrast, practical wisdom belongs to the second nature of human beings, and its acquisition *does* have this effect, for it allows us to think in moral terms and be responsive to the relevant requirements. It follows that the autonomy exhibited by these requirements:

> does not distance [them] from anything specifically human, as in rampant platonism. They are essentially within reach of human beings. We cannot credit appreciation of them to human nature as it figures in a naturalism of disenchanted[31] nature, because disenchanted nature does not embrace the space of reasons. But human beings are intelligibly initiated into this stretch of the space of reasons by ethical upbringing, which instils the appropriate shape into their lives. The resulting habits of thought and action are second nature.
>
> This should defuse the fear of supernaturalism.[32] Second nature could not float free of potentialities that belong to a normal human organism.[33]

---

[27] *Mind and World*, p. 83.

[28] The idea of second nature is exploited by Wiggins in the context of defending Hume's form of naturalism for rather similar purposes. See his 'Categorical Requirements: Kant and Hume on the Idea of Duty', in *Virtues and Reasons: Philippa Foot and Moral Theory*, ed. Rosalind Hursthouse, Gavin Lawrence, and Warren Quinn (Oxford: Clarendon Press, 1995), p. 310.

[29] *Mind and World*, p. 84.

[30] 'Response to Christoph Halbig' in *John McDowell: Experience, Norm, and Nature*, ed. Jakob Lindgaard (Oxford: Blackwell, 2008), p. 220.

[31] It will be a task of the following chapter to look more closely at McDowell's conception of disenchantment.

[32] Compare: 'The point of my appeal to second nature here is simply to help bring out that there is nothing "queer" (as J.L. Mackie claimed) about the idea of a capacity to know what there is a reason to do, if the capacity is understood as a result of being initiated into an ethical community', 'Response to Robert B. Pippin', *Reading McDowell on Mind and World*, ed. Nicholas H. Smith (London: Routledge, 2002), p. 275.

[33] *Mind and World*, p. 84.

And:

> Second nature acts in a world in which it finds more than what is open to view
> from the dehumanized stance that the natural sciences, rightly for their purposes,
> adopt. And there is nothing against bringing this richer reality under the rubric of
> nature too. The natural sciences do not have exclusive rights in that notion; and the
> added richness comes into view, not through the operations of some mysteriously
> extra-natural power, but because human beings come to possess a second nature.[34]

So morality is humanized in the sense that the domain it involves is essentially within reach of human beings. Our capacity to respond to this domain is
a rational capacity which stems from our human nature rather than from any
supernatural addition which gives us a 'mysterious separate involvement in
an extra-natural world'. But nature in this context is not to be comprehended
in the sense assumed by the scientific naturalist, for this sense cannot accommodate the moral, and, when applied to *human* nature, leads to the conclusion that, *qua* human, we are incapable of thinking and acting in moral terms.
The alternative is to expand the notion of human being to incorporate second
nature, and to allow that moral engagement requires nothing more mysterious
than an ordinary, ethical upbringing—an upbringing which, it should go without saying, takes place in the natural world. Once we have arrived at this point
we become *properly* human—we have, if you like, fulfilled our humanity—and
our conception of the natural world is expanded accordingly, for the 'demands
of reason are essentially such that a human upbringing can open a human
being's eyes to them'.[35] We have 'return(ed) to sanity',[36] and there is no longer
any need to be 'spooked' by the very idea of norms or demands of reason.[37]

3.5 BACK TO MORAL REQUIREMENTS

It is easy to think that the idea remains irredeemably weird, and that Plato's
heaven has been brought back down to earth at the cost of making the natural world intolerably odd. The charge is compelling if it is supposed that the
relevant norms or demands of reason 'waft by' in the natural world alongside tables, chairs, and human beings. We would be saddled with a naturalistic
transposition of the rampant platonist position, the only difference being that
there would be alien presences swarming in our midst rather than in some
second, supernatural realm.[38] This is not the picture, for there is no implication

---

[34] 'Two Sorts of Naturalism', p. 192.
[35] *Mind and World*, p. 92.
[36] *Mind and World*, p. 91.
[37] *Mind and World*, p. 95.
[38] Christine Korsgaard interprets the position in these terms, claiming that, according to the
moral realist, 'we have normative concepts because we've spotted some normative entities, as

that the demands of reason are, or are to be modelled on, material objects located in space. They are independent of us in the sense that they are there 'whether we know it or not' and impose demands upon us that we might fail to acknowledge. But reason is not some alien presence which dictates to us from outside our natural attitudes and character. Rather, it provides the shape of the practical intellect we come to possess by virtue of acquiring a second nature, and which gives us reason—*our* reasons—for both acknowledging and resisting the demands to which we become receptive.[39] To put it another way, we acquire the capacity to reason, this capacity transforms our nature, and it also transforms the world in which this transfiguring process takes place—an added richness comes into view.

There is no implication that moral requirements are irresistible, so the expansive naturalist can concede this much to Railton. However, they apply to us even if we ignore them, and we *can* ignore them for reason does not always prevail.[40] Are we irrational in such a situation? Railton is reluctant to draw this conclusion on the ground that a failure to be so motivated is not a rational deficiency. As he puts it, such a person is simply lacking in fellow-feeling, and because of this deficiency the reasons in question are not *his* reasons. Wiggins agrees that such a person has not renounced anything comparable to logic, denying that a commitment to morality is to be founded in anything like the 'narrowly' rational requirement, given that Socrates is a man and all men are mortal, to conclude that Socrates is mortal.[41] Rather, he finds a more fruitful direction to pursue in the Kantian idea that we should aspire to live with rational beings on terms that are worthy of them. Rational beings in this context do not, *pace* Kant, participate in some noumenal realm which stands apart from the natural world. Rather, they are human beings, and the envisaged solidarity is of human beings *qua* human.[42] Wiggins adds that it seems

---

it were wafting by'. On such a position, she continues, 'the world contains a realm of inherently normative entities or truths, whose existence we have noticed, and the business of ethics, or of practical philosophy more generally, is to investigate them further ... We have moral concepts because we have noticed some moral entities in the universe' (*The Sources of Normativity* (Cambridge: Cambridge University Press, 1996), pp. 44–45).

[39] McDowell insists that reason is no 'foreign power ... authoritative over us from outside our natural attitudes and inclinations' ('Two Sorts of Naturalism', p. 176), and that the practical intellect 'does not dictate to one's formed character—one's nature as it has become—from outside. One's formed practical intellect—which is operative in one's character-revealing behaviour—just is an aspect of one's nature as it has become' ('Two Sorts of Naturalism', p. 185). Railton claims likewise that '[p]rogress in treating the normative authority of moral discourse depends ... on understanding the free *aspiration* of our moral practices. Stevenson's identification of the "magnetism" of moral discourse is quite apt—we should be looking for an attractive pull rather than an unavoidable push' ('Précis of *Facts, Values, and Norms*', *Philosophical Studies*, vol. 126 (2005), p. 321).

[40] See Wiggins, 'Categorical Requirements', p. 313.

[41] 'Categorical Requirements', p. 326. Compare McDowell, 'Might There be External Reasons?', in *Mind, Value, and Reality*, p. 107.

[42] 'Categorical Requirements', p. 327. Wiggins's inspiration here is Hume. We might recall a similar focus in Railton.

unreasonable not to allow that reason itself is immanent in the moral practices of those who are united in this respect, grants that we have here an expanded conception of practical reason, and compares it to the 'enlarged' conception of reason that led C.S. Peirce to claim that 'logic itself', even the search for bare plain truth, is 'rooted in the social principle'.[43] Are we to conclude that the requirements of morality can be derived from this expanded conception of practical reason? Wiggins suggests that the claim is plausible provided that the derivation makes a 'manifest detour through considerations that are independently recognized as moral considerations'[44] and which are rooted in our humanity.[45] It is in this way, he claims, that we shall have arrived at a conception of practical reason—Aristotelian in origin—which 'subsumes within itself the ordinary norms of practical reasonableness, norms that both presuppose and involve (as Aristotelian *phronēsis* does, and Kantian practical reason does not) the actual human sentiments'.[46]

The territory is familiar from McDowell and Railton. There are reasons to respect moral requirements, they will fail to move those who lack fellow-feeling, and one commits no logical error in ignoring them. Moral obligation is not acknowledged apart from developed patterns of behaviour—in this respect we can agree with Railton that it is a 'social creature', or as Wiggins put it after Peirce, that practical reason is 'rooted in the social principle'. Crucially, however—and I find it difficult to decide whether Railton concedes this point—the relevant patterns of behaviour can be adequately comprehended only in terms which are irreducibly moral. That is to say that the reason they embody is the reason of those who are already party to the moral practices which find expression in such behaviour and who are motivated by the various considerations which become compelling once these practices take a hold.

Our practical rationality grants us the right to acknowledge the relevant demands and to think carefully about the considerations which tell in their favour. It is in this sense that we have the resources to scrutinize our thinking, albeit from a perspective which is irreducibly moral-involving.[47] McDowell

---

[43] 'Categorical Requirements', p. 329. The quote from Peirce comes from his *Collected Papers* (Cambridge, Mass.: Harvard University Press, 1932), ii, pp. 654–655.

[44] The relevant considerations are those that 'benevolence and its great progeny of other virtues ratify as authoritative'.

[45] McDowell makes a similar point when he rejects the (Kantian) idea that a rational motivation could be spun out of formal requirements without material motivational input ('Two Sorts of Naturalism', p. 196). Compare also James Griffin: 'We have a tendency to think of reasons as transcendent, as commands addressed to a resistant, or, at best, neutral human nature, whereas, on the contrary, they are reasons only because they incorporate a movement of the human will' (*Value Judgement: Improving Our Ethical Beliefs* (Oxford: Oxford University Press, 1996), p. 35).

[46] 'Categorical Requirements', pp. 329–330.

[47] As McDowell puts it, 'there need be no basis for critical scrutiny of one ethical concept except others, and the necessary scrutiny does not involve stepping outside the point of view constituted by an ethical sensibility' ('Projection and Truth in Ethics', in *Mind, Value, and Reality*, p. 162). Compare Charles Taylor who says of this form of evaluation that it is 'deep in a sense,

suggests that this second-order reflection applies not merely to our moral thinking, but also to those of our tendencies which belong to our first nature. As he puts it, we can step back from any motivational impulse we find ourselves subject to—a particular desire, for example—and question its moral credentials. It is in this sense that such reflection 'effects a kind of distancing of the agent from the practical tendencies that are part of what we might call his first nature'.[48] These tendencies no longer have exclusive authority, the subject is in a position to weigh them against other, moral, considerations, and to ask of a particular desire whether it should be pursued or whether it is good to have. She can do this because she is receptive to the requirements of morality, and no longer sees things and other people as mere opportunities for satisfying her desires.

3.6 QUEERNESS, AGAIN

There is no longer any need to be spooked by the idea of norms or demands of reason, but we need to make clear exactly where value fits into the picture, and to eliminate any residual weirdness that might be thought to accompany this aspect of the position. There is a sense in which the demand for an account of where value fits in is misguided, for it suggests that there is a separate issue to be tackled once we have clarified the nature of practical reason, and this leads all too quickly to the idea that values float free from our practices— that they exist in some second, supernatural realm. It should be clear from what has been said that this is not the picture, and that our practices—which embody practical reason—are already irreducibly value-involving. We come to appreciate these values by acquiring a second nature, and they give content to our practices, supplying us with appropriate ends to pursue and obligations to respect. So, for example, we are motivated by kindness, justice, and benevolence, appalled by cruelty and greed, and we shudder at the idea that someone

---

and total in a sense that the other less than radical ones are not. If I am questioning whether smuggling a radio into the country is honest, or I am judging everything by the utilitarian criterion, then I have a yardstick, a definite yardstick. But if I go to the radical questioning, then it is not exactly that I have no yardstick, in the sense that anything goes, but rather that what takes the place of the yardstick is my deepest unstructured sense of what is important, which is as yet inchoate and which I am trying to bring to definition. I am trying to see reality afresh and form more adequate categories to describe it. To do this I am trying to open myself, use all of my deepest, unstructured sense of things in order to come to a new clarity. Now this engages me at a depth that using a fixed yardstick does not. I am in a sense questioning the inchoate sense that led me to use the yardstick. And at the same time it engages my whole self in a way that judging by a yardstick does not. This is what makes it uncommonly difficult to reflect upon our fundamental evaluations' ('Responsibility for Self', in *The Identities of Persons*, ed. Amélie Oksenberg Rorty (Berkeley: University of California Press, 1976), p. 298).

[48] 'Two Sorts of Naturalism', p. 188.

could treat another person as a mere opportunity for satisfying their desires. It is in this sense that values make their demands on us and provide us with the relevant reasons for action, and it is in this sense that we come to find value in things, when, say, we are struck by the cruelty or kindness of a person or an act.

This latter point will strike some as problematic, for although there is no implication that values exist in some second, supernatural realm, there is a question to be raised about the nature of the influence that they have upon us, and, in particular, whether we are, or ought to be, committed to the idea that this influence is causal.[49] McDowell tells us that whereas there is a role for causation in scientific investigation—our conclusions are determined in part by our being causally receptive to the things we investigate—there is no such analogue in ethics.[50] The point is well taken if intended to put to rest some of the erroneous ideas which cloud our judgement in this area. For example, we can deny that values have the potential to interfere with the normal, causal run of things, and that ethical enquiry can license conclusions that pose a threat to the findings of science. We can deny also that we relate to values in just the way that we relate to tables, chairs, and indeed, coloured tables and chairs.

Much of this is familiar from what has been said already, but there is no need to conclude that we should abandon all talk of causation in a moral context. After all, we need to be able to make sense of the idea that values can have a transformative effect upon us, that they can lead us to reappraise what is and ought to be of importance to us, and that when this happens we are supplied with reasons to act. McDowell is happy to concede as much, and makes two important points in this context. First, he denies that the space of reasons is to be contrasted with the space of *causes*, doing so on the ground that such a position rules out the possibility that reasons might be causes. As he puts it, 'We need not see the idea of causal linkages as the exclusive property of natural-scientific thinking.'[51] Second, he is happy to allow that, in responding to reasons, we are being moved by a certain kind of cause. He claims further that the 'reasons can be causes' slogan which is operative here is more properly expressed by saying that '*someone's having a reason* can be causally relevant, for instance to their acting or to their forming a belief'.[52]

[49] Compare Railton: 'The idea of causal interaction with moral reality certainly would be intolerably odd if moral facts were held to be *sui generis*'. He adds in a footnote: 'Or if moral facts were supposed to be things of a kind to provide categorical reasons for action' ('Moral Realism', p. 171).

[50] 'Two Sorts of Naturalism', p. 187.

[51] 'Naturalism in the Philosophy of Mind', in *Naturalism in Question*, p. 92. This makes it clear that the relevant contrast for him is that between the space of reasons and the space of natural-scientific understanding.

[52] 'Reply to Charles Larmore', in *Reading McDowell on Mind and World*, p. 296. Compare Wiggins who denies that his position commits him to the claim that moral properties 'cannot cause anything or that they lie outside time. The goodness of nature of some Samaritan can have

This latter point makes it clear that the task is not the impossible one of explaining how a realm of weird non-spatial entities could be causally efficacious, or, to put it in Mackie's similarly pejorative terms, how such entities could have 'to-be-pursuedness' built into them. The point is, rather, that we can acquire reasons to act, or as Wiggins once put it, that considerations can hold sway. They hold sway when, for example, we are motivated to act courageously or kindly, or when we find reason to intervene in the face of cruelty. Finally, when we do find ourselves in such a situation, we can surely interpret the situation in the manner this mode of description suggests—we are responding to cruelty, the cruelty of the act makes itself manifest, it has an effect on us.[53]

All of this helps to deflect another aspect of the Argument from Queerness, for if we allow that our capacity to respond to value is a rational response, then there is a clear enough sense in which our moral responses *are*, after all, continuous with our ordinary ways of knowing about things. They are continuous with ordinary ways of knowing not simply by virtue of being *human* ways of knowing, but in the sense that they involve the exercise of reason. It should be clear from what has been said that this does not mean that moral reasons are reducible to non-moral reasons, nor that moral ways of knowing are the same as non-moral ways of knowing. So there is a difference between the moral and the non-moral, and one *could* argue that there is something about moral reasons and moral ways of knowing which makes them intolerably odd in comparison with their non-moral counterparts. I hope that I have said enough to temper the force of such a complaint. Alternatively, one could argue that there is something intolerably odd about reasons across the board, although the acceptance of such a position would have to be consistent with the possibility of articulating this form of scepticism. In any case, the idea that *moral* ways of knowing are peculiarly odd would have fallen by the way, and the Argument from Queerness would have been generalized. We would also have a rather worrying route to the conclusion that our openness to anything at all is intolerably odd, at least, this follows if

---

all sorts of effects, for instance. Some people may owe their life to it. Others may owe their life to the example that it set' ('Reply to Roger Crisp', in *Identity, Truth, and Value: Essays for David Wiggins*, ed. Sabina Lovibond and S.G. Williams (Oxford: Blackwell Publishers Ltd, 1996), p. 261).

[53] Compare Hilary Putnam: 'How could there be "value facts"? After all, we have no sense organ for detecting them... Consider the parallel question: "How could we come to tell that people are *elated*? After all, we have no sense organ for detecting elation". The fact is that we can tell that other people are elated, and sometimes we can even *see* that other people are elated. But we can only do so after we have acquired the *concept* of elation... Once I have acquired the concept of elation, I can see that someone is elated, and similarly, once I have acquired the concept of a friendly person, or a malicious person, or a kind person, I can sometimes see that someone is friendly, or malicious, or kind (*The Collapse of the Fact/Value Dichotomy* (Cambridge, Mass.: Harvard University Press, 2002), p. 102).

we accept, as McDowell does, that such openness is irreducibly conceptual. That, however, is another story.

3.7 UNMASKING ILLUSIONS

The expansive naturalist denies that value can be adequately comprehended in the terms dictated by the expansive scientific naturalist, so his approach is anti-scientistic, but it is not anti-scientific. He grants the significance of scientific enquiry, welcomes its role in expanding our knowledge and understanding of things, and applauds it for unmasking some of the illusions which seemed compelling in pre-modern times.[54] One such illusion is said to be the medieval idea that what we now see as the objects of scientific investigation are themselves imbued with meaning—that nature is 'a book of lessons for us'.[55] This idea is going to be important to the following chapter, and need not detain us here. More relevant to our present purposes is the example identified by Railton in a similar discussion of science's unmasking role, namely, the idea that moral requirements have a divine origin. The expansive naturalist agrees that this is an illusion to be unmasked, but denies that the relevant unmasking must proceed in scientific terms on the ground that moral phenomena escape the ambit of scientific enquiry. He allows therefore that science provides just one of several possible routes to knowledge and understanding, objecting that its unmasking pretensions in a moral context give rise to an equally implausible illusion which itself stands in need of unmasking. The illusion in question is that the scientist has the monopoly on ontology and explanation, and the unmasking comes with a rejection of this claim.

So science is to be respected, but not to the exclusion of other modes of enquiry. To return to the example at hand, we must resist the idea that moral requirements are to be constructed from the facts available to scientific investigation, and, more generally, that morality can be adequately comprehended in scientific terms. A rejection of these claims does not imply that scientific investigation has no role to play in moral theory, and the expansive naturalist is happy to concede its significance in this respect. It is allowed, for example, that there are questions to be asked about why people act as they do, why they have certain values or desires, what they need in order to do well and so forth, and that we can answer these questions with reference to 'facts about man and his environment' which remain morally neutral.[56] McDowell takes such enquiry to be pitched at the level of first-natural facts—i.e. facts concerning our biological nature and what we need *qua* beings with the relevant innate propensities. He grants that such

---

[54] See McDowell, 'Two Sorts of Naturalism', p. 181.   [55] *Mind and World*, p. 71.
[56] See McDowell, 'Two Sorts of Naturalism', p. 190.

facts have an important role to play in determining the shape our practical reason comes to assume. In this sense we can allow that our moral concepts would be different if the relevant first-natural facts were different, and that these facts make it intelligible that these concepts are as they are.[57] He claims also that there is room for making appeal to such facts from within the moral thinking which has thereby developed, when, for example, we seek reassurance about our moral practices, and look for a vindication of a more external kind.[58] In such a context, it may well be appropriate to make reference to the fact that morality promotes well-being, and that the values it involves are what we need in order to do well in a sense which is not itself shaped by ethical concerns.[59] McDowell would no doubt grant that an enquiry along these lines can incorporate the kind of social scientific focus which is so important to someone like Railton, and hence that the relevant facts to which we can appeal in this context are not confined to the purely biological.[60] What he denies, however, is that such an approach is sufficient to explain the nature of the practices which can be understood partially by reference to such considerations. In particular, he denies that such theorizing can take us all the way to the idea of moral obligation, and denies therefore that reflection of this kind can give one a moral reason to act.

The objection is familiar from Wiggins, and McDowell develops his argument in a similar direction. He claims that considerations of a (non-moral) kind operate at one remove from the rational will of the morally engaged person.[61] That is to say, they involve a stepping back. Not the stepping back at issue when the morally engaged person reflects upon the requirements of practical reason and subjects them to a critical scrutiny which is irreducibly moral-involving. Rather, it is a stepping back which involves a disengagement from the moral point of view and the concepts it involves. The expansive naturalist objects that this movement has the effect of severing us from the context in which the demands of morality come into view, and that the (non-moral) materials to which we are hereby confined provide an insufficient basis from which to comprehend our moral practices as they are conducted from within. In particular, it can make no sense of the idea that, say, a kind or courageous

---

[57] 'Two Sorts of Naturalism', p. 193.
[58] 'Two Sorts of Naturalism', p. 190.
[59] 'Two Sorts of Naturalism', p. 191.
[60] The social scientist is interested in how we satisfy our biological needs, and will grant that those needs are not dependent upon our social lives and the structures they involve. However, he is concerned also with propensities we have by virtue of being social animals, and is interested not simply in the question of how we satisfy them but why we have them. Are we to conclude that such enquiry exceeds the realm of the first-natural? It does so in the sense that we have gone beyond the purely biological. However, McDowell would deny that the relevant facts count as second-natural in the moral-involving sense with which he is concerned. We might deflate the worry that important distinctions are being progressively blurred by recalling Wiggins's anticipation of the humanization of social science.
[61] 'Two Sorts of Naturalism', p. 191.

act can be worth doing in its own right, and that this provides an adequate justification for so acting.[62] In a context of this kind, the relevant non-moral considerations drop out as irrelevant. As Wiggins puts it, 'one goes directly from the object as it affects one's moral judgement—and *sometimes* there is no room...for any other judgement about that object'.

3.8 CONCLUSION

The expansive naturalist takes himself to have combined the wisdom of Plato with the sanity of Aristotle. He exploits the wisdom of Plato by allowing that there is room within our ontology for value, and lends sanity to this move by granting that values are part of the natural world, albeit a world whose limits are no longer circumscribed by science. Aristotle plays an important role in this context, for his position allows us to make sense of the idea that our response to value is natural, and to do so whilst respecting its *sui generis* character. Such a position involves a concession to the supernaturalist in one respect, for it is agreed that values and our responses to them escape the ambit of scientific enquiry. So values are non-natural in this sense. However, they do not inhabit a second, supernatural realm, and our capacity to engage with them demands nothing extra-human on our part. On the contrary, it requires nothing more than the acquisition of a second nature—an acquisition which grants us the right to view the natural world in value-involving terms, and without which we should cease to be *properly* human.

All of this poses a serious challenge to the expansive scientific naturalist's position. The idea that such a position is the only alternative to speculative metaphysics is undermined, for we now have a non-scientific alternative which promises to be empirically respectable and genuinely explanatory. We have the resources for saying something intelligible about our moral practices, we can do so without severing those practices from our humanity, and we can give due weight to the relevant social scientific facts. So Plato's heaven has been brought back down to earth, but not at the cost of destroying the materials it promised, namely, materials which are irreducibly value-involving, and not at the cost of dispensing with the non-evaluative materials to which the expansive scientific naturalist makes appeal. There is room then for rejecting Randall's claim that the required combination of Plato and Aristotle has been effected only in the practice of scientific enquiry, for the scientific version of this combination is said to be deficient, and an expansive naturalist approach

---

[62] 'Two Sorts of Naturalism', pp. 190–191.

suggests a more satisfactory alternative. If this is right, then nature has become a more inclusive category, and it has become so in a manner which should be acceptable to one who seeks a plausible synthesis of the empirical and the normative without the baggage of worrisome ontological expansion. The question now is whether we can go any further.

4

Enchanted Nature

4.1 NATURE, ENCHANTMENT, AND DISENCHANTMENT

The expansive naturalist grants the significance of scientific enquiry, and applauds the role played by modern science in expanding our knowledge and understanding of things. He insists, however, that there is more to nature than what the scientist can comprehend, and seeks to unmask the scientistic conception of nature as an ideological prejudice. He takes this to amount to a 're-enchantment'[1] of nature, but emphasizes that the enchantment in question is only 'partial'.[2] The further claim is that science has performed a fundamental unmasking role in this context. It has done so in the sense that we no longer take seriously the idea that its subject-matter is 'filled with meaning, as if all of nature were a book of lessons to us'.[3] That is to say, we accept that its subject-matter is 'empty of meaning', that it is 'disenchanted'.[4] We are to suppose that a denial of this claim would amount to a total enchantment of nature, hence the caveat that the envisaged enchantment is merely partial.

There are two ideas at work here. First, the objects of scientific investigation are empty of meaning, and it is a mark of intellectual progress to conceive of them in these disenchanted terms. Second, it does not follow that nature itself is disenchanted, for this conclusion is forced upon us only on the assumption that we accept a scientistic conception of nature, and this assumption is unjustified. So there is room for allowing that nature is enchanted, but it is not enchanted in the way that it would be if nature were a book of lessons to us, and we are to suppose that we view it in these problematic terms when we enchant the objects of scientific investigation. The implication here is that

---

[1] See John McDowell, 'Reply to J.M. Bernstein, in *Reading McDowell on Mind and World*, ed. Nicholas H. Smith (London: Routledge, 2002), p. 298.
[2] John McDowell, *Mind and World* (Cambridge, Mass.: Harvard University Press, 1994), p. 85.
[3] *Mind and World*, p. 71.
[4] *Mind and World*, pp. 70–71.

there are good and bad ways of enchanting nature, and that modern science has prevented us from succumbing to the problematic version of this idea.

The term 'disenchantment' comes from Max Weber, and he introduces it in the context of describing the process of intellectualization and rationalization which arose in the wake of modern science. The meaning of this process, he tells us, is that:

> [w]e are not ruled by mysterious, unpredictable forces, but that, on the contrary, we can in principle *control everything by means of calculation*. That in turn means the disenchantment of the world. Unlike the savage for whom such forces existed, we need no longer have recourse to magic in order to control the spirits or pray to them. Instead, technology and calculation achieve our ends.[5]

It is no part of the expansive naturalist's position that we can control everything by means of calculation if this is taken to mean that we can comprehend all things scientifically, for he denies that the scientist has the monopoly on comprehension, and can accept also that there are limits to scientific comprehension even when it is appropriately directed. This latter concession grants us the right to allow that at least some mysterious, unpredictable forces are operative when we are engaged in scientific research—quantum phenomena being an obvious case in point. However, there are other such forces which the expansive naturalist *is* anxious to reject, namely, those which were postulated prior to the advance of modern science, and which may continue to hold us in thrall so long as we remain impervious to its intellectual lessons. It is in this context, we are told, that appeal is made to 'explanatory factors that are occult or magical factors that are, in a word that is very helpful in this context, supernatural'. The result is that we are thrown into 'the region of darkness... a region whose extent has shrunk for us with the advent of a modern scientific outlook, in the most extreme version of the outlook to nothing at all'.[6]

So the offending forces are occult and magical, and we are to suppose that they are on the same level as all the other supernatural phenomena which were detailed and questioned in chapter 1—gods, demons, ghosts, souls, and so forth. The picture is more complex, of course, for the scientific naturalist holds that the values which figure in the expansive naturalist's ontology warrant inclusion in this problematic category, and it is no part of the position under current consideration that such values are occult and magical. On the contrary, this conclusion is held to be a product of the assumption that the scientist has the monopoly on nature, the implication being that their metaphysical credentials can be challenged on scientific grounds only on pain of begging the question against an alternative and more appropriate mode of enquiry into

    [5] 'Science as a Vocation', in *The Vocation Lectures*, ed. David Owen and Tracy B. Strong, trans. Rodney Livingstone (Indianapolis: Hackett, 2004), pp. 12–13.

    [6] John McDowell, 'Reply to Fink', in *John McDowell: Experience, Norm, and Nature*, ed. Jakob Lindgaard (Oxford: Blackwell, 2008), p. 217.

the nature of their being. This point is going to be important when we look more closely at the grounds for classifying an item as occult or magical, for it may turn out that at least some of the offending items can be vindicated along similar lines to those which have been proposed for the case of value. We are to assume, however, that no such vindication is available for the magical forces at issue here, and we have a possible justification for this claim if it turns out that these forces *can* be challenged on scientific grounds, and that these grounds are sufficient to show that they are intolerably odd.

This seems to be part of what McDowell has in mind, for he suggests that the postulation of such forces was a product of 'pre-scientific superstition'.[7] The implication here is that they did fall within the province of scientific investigation, albeit a primitive version thereof which lacked the explanatory and predictive power of modern science and which is more properly described as a brand of superstition. He claims also that their postulation led to a problematic enchantment of nature—problematic in the sense that the objects of scientific investigation were imbued with a meaning they do not possess. We enchant nature in this problematic way when we approach the movements of the planets or the fall of a sparrow in the way that we approach a text or an utterance or some other kind of action.[8] It is when we do this that we are said to treat nature as a book of lessons.

4.2 THE MAGIC-MAKING GODS

One gloss on the idea that there are magical forces at work in nature is that these forces are the work of the gods. The picture is implicit in Weber's description of the worldview of the 'savage', and it is made explicit in Kenneth Miller's description of our ancestors who 'prayed as children, asking mercy from the gods of darkness, the demons of the night':

> Our gods did magic. They did the work of nature, and they ruled the lives of men. They warmed us some days, and on others they made us shiver. They healed us when they wished, and other times they struck us down with sickness and death. Most of all, they filled a need that all men have, a need to see the world as sensible and complete. Gods filled the voids in nature we could not explain, and they made the world seem whole.[9]

The gods do the work of nature in the sense that they make things happen,[10] and the things they do are determined by whim and mood. Their acts lend

---

[7] *Mind and World*, p. 72.

[8] *Mind and World*, p. 72.

[9] *Finding Darwin's God: A Scientist's Search for Common Ground between God and Evolution* (New York: HarperCollins, 1999), p. 192.

[10] Compare Pierre Hadot: '[Magic] relies originally on the belief that natural phenomena are brought about by invisible powers—gods or demons', *The Veil of Isis: An Essay on the History*

credence to the idea that nature has an underlying purpose, but this purpose remains unknown, and the only thing we can say about the forces which govern the behaviour of the things we observe is that they give expression to the gods' acts. It is in this sense that the gods fill the voids in nature which cannot be explained, and that its workings are to be approached in the way that we approach a text, an utterance, or some other kind of action. We can note also that the gods at issue here are open to manipulation—we pray to them as children, beg for their mercy, and hope that they will give us what we want. So they satisfy their own desires when they act in the world, but they also have the potential to satisfy our desires, assuming that they feel suitably pre-disposed. In this respect they are a lot like us—desiring beings, prone to moods and preferences, and susceptible to flattery and persuasion.[11]

At one level then, we have a paradigm of pre-scientific superstition. The workings of nature are viewed as acts of the gods, and this provides a primitive gesture in the direction of scientific explanation. It does so in the sense that reference to the gods is intended to provide some kind of answer—however inadequate—to the scientific question of why things happen. Nevertheless, their role exceeds these scientific terms, and it does so in two ways. First, we are given a sense that nature resists our attempts to control it—unlike Weber's scientist we cannot in principle control everything, although we are encouraged to respond to this predicament by developing our own more limited controlling tendencies. Second, we are led to suppose that nature has a purpose, albeit one which, as far as this particular picture is concerned, is driven primarily by the egoistic desires of the gods, and derivatively by the egoistic desires of men. In this respect, and *pace* Miller, we have a world which is egoistic and unpredictable rather than sensible and complete. To return to the terms which are familiar from Chapter 2: mindful action—whether of gods or men—is reduced to a kind of desire-satisfaction; things and men become opportunities for satisfying the desires of the gods; and the gods become opportunities for satisfying the desires of men.

---

of the Idea of Nature, trans. Michael Chase (Cambridge, Mass.: The Belknap Press of Harvard University Press, 2006), p. 107.

[11] Compare Herbert McCabe: 'The gods are more powerful than we are, but they can be manipulated by presenting gifts of a kind they are known to like or by flattering their vanity and so on. For the gods, powerful as they are, are still fellow members of the universe', 'The God of Truth', in *God Still Matters* (London: Continuum, 2002), p. 30. It is not ruled out, however, that we ourselves can modify the relevant phenomena by *forcing* the gods to do what we want. As Weber puts it, we can 'control the spirits' by means of magic, although we are to suppose that our controlling capacities in this context are compromised by the more powerful gods. Hence Hadot: 'One acts on the god or demon by calling it its true name, and then by performing certain actions and rituals, using plants or animals that are considered to be in sympathy with the invisible power one wishes to constrain. The god then becomes the servant of the person who carries out the magical practice, for magic claims to be able to dominate this power in order to have it at its disposal to carry out what it desires', *The Veil of Isis*, p. 107.

Having described the way in which our ancestors submitted to the authority of the 'gods of darkness', Miller continues as follows:

> Then something happened. Something wonderful. A few of our ancestors began to learn the rules by which nature worked, and after a while, we no longer needed Apollo to pull the sun's chariot across the sky. We no longer asked Ceres to waken seeds from winter sleep. The movements of the sun and moon became part of a mechanism, a celestial machine in which each motion could be calculated and explained...In a word, we learned to explore nature in the systematic way we now call *science*...the gods are gone, and we are no longer subject to their tyranny.[12]

So science provides a framework for learning the rules by which nature works, the relevant workings are approached accordingly, and there is no longer any need to view them as the acts of capricious gods, or indeed, as acts of any kind at all. Rather, they are processes or events which, as McDowell stresses, exhibit a different kind of intelligibility from that which characterizes texts, utterances, and other kinds of action. That is to say, they belong to the realm of 'natural-scientific intelligibility', and one of the paradigmatic ways in which natural science makes things intelligible is by subsuming them under natural laws.[13] It is in this sense that it can be said to provide the rules by which nature works. The upshot is that the relevant phenomena are emptied of the kind of meaning they were thought to possess when the gods were on the scene, and the realm of scientific investigation is suitably disenchanted.

All of this provides one way of rejecting the idea that the movements of the planets and the fall of a sparrow are to be approached in the way that we approach a text, or an utterance, or any other kind of action, for they are no longer to be viewed as acts of the gods. Furthermore, we can allow that the offending approach involves appeal to explanatory factors which are 'occult or magical', for the idea is that the gods do magic. They do magic in the sense that they manipulate the workings of nature according to whim or mood, and this magic is supernatural in the sense that it escapes the ambit of modern natural science and, indeed, is called into question by it. However, it was once thought to be an appropriate object for scientific investigation, albeit a science which lacked genuine explanatory and predictive power. Viewed from the perspective of such a 'science', these magical forces are an intrinsic part of nature—they constitute its very workings. So they count as natural in this sense. Furthermore, the authors of these forces—the gods—although unobservable at one level, are themselves taken to be a part of nature. They are a

---

[12] *Finding Darwin's God*, p. 193.

[13] McDowell concedes that the idea of the realm of law needs refining if we are to accommodate biological intelligibility, and modifies his earlier talk of phenomena being 'subsumable under natural law' for the idea that they are 'explicable in a natural-scientific way', 'Response to Christoph Halbig', in *John McDowell: Experience, Norm, and Nature*, ed. Jakob Lindgaard (Oxford: Blackwell, 2008), pp. 220–221.

part of nature in the sense that they are beings amongst beings. To be sure, they are more powerful than other beings and lack our mortal limitations. However, they are firmly situated within the natural world, and there is no implication that they could exist in its absence. In the version under current consideration, they give primitive[14] expression to the necessities which govern the workings of nature, and, as such, function as placeholders for the explanations to be supplied by modern science. These explanations take the magic out of the relevant forces, allowing us to retain the idea that they form an intrinsic part of nature but without any implication that they are the acts of the gods. It is in this sense that the objects of scientific investigation are disenchanted.

4.3 FURTHER CLARIFICATIONS

We can agree that there is a distinction to be drawn between behaviour which is mindful and behaviour which is not, that the movements of the planets and the fall of a sparrow fall into the latter category, and that we do not approach these phenomena in the way that we approach texts, utterances, or any other kind of action. We can agree also that modern science provides a framework in terms of which to comprehend behaviour of this kind—one which puts to rest the idea that it is on the same level as that which is operative when somebody is doing or has done something. More generally, the point is that there are large-scale entities that have minds and thoughts and lots of entities that do not because they are too small and/or they are not composed of the right kind of stuff. Modern science has 'disenchanted' these latter entities in the sense that they are no longer to be viewed in mind-involving terms, and it is a mark of intellectual progress that we have moved beyond this 'enchanted' conception of their nature and behaviour.

This much is indisputable, but there is a question about whether we should accept that all of the objects of scientific investigation are disenchanted in this sense. The claim seems plausible enough if we restrict ourselves to the natural sciences, but it becomes more contentious when the human sciences are brought into the equation, for these sciences precisely do involve an investigation of mentally endowed entities and their mindful behaviour. To return to the example which is familiar from Chapter 2, they study the kind of behaviour at issue when human beings are practically engaged with the world. So the objects of scientific investigation are enchanted to this degree at least, and such

---

[14] It would be natural to say that the gods give *mythical* expression to the relevant necessities. However, there are questions to be raised about the meaning of the term 'myth', and we should hesitate before concluding that myths are pre-scientific superstitions in the sense at issue here. I shall be returning to this issue in the final chapter.

a concession raises no obvious scientific or philosophical difficulties provided that we resist the lure of physicalist reductionism and grant the explanatory pretensions of the human sciences.

The expansive naturalist can concede this much. Nevertheless, he has serious doubts about whether such an approach can accommodate all that needs to be said about the human behaviour at issue, and, in particular, whether it provides an adequate account of our moral responses. He argues that we can rectify this deficiency only by ascending to a different, non-scientific level of explanation which can make sense of what is really at issue when values make their demands on us and provide us with appropriate reasons for action. The further claims are that once we grant the possibility of this non-scientific form of understanding and explanation, we shall be granted access to a range of values which are *sui generis* with respect to scientific explanation, and that the resultant ontological expansion could appear to be worrisome only on the misguided assumption that the scientist has the monopoly on ontology and explanation. The expansive naturalist concludes that this amounts to a partial re-enchantment of nature. It is partial in the sense that it leaves room for the disenchanted objects of scientific investigation, and it is a *re*-enchantment in the sense that we have moved beyond a scientistic conception of nature. We have moved beyond it by introducing into our ontology a level of value which eludes the perspective of the scientist.

So there are various conceptions of enchantment and disenchantment at work here. According to one conception of enchantment, something counts as such if it is mind-involving and purposive. The behaviour of the gods is enchanted in this sense, but this behaviour is not an appropriate object of scientific investigation and science calls into question the idea that the workings of nature are to be comprehended in these mind-involving terms. We have noted also that this behaviour is confined to a kind of desire-satisfaction. Thus, the gods do not consider the question of whether a particular desire is good to have, and we are to suppose that any reflection on their part remains at the instrumental level of a purely self-interested being.[15] In this respect, we have a position in which value is reducible to desire, inclination, and causal tendency—one which, as Bilgrami sees it, fails to accommodate the normativity of value and merits the label 'scientistic'. If this is right, then there is a sense in which the mindful behaviour which is operative at the level of McDowell's picture of total enchantment can also be described as disenchanted. It is disenchanted in the sense that it can be characterized in the absence of any reference

---

[15] I am not ruling out the possibility that there are more sophisticated gods whose behaviour exceeds these egoistic parameters, and it will be a task of the final chapter to consider how McDowell's own position might be situated within such a framework. It is a more general task of the book as a whole to comprehend the transition from gods to God, and the implications of this move for the question of value will become clear as the argument proceeds.

to a conception of value which exceeds the aforementioned desire-involving terms. To put it in terms which are familiar from the previous chapter, the gods lack a second nature.

This latter point is important for an understanding of the behaviour which provides the focus of the human sciences. This behaviour counts as enchanted in the sense that it is mind-involving and purposive. Furthermore, unlike the behaviour of the gods, it does serve as an appropriate object of scientific investigation provided that our conception of science is expanded accordingly. The behaviour at issue here is that which is operative when we are practically engaged with the world. The expansive naturalist can allow that at least some of this behaviour is adequately comprehended by the human sciences. He can allow also that it exceeds the parameters assumed by Bilgrami's human scientist, doing so, for example, by granting Railton's preferred approach. What he denies, however, is that such an approach—in so far as it remains faithful to its reductive aims—can cover all of the explanatory ground. In particular, it fails to accommodate our capacity to engage with moral value. He concludes that there is more to explanation than scientific explanation, more to nature than what the scientist comprehends, and that once we concede these points we arrive at a partially re-enchanted conception of nature.

The enchantment at issue here is a morally evaluative enchantment, and there are two related senses in which nature can be said to have been enchanted in this way. First, it incorporates natural beings who can think and act in moral terms. As such, they are to be distinguished from those who lack such a capacity, like, for example, the aforementioned gods and Bilgrami's purely desire-driven beings. So there is an evaluative enchantment at the level of the human subject. However, it counts equally as an evaluative enchantment of the world, for the relevant habits of thought and action involve a responsiveness to a range of moral norms which are part of the natural world, albeit a world whose limits are no longer circumscribed by science and whose evaluative aspect can be appreciated only by suitably endowed natural beings.

It should be clear from what has been said that this is no recommendation to retreat into the realm of pre-scientific superstition. On the contrary, the envisaged enchantment of nature is intended to be compatible with the findings of modern science, and acceptable to those who take seriously the scientific worldview. So it is not a matter of enchanting the world with the magical interventions of the gods, for these interventions *are* called into question by science. Rather, it is a matter of allowing that there are things in the world—values—which are compatible with the findings of science, and which are irreducible to the things it can explain. The further claim is that there is a perfectly satisfactory ontology and epistemology for these things provided that we resist the lure of scientism, and that we succumb to this restriction only at the cost of courting a conception of nature for which there is no good philosophical or scientific justification.

4.4 DIVINE ENCHANTMENT?

Bilgrami notes that the notion of an evaluatively enchanted natural world was once inextricably linked to the idea that this enchantment has its source in a divinity—a divinity which 'was, in many a view, itself immanent in the world'. He claims also that this source was undermined in the modern period that Weber describes with reference to the notion of disenchantment, that this sceptical response has tended to be lumped together with Nietzsche's announcement of the death of God, and that those who oppose this modern picture are treated with disdain and suspicion—their beliefs are immature and irrational.[16]

Bilgrami takes all of this to be a gross oversimplification, and he is right about this. I want, however, to leave on one side most of the grievances he expresses in this context, and lend justice to his criticism by trading upon considerations which are more germane to the issues at hand. Let us begin with the idea that an evaluatively enchanted world has its source in a divinity, and the suggestion that such an idea is immature and irrational. One is reminded immediately of McDowell's picture of a totally enchanted world, and his claim that 'it is a mark of intellectual progress that educated people cannot now take that idea seriously'.[17] We can agree that there is a version of this idea which cannot be taken seriously, namely, that according to which the workings of nature are to be viewed as the acts of capricious and egoistic gods. We can agree also that this picture promises to deliver a version of the idea that the relevant source of value is immanent in the world—after all, these gods are fellow members of the universe. However, there are several reasons for denying that it provides an appropriate model for the idea that an evaluatively enchanted world has its source in a divinity. First, the values which figure in McDowell's evaluatively enchanted world have no place in this scheme of things, for it is driven purely by the gods' desires, and things acquire a value only to the extent that they satisfy these desires, or, alternatively, if they satisfy the desires of those who remain beholden to the gods. In this respect, we have a primitive analogue of the scientistic position detailed and criticized by Bilgrami—a conception against which McDowell's preferred alternative is defined. Second, although some of the values to which we are confined on this picture can be said to have a divine source in the sense that they are generated by the desires of the gods, there are others which do not, namely, those which are generated by the desires of those who pray to the gods in the hope that they will get what they want. Finally, given that the beings at issue here are motivated purely

---

[16] 'The Wider Significance of Naturalism: A Genealogical Essay', in *Naturalism and Normativity*, ed. Mario De Caro and David Macarthur (New York: Columbia University Press, 2010), p. 35.
[17] *Mind and World*, p. 71.

by egoistic desires and distinguished only by virtue of the fact that some of them are more powerful than others, it seems inappropriate to describe the picture as one in which the source of value is divine. At least, this is so if we accept, as we surely must, that there is more to divinity than being able to get what you want. We can conclude that this picture cannot capture what it means to say that an evaluatively enchanted world has its source in a divinity, and we can agree also that it is irrational and immature. It is irrational in the sense that there is no good reason for viewing the workings of nature in these god-involving terms. It is immature in the sense that it involves a projection of the infantile wish to make the world conform to one's own desires, and leaves no room for a conception of value, humanity, or divinity which exceeds these egoistic terms.

So there may be an alternative notion of divinity to exploit in this context—one which is better placed to accommodate the values which figure in the expansive naturalist's position, and which can lend justice to the idea that they have a divine source. Let it be said immediately that the expansive naturalist would reject such a possibility. His notion of evaluative enchantment is resolutely secular, and he believes that any move in the direction of a divinity would be a quick route back to pre-scientific superstition. To revert to McDowell's imagery, we would be transported into 'the region of darkness'—the region occupied by occult and magical phenomena. It should be clear from what has been said that the issue is rather more complex. Indeed, this complexity emerges if we examine the context in which McDowell employs the imagery of darkness. The context is familiar enough, for it concerns the question of whether it is philosophically acceptable to introduce into our ontology phenomena which lie beyond the reach of scientific understanding, and he takes this question to be equivalent to that of whether we can make this move without relegating the relevant phenomena 'to the sphere of the occult or the supernatural'. It is equally familiar that his expansive naturalist framework is intended to vindicate this possibility as far as the case of value is concerned. Thus—and in this particular context the focus is natural science—we are told that value is 'exempt from natural-scientific intelligibility', and that we can grant this concession without 'being required to push it back into the region of darkness, the region supposedly occupied by phenomena that resist the light cast by natural science because they are occult or supernatural'.[18]

So things can be exempt from natural-scientific intelligibility without being philosophically disreputable, and the point can be generalized to include modes of scientific explanation which exceed the parameters of natural science. The relevant things remain philosophically reputable because there are other ways of rendering them intelligible—ways which, to continue the

---

[18] 'Reply to Fink', p. 217.

imagery, can cast a different, non-scientific, light upon them and rescue them from the region of darkness. Thus, they are not bound to be occult in the way that the magical forces of the gods count as such, but, *pace* McDowell, they *can* be described as supernatural if this label is just another way of capturing the sense in which they resist scientific explanation, that is to say, if 'natural' in this context is comprehended in the offending scientistic terms and 'supernatural' becomes the logical complement of 'natural' so understood. But how are we to interpret the force of his claim that the region of darkness has shrunk for us with the advent of a modern scientific outlook, and that, in the most extreme version of the outlook, it has shrunk to nothing at all? The extreme version of the outlook calls to mind the reductive picture which is forced on us if we remain wedded to scientism. At least, this reading becomes plausible once it is remembered that, as far as the scientific naturalist is concerned, McDowell's evaluatively enchanted world merits inclusion in the region of darkness. It seems clear from what he goes on to say, however, that any residual darkness is to be reserved for items which are supernatural not just in the sense that they resist scientific explanation, but in the sense that they escape the ambit of an expansive naturalist framework. Hence we are told that:

> (i)t is tendentious to use the term 'superstition' for continued belief that that region is not empty, and to use the imagery of darkness for what would supposedly occupy that region. But someone who continues to believe the region is not empty, rejecting that tendentious description of it, might nevertheless acknowledge how unattractive it is to suppose that the supernatural includes human responsiveness to reasons...What 'natural' means, as the root of 'naturalism' in, say, 'relaxed naturalism' as I use that phrase, is: not supernatural (not occult, not magical,...). And there is no need for me to take a stand on whether *everything* is natural in that sense (thereby, among other things, giving needless offence to people who think respect for modern science is compatible with a kind of religious belief that preserves room for the supernatural).[19]

So McDowell is prepared to allow that there are phenomena which are not natural in the more liberal, non-scientific sense of that term, and that these phenomena count as supernatural. He claims also that 'supernatural' in this sense is equivalent to 'occult' and 'magical', even whilst conceding that it is tendentious to use the word 'superstition' for the belief that such items exist. We can applaud McDowell's attitude to superstitious beliefs if the point is simply to reject those which are called into question by modern science, and we can agree that their elimination underlies the attractiveness of scientific naturalism.[20] This much is familiar from what has been said about the occult and magical forces which were equated with the workings of nature when pre-scientific superstition ruled the day. We can agree also that the religious belief at issue

---

[19] 'Reply to Fink', p. 218.   [20] 'Reply to Fink', p. 218.

here—that the workings of nature are controlled by capricious and egoistic gods—stands also to be eliminated. It remains open, however, that there is a kind of religious belief which survives such criticisms, and furthermore, that the imagery of darkness stands to be exploited in this context, albeit without the accompanying pejorative tones. If this is right, then there may yet be room for allowing that belief in God is intellectually respectable, and that there is sense to be made of the idea that the natural world is *divinely* enchanted.

4.5 EXPANDING EXPANSIVE NATURALISM

I want to make a case for these possibilities by exploiting arguments which have a similar structure and content to those which are used by the expansive naturalist to defend his own preferred stance. So the position I arrive at is intended to be compatible with an expansive naturalist framework, albeit one which has been expanded beyond its currently envisaged limits. The structure of the approach will concern me initially, and we can get a sense of its relevance to the present set of issues by returning to the scientific naturalist's worries about the expansive naturalist's evaluatively enchanted world.

The enchantment at issue here carries no reference to a divine source, so it is rescued from any 'region of darkness' as far as the expansive naturalist is concerned. Nevertheless, the scientific naturalist objects that it involves a 'worrisome' ontological expansion, and takes such a position to be on the same level as any other which has undertakings in the noumenal realm. As he sees it then, secular evaluative enchantment is just as problematic as its theistic counterpart. At least, this is so provided that it is to be comprehended in the envisaged non-scientific terms.[21] The expansive naturalist objects that these worries stem from a commitment to a scientistic framework, that this framework is open to challenge, and that its rejection puts us in a better place to accommodate the phenomenon of value. An evaluatively enchanted world is not intolerably odd, and our dealings with it do not transport us into the realm of the noumenal, unless this is just a fancy way of saying that we have moved beyond the parameters of science. On the contrary, such a world is perfectly natural, as is our capacity to respond to it, and we can concede these points by allowing that there is more to nature—and indeed, human nature—than what is revealed at the level of scientific investigation.

The expansive naturalist grants an ontological expansion which, from the scientific naturalist's point of view, is philosophically inadmissible. The expansion is held to be legitimate provided that we reject scientism, and it is denied that it involves reference to anything which could offend the sensibilities of an

---

[21] I make this caveat to accommodate the possibility of there being a form of evaluative enchantment which remains philosophically permissible to the (expansive) scientific naturalist.

anti-scientistic naturalist. McDowell is prepared to allow that the limits of reality exceed these broader naturalistic terms, doing so out of respect for a 'kind of religious belief that preserves room for the supernatural'. We are led to suppose, however, that such belief is problematic, and that the expansion at issue is worrisome in the extreme. So both the scientific naturalist and the expansive naturalist agree that there are problematic ontological expansions, and that they involve reference to a supernatural realm. They would agree also that such a realm is presupposed when we introduce God into our ontology. The scientific naturalist objects that the expansive naturalist's evaluatively enchanted world is problematic in the relevant sense, and that the values he postulates count as supernatural. As he sees it then, belief in such values is on the same level as belief in God. The expansive naturalist denies that this is so, but he believes that whereas there is room for allowing that value can be naturalized by broadening the limits of nature accordingly, there is no such move to be made on the part of God.

There is something absolutely right about the expansive naturalist's response here if the point is simply to deny that God is part of the natural world. For God is on a different ontological level from anything that is to be found within the world—He is not, and could not be, a being amongst beings. This much sets God apart from the gods who lurk within McDowell's totally enchanted world, and we shall see that He is to be distinguished from them in certain other fundamental ways, but more on that later. What I want to emphasize here is that even if we grant, as we surely must, that God cannot be naturalized in *this* sense, it does not have to follow that the natural world is not divinely enchanted. To put it another way, it does not follow from the fact that God is not a god—or any other finite being for that matter—that He must be squeezed out of the picture. To suppose that this *does* follow is surely to commit a structurally similar error to that which is operative when value is eliminated on the ground that it does not conform to a scientific paradigm. There may yet be scope then for allowing that God *can* be accommodated from within an expansive naturalist framework, and that the expansive naturalist can help us to see how this could be so.

We can begin to spell out this latter possibility by returning to the expansive naturalist's response to the complaint that an evaluatively enchanted world is intolerably odd. His response is to challenge the scientistic framework which is presupposed in such a complaint. This framework is not mandatory, and once it is rejected, the limits of nature can be expanded accordingly. Now take the complaint that a divinely enchanted world is intolerably odd. The complaint has a point if we insist upon a scientistic framework, for, as I shall spell out in more detail below, God does not and could not fall within the province of scientific investigation,[22] and there are good reasons for thinking that an

---

[22] It is misguided therefore to say, as Richard Dawkins does, that 'the presence or absence of a creative super-intelligence is unequivocally a scientific question', *The God Delusion* (London: Bantam Press, 2006), pp. 58–59.

alternative approach is required if we are to make sense of a divinely enchanted world. The idea that God cannot be comprehended in scientific terms provides a further sense in which He is to be distinguished from the gods, which latter were at least potential candidates for such investigation, albeit a primitive version thereof which modern science has called into disrepute.[23] The further idea that these terms cannot capture what it means to say that the world is divinely enchanted can be related to an analogous claim which has been made about evaluative enchantment.

The expansive naturalist remains sceptical about the possibility of extending his arguments in a theistic direction, doing so on the ground that it involves a worrisome ontological expansion—God is too spooky to be part of our ontology, and there are no divine traces to be found in nature. He would doubtless add that such an expansion brings insuperable epistemological difficulties—to revert to Mackie's terminology, we would be saddled with a mysterious faculty in terms of which to relate to God, one which is 'utterly different from our ordinary ways of knowing about anything else'. The move is structurally similar to that which is used by the scientific naturalist to block the ascent to value. The expansive naturalist challenges this injunction on the ground that it involves a commitment to an unjustified scientistic framework, claiming that the relevant epistemological and metaphysical difficulties evaporate once this framework is relinquished. He would insist, however, that an analogous vindication is unavailable for the case of God. The conclusion is indisputable if the task is that of superimposing onto the world an additional appendage whose only effect is to spook its boundaries and those of the beings who are said to relate to it. Furthermore, it is easy to be persuaded that such a conception of the task is mandatory if we continue to insist that divine enchantment is either a contradiction in terms or the preserve of superstitious minds. The alternative is to question these loaded terms by objecting that this conception of God and of our relation to Him stems from a framework we have no reason to accept.

The move is familiar from the case of value, for the expansive naturalist encourages us to reject the assumption that the values with which he is concerned are intolerably odd, and offers a conception of our relation to them which could invite this charge only on the assumption that science is the measure of reality. More specifically, he claims that values engage us at a practical level which is irreducibly moral. The further claim is that the scientist has a difficulty capturing this level of engagement, and that we can do justice to it if we ascend to a non-scientific level of explanation. This level of engagement is different from that which is at issue in a non-moral context, but it is not *spookily* different. On the contrary, it is perfectly natural, and it opens our eyes to an

---

[23] Compare McCabe's claim that '(t)here is no quarrel between the scientific project and worship of the creator; there is only sometimes a quarrel between science and the religion of the gods', 'The God of Truth', p. 34.

aspect of nature which is concealed so long as we remain within the confines of the aforementioned scientific stance.

So the expansive naturalist does not need to be persuaded that there are aspects of the world which elude scientific investigation and which demand for their discernment and understanding a rather different approach. What he objects to is the idea that this move can be generalized in a theistic direction. We are to suppose then that there are no prospects for showing that our responsiveness to God is natural, even if 'natural' is comprehended in the more liberal sense of that term. That is to say that it is on a very different level to our responsiveness to value, and cannot be shown to be part and parcel of our natural human being. It is different in two related senses. First, its object lies beyond anything which is to be found in the natural world (as broadly conceived); second, and consequently, the responsiveness in question requires that we are partly in nature and partly outside of it. To revert to the terminology McDowell employs in the context of criticizing the rampant platonist's position, we would be committed to claiming that we have a 'foothold in the animal kingdom and a mysterious separate involvement in an extra-natural world', that 'our lives are mysteriously split, somehow taking place both in nature and in some alien realm...in "Plato's Heaven", perhaps'.

The expansive naturalist is happy to allow that we are partly in nature and partly outside of it if nature is understood in the narrow, scientistic terms he is concerned to reject. What he takes issue with is the idea that the relevant 'non-natural' aspect is utterly divorced from our human being, and that it puts us in touch, who knows how, with some 'alien realm'—'alien' in the sense that it is to be set apart from anything to which we could relate by virtue of being human, and can have no bearing upon our humanity. It is for this reason that he resists any such treatment of our responsiveness to value, even whilst insisting that a correspondingly alienating conception lies in wait for those who respond to these metaphysical and epistemological excesses by retreating into the scientistic camp.

The familiar message is that we must reject the assumption that the scientist has the monopoly on nature and broaden its limits accordingly. The message I have been building up to here is that we must be prepared also to question the assumption that these limits are to be monopolized by the form of expansive naturalism under current consideration. That is to say, we must consider the possibility that there is an intellectually respectable version of the claim that the natural world is divinely enchanted, that our responsiveness to such a world is continuous with our natural being, and that this responsiveness precisely *does* have a bearing upon our humanity. Such a position promises to lend justice to the scientific naturalist's assumption that divine enchantment and evaluative enchantment come as a joint package, although the precise nature of the relation between God and value remains to be seen. For the moment I want to consider the general shape of the position at issue, and to make explicit the relation it bears to its secular expansive naturalist counterpart.

4.6 THE NATURAL AND THE SUPERNATURAL IN THEOLOGY

Theologians have long been interested in the question of how we are to understand the concept of the supernatural, and have sought to reject what they take to be flawed conceptions thereof. Indeed, E.L. Mascall goes so far as to claim that this concept has been either disowned or pushed into the background in much recent theological writing, and that in John Robinson's book *Honest to God* 'it is disowned in scornful terms, usually under the still more contemptible form of "supra-natural"'. Mascall complains that this has led to a neglect of the classical theological distinction between the natural and the supernatural, and responds as follows:

> I do not think, however, that we can afford to do without the distinction, though I think that Catholic theology has tended in the past to formulate it in a very rigid and unsatisfactory manner, especially in the textbooks, and that it needs a good deal of reformulation and development.[24]

Robinson's reservations about the supernatural are not reservations about God, and he is in broad agreement with Mascall. He prefers to use the term 'supranatural' to refer to the object of his attack not simply because the word 'supernatural' tends to be used interchangeably with 'the divine' (when it does not mean 'the spooky'), but because this less familiar word will allow us to see that the issue is not the reality of God as such, but, rather, a particular way of representing or describing it.[25] The caricature of this approach, we are told, is the deist conception of God: God as the 'remote watchmaker' who starts it all up and then leaves us to our own devices. However, it is not enough to shoot down this deist picture by insisting that God's relation to the world is personal, for it is not just the *quality* of the relationship that requires to be amended, but also its *structure*. According to the offending structure, God is 'a *being* whose separate existence over and above the sum of all things has to be demonstrated and established';[26] 'a "divine Person behind the scenes"...for whose existence the evidence was to say the least doubtful'.[27]

Robinson's target then is an approach which makes it difficult to suppose that we could stand in a personal relation to God, and which implies that His reality is, at best, a hypothetical super-addition to the world—something whose existence we might seek to establish by citing as evidence the experiential materials at our disposal, but whose postulation remains doubtful and, in any case, peripheral to the stuff of human life. As he puts it, God is banished to the edges of life, to become an extra, spooky storey to which we might or might not ascend when the business of living is over.

---

[24] *The Openness of Being: Natural Theology Today* (London: Darton, Longman, and Todd, 1971), p. 151.
[25] *Exploration into God* (London: SCM Press, 1967), p. 22.
[26] *Honest to God* (London: SCM Press, 1963), p. 15.
[27] *Exploration into God*, p. 22.

Mascall shares some of these worries. He bemoans a position which rules out the possibility of there being any 'real self-communication of God to man, any real elevation of man into the life of God', claiming that it involves an inadequate understanding of the relation between God and man:

> This relation has only too often been thought of solely in terms of a comparison of the respective natures or essences of God and man, to the neglect of the concrete existential activity uniting them...Sometimes we are told that God is *das ganz Anderes*, the 'wholly other', and both these assertions are true. They neglect, however, the basic fact in which the mutual otherness of God and man consists, namely that man is totally dependent for his existence on the incessant creative activity of the self-existent God. And the importance of this, as I have previously emphasized, is that while it involves the greatest conceivable contrast between God and man, it simultaneously places them in the most intimate connection.[28]

Like Robinson, he sees a deistic influence at work in the idea that man is isolated from God,[29] objecting likewise that such a framework encourages us to view the move from created world to creator as consisting of discursive argument to the concept of a 'remote and glacial deity'. The result of such an approach is that 'in the very act of affirming God's existence' we end up losing hold of 'the intuition of God and finite being together without which the argument could never begin'.[30] This intuition involves an awareness 'of the creature as dependent upon its creator', and it is 'closely linked with the capacity for contemplative wondering'.[31] By contrast, if we hold to a deistic conception of creation, we shall think of men as:

> incapsulated in their finitude in such a way as to make them incapable of receiving anything more than purely external manipulation by God. He can push them around, but he cannot bring about any inner transformation in them; at least he cannot do this without destroying their natures and making them into other beings than they are.[32]

He describes as follows the offending 'rigid and unsatisfactory' formulation of the natural/supernatural distinction. It has:

> tended to see man's natural constitution as rounded off and complete in itself, and as concerned entirely with his life in this world and sustained by the forces of nature. On top of this there has been superimposed a supernatural constitution, in virtue of which man is orientated to the supernatural end of the vision of God...Although nature is held to possess a *potentia oboedientialis* for grace and

---

[28] *The Openness of Being*, p. 150.
[29] *The Openness of Being*, p. 150.
[30] *The Openness of Being*, p. 141.
[31] *The Openness of Being*, p. 141.
[32] *Via Media: An Essay in Theological Synthesis* (London: Longmans, Green and Co., 1956), pp. 152–153.

the supernatural, this consists of little more than a lack of antagonism towards it, and the orders are thought of rather as if they were two apartments on adjacent floors, with a layer of soundproof packing between the natural ceiling below and the supernatural floor above.[33]

The claim then is that the relation between the natural and the supernatural has been distorted. The terms of this relation have not been spelled out in any detail, but the supernatural is said to denote a dimension of reality which involves God and His action, and the natural includes man as he exists in this world 'sustained by the forces of nature'. These terms are not to be conflated, for there is the 'greatest conceivable contrast' between them. However, they also stand in the most intimate connection, and the distortion occurs when this connection is lost. It is lost when the supernatural defines the divine in separation from the human and is located in an inaccessible, incommunicable beyond. As such, it is 'spooky' and 'uncanny'. God ceases to be the 'most real thing in the world' and becomes something whose existence is doubtful and, in any case, irrelevant to our humanity. Human life, on this picture, is played out within the natural world and sustained by its forces. It involves a concern for this world alone, and this world is closed off from the supernatural, as is man's natural constitution: he is 'incapsulated in his finitude'. Incapsulated in his finitude, man can, at best, be externally manipulated by God—a manipulation which falls short of the kind of inner transformation which occurs when the relation between the supernatural and the natural is understood aright. The further claim is that, provided we remain within the offending framework, this transformation could be effected only with a destruction of man's (natural) being.

4.7 EXPANSIVE NATURALISM, AGAIN

How does all of this relate to what the expansive naturalist is saying? In both cases we are faced with the question of how to comprehend the limits of nature. The expansive naturalist argues that the scientific naturalist is working with an unduly restricted conception of these limits, and that provided we remain within such parameters we shall have a difficulty accommodating phenomena which cannot be comprehended in scientific terms but which are central to how we think about ourselves and the world. We shall end up concluding that such items are irreducibly mysterious, and there will be no way of explaining how we relate to them. Mascall and Robinson see a similar line of argument at work in a theistic context. In this case, the phenomenon in question is God, and according to the offending framework, He belongs to a dimension of reality which is

---

[33] *The Openness of Being*, p. 151.

'other-worldly' and 'supernatural'. They allow that there is an acceptable inter-pretation of such a claim—compare an analogous move which is available to our expansive naturalist—and are anxious to preserve a sense in which God is 'wholly other' with respect to nature and man. So there is no concession in the direction of anti-realism. What they object to, however, is a picture which severs all connection between God and nature, and, thereby, the connection between God and man. According to this picture, nature can be adequately compre-hended in non-God involving terms, and man *qua* natural being bears no rela-tion to God. He can perhaps be externally manipulated by Him, and it is not ruled out that he can use his rational resources to construct an argument for His existence. We are led to suppose, however, that such an endeavour is bound to misfire, and that it is no better than an analogous move that might be made by the scientific naturalist when he tries to convince us that he can, after all, accom-modate the possibility of value.[34] The implication here is that we have been left with an impoverished conception of man and of nature, and that the offending framework rules out the possibility of incorporating the vital missing ingredient. It has become 'other-worldly' in the pejorative sense, and we are led to suppose that, working within such a framework, the rational response is atheism.

The alternative is to reject the offending conception of the relation between nature and God so as to allow that we ourselves, *qua* natural beings, are already open to God. That is to say that the supernatural—which here embraces both God and His communicative action—is not a spooky superstructure, extrinsic or added on to a nature which is complete in itself. Rather, it is a quality or dimension which enriches or perfects the natural world. This grants us the right to allow that man can be inwardly transformed by God. And precisely because this transformation serves to enhance his natural being—given that we are now working with a broader conception of nature—we avoid the impli-cation that such divine action spells the destruction of man, severing any con-nection he might have with ordinary human life. I think it is fair to say at this preliminary stage that we have arrived at a theistic version of McDowell's con-ception of second nature, and a suitably modified interpretation of the claim that it brings a richer reality into view.

4.8 CONCLUSION

The modification will not suit our expansive naturalist, of course, and it will be the task of the following chapters to spell out further details of the position and

---

[34] It should go without saying that I am thinking here of the kind of scientific naturalist who has not made the 'humanizing' gestures which, from Wiggins's point of view, situate him more properly in the non-scientistic camp.

to extend the case for showing that at least some of his worries are unfounded. For the moment, I want to sum up my present conclusions, making clear where things stand as far as the notion of enchanted nature is concerned. I began with McDowell's idea of a partially enchanted nature, and agreed with him that there are conceptions of total enchantment which stand to be rejected. In particular, we must reject the idea that nature is controlled by the gods, and that its workings give expression to their capricious acts. It has been granted that such a framework involves a primitive gesture in the direction of scientific explanation, and that it also gives expression to the sense that nature has a purpose, and that we are not its measure. We can note, however, that the purpose in question is defined in terms of the mastering tendencies of the gods, and it is these tendencies that we are encouraged to cultivate in ourselves. These points will be important in what follows.

The scientific limitations of this picture are remedied by modern science, and this provides one interpretation of the claim that it has disenchanted its objects, although the claim is too strong if it is taken to rule out the mindful action which forms the focus of the human sciences. So the objects of science can be enchanted to this degree at least, although the minds in question belong to human beings rather than to gods. We have not yet arrived at the idea that the natural world is enchanted in a morally evaluative sense, and the expansive naturalist argues that we can capture this mode of enchantment by ascending to a non-scientific level of explanation which is better placed to accommodate our moral responses. I noted that there is no place for such responses in McDowell's totally enchanted world, and that the 'godly' behaviour it involves is reducible to the kind of desire-satisfaction which exhausts the investigative limits of Bilgrami's human scientist. That is to say, this world does not count as evaluatively enchanted in McDowell's sense.

An evaluatively enchanted world incorporates beings like ourselves who are capable of responding to value. This capacity is natural, and it opens our eyes to an aspect of nature which is missing from the totally enchanted world with which McDowell takes issue. It has been common in the tradition to trace this evaluative enchantment to a divine source, albeit one which has little in common with the aforementioned gods. The expansive naturalist resists this theistic move, and, more generally, the idea that the natural world is divinely enchanted. I have argued that his objections serve more properly to undermine a version of the position we have no reason to accept, and that there may be scope for exploiting his approach in the context of defending a more satisfactory conception of divinity and divine enchantment. To this end, I turned to the distinction between the supernatural and natural as it arises in a theological context, and considered a way of conceiving of this distinction which has structural affinities to the expansive naturalist's conception of the relation between value and nature. On this way of thinking, God is no longer a spooky and irrelevant something else, and our capacity to *engage* with Him becomes fundamental to our natural human being.

Thus far, the focus has been upon the structure of the relation between God and nature, and although vague reference has been made to the idea of a divinely enchanted world, the details of the position remain unclear. In particular, we need to spell out what it could mean to say that the natural world has its source in a divinity, and what the relation is between this divine source and the world it supposedly enchants. We must consider also how the resultant picture is to be squared with McDowell's insistence that enchantment can only ever be partial, and whether we have the resources for vindicating a picture of divine enchantment which escapes his objections. Divine enchantment may or may not be total, but there seems to be a clear sense in which we ourselves are susceptible to it—such, at least, is the implication of the claim that we can be inwardly transformed by God. Can this claim be defended? What does it really mean? And does it have a suitable analogue in the value case? Finally, there is the question of whether the possibility of divine enchantment—both at the level of the subject and of the world—can be squared with the idea that God is irreducibly other. This idea suggests a clear sense in which God belongs firmly and squarely within the region of darkness—a point which would lead our expansive naturalist to reject the naturalistic aspirations of the position. Mascall, by contrast, insists that we stand in the most intimate contact with this wholly other Being, and that it belongs to our natural endowment to do so. Do we have the naturalistic resources for making sense of such a position? And can we do so without compromising God's reality, or indeed, our humanity? It is to these questions that I now turn.

5

God's Otherness: Some
Problematic Models

5.1 GOD IS NOT A GOD

According to the position under consideration, the limits of nature can be expanded in a theistic direction, but there is a fundamental sense in which God must remain wholly other. This latter claim has not been spelled out in any detail, but it involves the thought that there is the greatest conceivable contrast between God and world (and God and man), and this, we have been told, is compatible with the idea that they stand in the most intimate connection. The idea that there is the greatest conceivable contrast between God and world provides convenient grist for the mill of our expansive naturalist, for it suggests that there are no prospects for allowing that God is part of the natural world—a conclusion which provides a seemingly compelling ground for resisting the idea that the limits of nature can be expanded in a theistic direction. It does so in the sense that such a move threatens to reduce God to just one more item within the world, in which case His otherness is compromised. This suggests that if we have any religious sympathies at all—and our expansive naturalist does not—we would do better to consign God's reality to a quite different 'supernatural' realm. The question of what such a move amounts to remains unclear, and I shall be claiming eventually that there is an interpretation which accommodates God's otherness whilst being compatible with an expansive naturalist framework. On the face of it, however, it stands opposed to such a framework, implying that God is to be situated in a second, supernatural world. I shall argue that we accept this implication at the cost of compromising God's otherness.

I suggested in the previous chapter that a refusal to take seriously the possibility of a theistic form of expansive naturalism may involve a similar error to that which is operative when the scientific naturalist eliminates the expansive naturalist's values on the ground that they do not conform to his preferred paradigm. The implication here is that there is a legitimate and potentially comparable sense in which values can be described as 'other', and that we can trade upon this similarity to shed light upon the case of God. Values can be described as 'other' in two senses. First, they do not conform to the scientific naturalist's paradigm. This is what the expansive naturalist is getting at when he insists that they are *sui generis* with respect to scientific explanation. His further claim is that this otherness provides no ground for concluding that values are intolerably odd—that they inhabit some weird, non-natural realm which has no bearing upon our moral practices and to which we could relate only by virtue of possessing some equally weird non-natural faculty. On the contrary, they are part of the natural world, our capacity to engage with them is continuous with our natural being, and it is by so relating that we can be said to fulfil our humanity. The values in question are no mere creatures of our desires, and this provides a further sense in which they can be described as other. They are other in the sense that they are irreducible to what happens to be desired, serving, rather, to provide a normative constraint upon desire. If Bilgrami is right, the denial that values are *other* in this second sense likewise goes hand in hand with a commitment to scientism, a brand thereof which restricts our understanding of value to the desire-satisfying behaviour of human beings.

The gods described in the previous chapter are limited to behaviour of this kind, and the world serves as an opportunity for satisfying their desires. These gods are a part of the world they manipulate, for they are beings amongst beings, distinguished only by virtue of their immortality and their superior magical powers. Furthermore, they themselves can be manipulated by us provided that we appease them in the right way, and provided that they are in the mood for giving us what we want. So gods and men are alike in exhibiting desire-satisfying behaviour, but they differ with respect to their capacity to satisfy the relevant desires. We have noted already that there is no room in this picture for a conception of value which exceeds these desire-driven terms. That is to say, there is no room for any more intrinsic normative element which would grant us the right to evaluate the relevant desires, and to make sense of the idea that an existence which is purely desire-driven in this respect is deficient.

God is not a god in this sense. First, He is not an egoist, to be distinguished from the gods only by virtue of possessing an unrivalled power to get what He wants. Second, He is not there to satisfy our egoistic desires. Third, He is not a part of the world. The idea that God is not a part of the world suggests that He is to be distinguished not merely from the gods, but also from anything which is to be found in the natural world, even on a suitably expanded conception of its nature. So God possesses an otherness which outstrips the otherness of value, for although values can be described as other in the two aforementioned senses, they are still a part of the natural world. At least, this is so if we accept the expansive naturalist's framework.

The expansive naturalist believes that God must either be eliminated from our ontology or relegated to a supernatural realm. Politeness and tolerance notwithstanding, we are left in no doubt that the first of these options is the intellectually respectable one, and that the second one leaves us with a worrisome ontological addition which has no bearing upon the natural world and the beings within it. God becomes 'other' in a pejorative sense, for He is consigned to a realm which lies beyond anything to which we could intelligibly relate *qua* natural beings, and it is implied that we are multiplying entities beyond necessity. To revert to Robinson's terminology, He becomes a divine person behind the scenes for whose existence the evidence is to say the least doubtful. That is to say, He is on a level with the values which form the target of the scientific naturalist's attack and the gods rejected by the expansive naturalist—weird, unnecessary, and tempting only to one who remains in the thrall of superstition and magic.

The sensible theologian rejects this conception of God's otherness for two reasons. First, it turns Him into just one more being, albeit a being who stands 'over and above' rather than 'alongside' everything else. In this respect the idea that there is the greatest conceivable contrast between God and man— and, more generally, God and nature—is lost, and we fail to accommodate the kind of otherness at issue here. As Karl Rahner has put it, God becomes 'one object among other objects', something 'to be situated within our system of co-ordinates', 'to be defined by being distinguished from something else'.[1] So the distinction between God and world is lost, for He is reduced to just one more being. Second, this position neglects any reference to the idea that, such contrast notwithstanding, God and nature—and God and man—are intimately connected. The nature of this connection has not been spelled out, but, as far as the God/man relation is concerned, we have been told that man can be inwardly transformed by God. A God who is *other* in the aforementioned pejorative sense could not enact anything like this, for He lies beyond anything to which we could intelligibly relate. He is confined, at best, to an external manipulation of man—a pushing around which seems more appropriate to the behaviour of the aforementioned gods, or to the cosmic coercive forces which Railton seeks rightly to eliminate in the context of discussing the nature of moral requirements.

The idea that God is a cosmic manipulator suggests that, in one important sense, He is on a level with any other cause in the natural world. To be sure,

---

[1] *Foundations of Christian Faith: An Introduction to the Idea of Christianity*, trans. William V. Dych (London: Darton, Longman and Todd, 1978), p. 61. Compare Brad S. Gregory who rejects the idea that God is to be conceived as 'part of, alongside, or in competition with the natural world—that is, perhaps God is not a "highest being" or a "supernatural entity" that can in any sense be properly conceived within or as a component of a more comprehensive reality' ('No Room for God? History, Science, Metaphysics, and the Study of Religion', *History and Theory*, vol. 47 (December 2008), pp. 502–503).

we could endeavour to capture the essential difference by insisting that God has the magical power to interfere with the natural run of things by producing the occasional 'special effect' to awaken us from our atheistic slumbers. However, such a caveat leaves intact the idea that God's activity—magic notwithstanding—is similar to other, more mundane, interactions, for as Herbert McCabe has put it, 'to interfere you have to be an alternative to, or alongside, what you are interfering with'.[2] The further worry is that we are landed with a conception of God's activity which provides instant cannon fodder for the secular naturalist, for it suggests that a theistic framework is bound to lead us back to the gods of pre-scientific superstition. It threatens also to inherit the egoistic strand of this picture, for it is an obvious extension of the position that at least some of these divine interventions are intended to give us what we want, and that God serves as a means for satisfying our desires when He is not satisfying the desires of others or simply doing His own thing. Again, we are left with a cosmic manipulator—this time with a propensity towards favouritism—and an instant route to the conclusion that God is simply a product of childish wishful thinking.[3] His status is reduced to that of an over-indulgent parent—dishing out rewards from on high—and the idea that we could be inwardly transformed by God rather than simply using Him as a means for getting what we want is again lost. He becomes an opportunity in Bilgrami's sense of that term.

This is how Karl Rahner sums up the position under criticism:

> *That* God really does not exist who operates and functions as an individual existent alongside other existents, and who would thus as it were be a member of the larger household of all reality. Anyone in search of such a God is searching for a false God. Both atheism and a more naïve form of theism labour under the same false notion of God, only the former denies it while the latter believes that it can make sense of it. Both are basically false: the latter, the notion that naïve theism has, because this God does not exist; and the former, atheism, because God is the most radical, the most original, and in a certain sense the most self-evident reality.[4]

The idea that both the atheist and the naïve theist are labouring under the same false notion of God is familiar from what has been said. They both end up treating God as a god, and this conception serves not merely to compromise

---

[2] 'Creation', in *God Matters* (London: Continuum Press, 1987), p. 6.

[3] Levinas attacks this 'infantile' conception of God, claiming that it is 'a fairly primary sort of God' who 'dished out prizes, inflicted punishment or pardoned sins—a God who, in His goodness, treated men like children'. He goes on to ask, 'But with what lesser demon or strange magician have you therefore filled your heaven, you who claim that it is empty?', and claims that 'The adult's God is revealed precisely through the void of the child's heaven' ('Loving the Torah More Than God', in *Difficult Freedom*, trans. Seán Hand (Baltimore: Johns Hopkins University Press, 1990), p. 143). I shall be considering Levinas's position in the following chapter.

[4] *Foundations of Christian Faith*, p. 63.

God's otherness, but to encourage the conclusion that He is a superfluous and ultimately unintelligible addition to our ontology rather than being 'the most radical, the most original, and in a certain sense the most self-evident reality'.

How then is God's otherness to be understood? Our answer to this question must give due weight to the claims that God is not a member of the larger household of all reality, that He stands in the most intimate connection with things, and that He has the power to inwardly transform those beings who are human. Rahner's claim that God is 'in a certain sense the most self-evident reality' distinguishes Him from the god who serves as the object of the atheist's attack, for this god is such that the evidence for his existence is 'doubtful to say the least'. The implication here is that the atheist is right to reject this false god, but wrong to conclude that there is no God. We are led to suppose also that there is something incoherent about atheism—after all, if God is the most radical, the most original, and in a certain sense the most self-evident reality, then his existence *cannot* be denied. It is unclear how we are to interpret the force of the caveat that it is only 'in a certain sense' that His reality is revealed as self-evident, but we are to assume that, at one level at least, atheism constitutes the perfectly natural response.

5.2 GOD AS SOURCE

Robert Sokolowski tells us that 'God himself, as God, does not appear in the world or in human experience. He is not the kind of being that can be present as a thing in the world.'[5] The claim is commonplace in (sensible) theology, it finds biblical expression in God's response to Moses that 'you cannot see my face',[6] and is emphasized by those who have sought to undermine the idea that God might offer himself for observation.[7] This much puts paid to the idea that God is a part of the world, but it suggests also that atheism might be both the natural and the rational response. For if God is necessarily absent from the world, then

---

[5] *The God of Faith and Reason: Foundations of Christian Theology* (Washington, DC: The Catholic University of America Press, 1982), p. 1.

[6] Exodus 33:20.

[7] Hegel tells us that 'God does not offer himself for observation' (*Lectures on the Philosophy of Religion, I: Introduction and Conception of Religion*, ed. Peter C. Hodgson (Berkeley: University of California Press, 1984), p. 258). Nicholas Lash quotes this claim in the context of criticizing what he calls 'Loch Ness Theology'. Loch Ness Theology, we are told, is 'a story, a construct of modern rationalist impertinence, of plucky little *homo sapiens* striding out into the great unknown, anxiously seeking for some evidence that, somewhere out in all this darkness, deity may be discerned' ('Thinking, Attending, Praying', in *Philosophers and God: At the Frontiers of Faith and Reason*, ed. John Cornwell and Michael McGhee (London: Continuum, 2009), p. 42). See also 'The Impossibility of Atheism', in *Theology for Pilgrims* (London: Darton, Longman and Todd, 2008), p. 27.

it is unclear how we could make a case for claiming that He exists, and even less clear how Rahner's suggestion that His reality is self-evident could be vindicated.

The sensible theologian will insist that God's necessary absence in this sense guarantees that we are dealing with the Real Thing rather than some lowly surrogate. Indeed, Levinas goes so far as to claim that atheism provides the first essential step towards God, doing so on the ground that an acknowledgement of His absence from the world is an indication that one has moved beyond the false and infantile gods of superstition. As he puts it:

> The path that leads to the one God must be walked in part without God...The adult's God is revealed precisely through the void of the child's heaven. This is the moment when God retires from the world and hides His face.[8]

So God is absent from the world and could be present as a thing within it (or alongside it) only by ceasing to be God. An acknowledgement of this absence can be described as a form of atheism, but it is more properly understood as the attitude which clears the ground for a proper revelation of God. We are to suppose that a proper revelation reveals Him as 'the most self-evident reality', albeit not a reality which is a mere part of the world.

Sokolowski continues as follows:

> Despite this necessary absence, he is believed to be that which gives the definitive sense to everything that does appear in the world and in experience...God is not a part of the world, and yet the world has its being and definitive sense from him. [9]

The implication here is that God is the ontological source of the world rather than something within or beyond it, and further, that the world is not ultimately separable from Him—He gives everything its 'definitive sense'. So, rather than being a member of the larger household of reality, He is that without which reality would cease to be. It is in this sense that He can be said to make a difference. That is to say, He makes a difference not by tinkering with the workings of nature in the manner of a god, nor by adding to the inventory of things. Rather, He does so by making it the case that there is something rather than nothing. That is to say, He provides an answer to this fundamental question of being. As McCabe puts it:

> If God is whatever answers our question, how come everything? Then evidently he is not to be included amongst everything. God cannot be a thing, an existent among others. It is not possible that God and the universe should add up to two.[10]

God and the universe cannot add up to two because God is not a part within a larger whole, and it is not a matter of there being 'two things alongside each other'.[11] This, Rahner tells us, is the truth in pantheism. The pantheist goes

---

[8] 'Loving the Torah More Than God', p. 143.   [9] *The God of Faith and Reason*, p. 1.
[10] 'Creation', p. 6.   [11] Rahner, *Foundations of Christian Faith*, p. 62.

wrong, however, when he eliminates God from the picture, leaving us with just one thing—the world—rather than two. This is a mistake for several reasons. First, it plays into the hands of the offending conception of God by assuming that if He is not a something, then He must be banished from the equation. Second, it assumes that the world can exist in the absence of God, contravening the claim that He is its *sine qua non*. Third, it fails to acknowledge that God and the world are different. They are different not in the way that two things alongside each other are different. This, Rahner tells us, would be to comprehend the distinction in dualistic terms.[12] Rather:

> The difference between God and the world is of such a nature that God establishes and is the difference of the world from himself, and for this reason he establishes the closest unity precisely in this differentiation. For if the difference itself comes from God, and, if we can put it this way, is itself identical with God, then the difference between God and the world is to be understood quite differently than the difference between categorical realities. Their difference is antecedent to them because they presuppose as it were a space which contains and differentiates them, and no one of these categorical distinct realities establishes its difference from the other or is this difference.[13]

This position occupies the conceptual space between dualism and pantheism, and it is intended to accommodate their respective insights whilst avoiding their difficulties. The insight of dualism is that there is a distinction between God and the world; the insight of pantheism is that it is unlike any distinction within the world. It is unlike any distinction within the world because God is not a part of the world. The idea that God is not a part of the world suggests that He cannot be distinguished from things in the way that we distinguish *between* things—a point which rules out the possibility that He hovers beyond the world in any spatial sense.[14] So He is not outside His creation in this sense, and could be so only at the cost of being reduced to an item within it. Rather, He is the *source* of the distinction between God and world. It is in this sense that we can say that God establishes the difference of the world from Himself.[15] The further claim—implicit in the suggestion that He *is* this difference—is that the closest unity is established in this differentiation. That is to say that the reality God creates is not ultimately separable from Him. It is not ultimately separable from Him, but Rahner makes it clear that God cannot be known in Himself. He is the ultimate measure which cannot itself be measured:

---

[12] *Foundations of Christian Faith*, p. 62.

[13] *Foundations of Christian Faith*, pp. 62–63.

[14] See Gregory, 'No Room for God?', p. 503, and Brian Davies, 'The Doctrine of Divine Simplicity', in *Language, Meaning and God: Essays in Honour of Herbert McCabe OP*, ed. Brian Davies (Eugene, Oregon: Wipf and Stock, 2010), p. 62.

[15] Compare Sokolowski: 'God is understood not only to have created the world, but to have permitted the distinction between himself and the world to occur', *The God of Faith and Reason*, p. 33.

The infinite expanse which can and does encompass everything cannot itself be encompassed…it presents itself to us in the mode of withdrawal, of silence, of distance, of being always inexpressible, so that speaking of it, if it is to make sense, always requires listening to its silence…We do not know God by himself as one individual object amongst others, but only as the term of transcendence…the term of this transcendence is mystery.[16]

5.3 THE GOD OF THE PHILOSOPHERS

The idea that God is the source of reality promises to accommodate the claim that there is the greatest conceivable contrast between God and world (and God and man), although it remains to be seen how this contrast is to be squared with the idea that we stand in the most intimate connection with Him. I shall return to this problem in the following chapter, but we can begin to pave the way towards its resolution by considering a rather different complaint, namely, that such a position is in danger of *compromising* God's otherness in some sense, and that this has the effect of isolating us from God. The implication here—paradoxical though it may seem—is that God's otherness is a condition upon our being able to relate to Him.

A version of this complaint is to be found in Heidegger, and it begins from the thought that if God is the source of reality, then it follows that reality is to be understood with reference to this source. The idea seems innocuous enough as it stands. After all, if God is the source of reality, then it can scarcely be denied that, at some level of understanding, reality demands reference to this source. The worry, however, is that we become susceptible to a similar error to that which is operative when we seek to comprehend the world from the perspective of our all too human values—a perspective which, Heidegger believes, has the effect of robbing things of their intrinsic worth. The theme is familiar from Chapter 2, the question there being whether we should grant the possibility of there being a dimension of reality whose worth is not a mere function of its capacity to satisfy.

Our previous discussion of these claims was focused upon their relevance to the problem of value, and their theistic significance was left on one side. Heidegger makes it clear, however, that the offending approach gains a foothold when we seek to comprehend God. Thus, we are told that:

When one proclaims 'God' the altogether 'highest value', this is a degradation of God's essence. Here as elsewhere thinking in values is the greatest blasphemy imaginable against being.[17]

---

[16] *Foundations of Christian Faith*, pp. 64–65.
[17] 'Letter on Humanism', trans. F.A. Capuzzi, in *Basic Writings*, ed. D.F. Krell (London: Routledge Press, 1978), p. 251.

He claims also that this way of thinking finds expression in the idea that God is the 'highest being in the sense of the first cause of all beings', and that, considered as such, He becomes 'the transcendent' or 'supersensible being'. We are left in no doubt that such a conception leaves us 'cut loose' from God. We become merely 'worldly' creatures, 'turned away from God'.[18] Elsewhere, we are told that this is the 'god of philosophy', that 'man can neither fall to his knees in awe nor can he play music and dance before this god', and that 'the god-less thinking which must abandon the god of philosophy, god as *causa sui*, is thus perhaps closer to the divine God'.[19]

Heidegger describes the offending approach to God as 'onto-theological',[20] 'onto-theology' now being a rather convenient and generic term of abuse which, as Merold Westphal puts it:

> becomes the abracadabra by which a triumphalist secularism makes the world immune to any God who resembles personal creator, Lawgiver, and Merciful Savior of Jewish, or Christian, or Muslim monotheism. The only religion that escapes the Lord High Executioners who speak as Heidegger's prophets is religion that is pagan/polytheistic, pantheistic, or a/theistic (with or without the slash).[21]

Our previous arguments suggest that pagan religion can be of little help to those who seek to transcend the kind of thinking with which Heidegger takes issue, at least, not so long as it assumes the 'egoistic' form with which we have been concerned, and that pantheism simply plays into the hands of the conception according to which God is a god by assuming that if He is not like this, then He must be banished from the picture. This much is familiar enough, but where does it leave the idea of God as ontological source? Are we to suppose that such a conception likewise turns us away from the true God? And what does any of this have to do with the putative sins of onto-theology?

Heidegger does not take issue with the god before whom we can fall to our knees with awe. Perhaps he takes this to be the truth in pagan religion, for these gods are nothing if not objects of worship.[22] Rather, it is the god of philosophy we are required to abandon, the god who is identified as 'the first cause of all beings'. Talk of the god of philosophy is liable to mislead, for it suggests that we have a clearly defined target whose shortcomings are, or at least

---

[18] 'Letter on Humanism', p. 252.

[19] *Identity and Difference*, trans. Joan Stambaugh (Chicago: HarperCollins Inc., 1969), p. 72.

[20] *Identity and Difference*, p. 71.

[21] 'Overcoming Onto-theology', in *Overcoming Onto-theology: Towards a Post-Modern Christian Faith* (Fordham: Fordham University Press, 2001), pp. 3–4.

[22] McCabe goes so far as to say that they are nothing but objects of worship: 'It is characteristic of false gods that they are nothing but *objects of worship*. They have no other reality. The God of truth has to exist in its own right whether we worship her or not; talk about the gods has to be talk about human belief and cultures' ('The God of Truth', in *God Still Matters* (London: Continuum, 2002), p. 29). Of course, it is a further question whether these gods are *worthy* of worship. Paul Moser argues that they are not: 'morally deficient beings don't merit worship...because their moral deficiency recommends against full trust in them. A worshiped

ought to be, obvious to all, and that any attempt to philosophize about God is bound to misfire. A cursory look at the history of philosophy suggests that the very idea of identifying such a target is a pipedream for those who substitute caricature for genuine engagement. To be sure, we can seek to impose the required restriction by focusing upon the God of certain key figures, for example, those who have a penchant for the idea that God is the first cause of all beings. However, such an idea supports a variety of positions, not all of which rule out the possibility that He is an appropriate object of worship. It is clear also that the danger of caricature looms large in this context too, for the positions of those who stand accused of propagating the offending god often bear little resemblance to the versions with which we are presented.[23] Again, we are left wondering what the target in question is supposed to be, whether it admits of any genuine instances, and whether the surrounding rhetoric isn't just a cheap way of imposing an a priori ban upon any attempt to philosophize about God.

Westphal suggests that the real error of the onto-theologian is to suppose that philosophy can render the whole of reality intelligible to human understanding, and that God can be put to the service of this project—a project which involves 'human mastery of the real'.[24] The pejorative tones are obvious,

---

being should thus be without moral deficiency, and, therefore, we ourselves are immediately disqualified as candidates for (worthiness of) worship. That shouldn't come as breaking news to anyone...Polytheism suffers gravely from the fact that it's difficult to find even *one* being worthy of worship' (*The Elusive God* (Cambridge: Cambridge University Press, 2008), p. 18).

[23] Hegel is the culprit in Heidegger's *Identity and Difference* (p. 56), but Hegel takes himself to be providing a philosophical defence of the Christian conception of God—a defence which is intended to accommodate the God 'before whom man can fall to his knees in awe'. Perhaps he fails to bring off this feat, but there has been no a priori demonstration of this. For a sympathetic account of Hegel's conception of God see Quentin Lauer SJ, *Hegel's Concept of God* (Albany: State University of New York Press, 1982). See also Anselm K. Min, 'Hegel's Absolute: Transcendent or Immanent?', *The Journal of Religion*, vol. 56, no. 1 (Jan 1976), pp. 61–87; 'The Trinity and the Incarnation: Hegel and Classical Approaches', *The Journal of Religion*, vol. 66, no. 2 (April 1986), pp. 173–193. Aquinas is identified as a culprit by Heideggarian scholars. For responses to this charge see Jean-Luc Marion, 'Thomas Aquinas and Onto-theo-logy', in *Mystics: Presence and Aporia*, ed. Michael Kessler and Christian Sheppard (Chicago: University of Chicago Press, 2003), pp. 38–74; Merold Westphal, 'Aquinas and Onto-theology', *American Catholic Philosophical Quarterly*, vol. 80, no. 2 (2006), pp. 73–91; Fergus Kerr, *After Aquinas: Versions of Thomism* (Oxford: Blackwell Publishing, 2002); A.N. Williams, *The Ground of Union: Deification in Aquinas and Palamas* (Oxford: Oxford University Press, 1999). For a defence of another figure who tends to be criticized in this context, namely, Descartes, see John Cottingham, 'Sceptical Detachment or Loving Submission to the Good? Reason, Faith, and the Passions in Descartes', *Faith and Philosophy*, vol. 28, no. 1 (January 2011). Levinas seeks to rescue Descartes from the charge of treating God as a mere inferential product, claiming that his arguments give expression to a profound religious experience (*Ethics and Infinity: Conversations with Philippe Nemo*, trans. R.A. Cohen (Pittsburgh: Duquesne University Press, 1985), pp. 91–92; *Otherwise than Being or Beyond Essence*, trans. Alphonso Lingis (Dordecht: Kluwer, 1991), p. 146). See also Hilary Putnam, *Jewish Philosophy as a Guide to Life: Rosenzweig, Buber, Levinas, Wittgenstein* (Bloomington: Indiana University Press, 2008), ch. 4.

[24] 'Overcoming Onto-theology', p. 4.

and we are to suppose that such mastery serves in some sense to compromise the reality of that which is mastered. Heidegger's worry about 'thinking in values' comes to mind, in particular, his claim that we commit the greatest blasphemy imaginable against Being if we approach it in these terms. We commit this blasphemy because such thinking leaves us blind to the intrinsic worth of things. Their value becomes a mere function of their capacity to satisfy and we fail to acknowledge a level of worth which exceeds such terms. It seems fair to say that we 'master' God in this sense when we treat Him as the ultimate satisfier. Thus understood, He becomes the supreme opportunity for giving us what we want—a grander and more user-friendly version of the gods of pre-scientific superstition, the 'highest value' in Heidegger's sense of that term.

The idea that God is the ultimate satisfier serves to compromise His otherness in one respect, for He is reduced to the status of a self-indulgent parent. However, such a conception seems a far cry from that according to which God is the ontological source of all things, which latter is a more obvious candidate for a philosophical God. Given, however, that the idea of God as source imposes no immediate philosophical constraints, it is unclear that it has to involve any kind of 'human mastery of the real'. At least, this is so if we interpret such mastery in cognitive terms, and take heed of Rahner's claim that God is the ultimate measure which cannot itself be measured. So there is room for allowing—or indeed, insisting—that God cannot be 'mastered' in this sense. It remains open, however, that there are versions of such a position which fail to respect this constraint.

Cognition returns us to theory, and theory to the idea that God could be an object of theoretical interest. We know from previous chapters that the notion of a theoretical interest is fairly broad as it stands, that approaching something in this manner is not bound to compromise its reality, but that this *can* follow if the theorizing in question turns out to be inappropriate to the phenomenon at hand. So, for example, it is inappropriate to approach human behaviour in the way that we approach the behaviour of electrons, and to approach our moral responses in the way that we approach our responses to things whose value is a mere function of their capacity to satisfy. If this is right, then the idea that God could be an object of theoretical interest imposes no immediate constraints other than to allow that we can reflect upon Him. In particular, there is no requirement that He be approached in the way that we approach other objects of theoretical interest, whether those objects are those which provide the focus of scientific interest or those with which we are concerned at the level of non-scientific explanation. Nor need it follow that we could ever know everything about God—that we could get the 'measure' of Him in this sense. So it is not ruled out that we can make some theoretical progress in this context, but we are to suppose that there are ways of proceeding which rule out this possibility—that our theorizing about God can miss its mark, and that we can become isolated from Him in the way that we become isolated from value when we abstract from the kind of perspective which must be operative if it is to be discerned and thought about in the first place. We are to suppose also that the required perspective upon God must concede something to Heidegger's worshipful attitude—that it is at this level of response that we can be said to 'find' God.[25]

5.4 GOD AS ULTIMATE EXPLAINER AND MAN AS ULTIMATE MEASURE

Westphal has told us that the real error of the onto-theologian is to suppose that philosophy can render the whole of reality intelligible to human understanding, and that God can be put to the service of this task. He spells this out further by claiming that, on this way of thinking, God is at the beck and call of human understanding—He becomes the means to our end of making the whole of being intelligible.[26] He is the ultimate explainer. We are returned to the idea that God *qua* source is that in terms of which reality is to be understood. I have suggested already that *if* God is the source of reality, then it makes perfect sense to accept this claim. We can allow also that He serves as ultimate explainer in this context, for the point could simply be that He provides a placeholder for an explanation we could never attain.[27] So there is no immediate implication that God is at the beck and call of human understanding. Nor is it clear that such a conception serves to compromise His otherness. On the contrary, the idea that the relevant explanation is unavailable to us serves more properly to *guarantee* that there is the greatest conceivable contrast between God and man. It might be thought also to put paid to the idea that these terms could be intimately connected.

The position with which Westphal takes issue involves a rather different interpretation of the claim that God *qua* source is ultimate explainer. According to this interpretation, God precisely *is* at the beck and call of human understanding, for He becomes the means to the end of making the whole of being intelligible to ourselves—an end which is said to involve human mastery of the real. Now there is absolutely nothing wrong with wanting to explain things, and it is for this reason that we can applaud the rise of modern science.

---

[25] Compare Nicholas Lash who, having conceded that there is important academic work to be done on the question of God, insists that if this work is not done, at least metaphorically, 'on one's knees, with one's shoes off, then it will miss the mark' ('The Impossibility of Atheism', p. 28). We might also bear in mind Wiggins's insistence that the philosopher of value remove her rubber gloves (*Ethics: Twelve Lectures on the Philosophy of Morality* (London: Penguin, 2006), p. 320). I shall return to Lash's claim in the final chapter.

[26] 'Overcoming Onto-theology', p. 12.

[27] See Westphal, 'Overcoming Onto-theology', p. 7.

Science can be said to involve a kind of mastery of the real if this is just a fancy and needlessly pejorative way of saying that it puts us in a position to get the measure of things. So we are capable of mastering things in this sense, but there is no reason for thinking that such mastery compromises their reality, and every reason for thinking that it has an emancipatory effect at the level of both explainer and explained.[28] This much should be clear from the previous chapter. It should be clear also that there are forms of explanation which render intelligible phenomena that resist scientific treatment. Again, there is no implication that our explanatory pretensions in this context are dubious. On the contrary, they promise a way of vindicating the reality of phenomena which tend to be squeezed out of the picture if we succumb to scientism.

So the problem is not with the explanatory drive per se. The difficulty arises, rather, when this drive assumes a distorted form. It becomes distorted when we fail to explain things on their own terms, and one way of committing this error is by committing to scientism. It is in this context that we can be said to master things in the pejorative sense. We do so by squeezing them into an inappropriate straitjacket which has the effect of compromising their reality. Failing to explain things on their own terms suggests that the terms in question are ours, and Heidegger takes this to be an expression of our tendency to control and to possess. We want the measure of things, and we shall stop at nothing to get it. There is obviously *some* truth in this claim, evidence for which can be found in the fundamentalist tones which accompany the message of those naturalists who remain unduly dazzled by science.[29] However, it is not the whole truth, for we are motivated also by the desire to explain things on their own terms. Such a motivation involves the desire to get the measure of things in some sense, but it goes hand in hand with a preparedness to give due weight to the reality of the relevant phenomena, and to question those approaches which fail on this score. It also involves a willingness to acknowledge our human standpoint, and it is in this respect that equal weight must be given to the terms—our terms—which define our explanatory endeavours. So we must enquire on our own terms to this degree at least, these terms will vary depending upon the nature of the phenomena we are seeking to comprehend, and there need be no implication that this involves anything remotely pernicious or controlling. The points are familiar from the case of value.

---

[28] Of course, we can challenge this picture by insisting that our concepts function as distorting instruments. There is no doubt an insight lurking in such a position, namely, that our concepts *can* function in this way. Perhaps we must also allow that there is a dimension of reality which is in principle inhospitable to conceptualization—Rahner's measure which cannot be measured is an obvious case in point. However, none of this suffices to show that all conceptualization involves distortion, and I know of no good arguments—Kantian or otherwise—to warrant such a conclusion.

[29] Compare Weber's description of the process of rationalization which arose in the wake of modern science: 'we can in principle *control everything*'.

So we can fail to explain things on their own terms, and one way of under-standing the offending approach to God is to say that it involves a version of this error. That is to say that when we treat God as a means to the end of mak-ing the whole of being intelligible to ourselves we are approaching Him on our terms alone and failing to give due weight to His reality. We are mastering Him in the aforementioned pejorative sense. Such an approach to God is theoretical in one obvious sense, for He promises to satisfy our desire to get the measure of everything. But what could it mean to exploit God in this way? Surely the very idea that we could succeed in this aim involves a failure to acknowledge our human standpoint. This is true, but the position at issue is intended to give expression to our desire to get the measure of everything and our belief that this desire can be satisfied. So God is at the beck and call of human understand-ing in the sense that we aspire to the position of ultimate measure and claim to be able to occupy it. Westphal accepts this interpretation, citing Heidegger's claim that 'man contends for the position in which he can be that particular being who gives the measure and draws up the guidelines for everything that is'.[30] He claims also that, on this way of thinking, 'God is part of this world that revolves around "man"', and, returning again to Heidegger, tells us that God loses 'all that is exalted and holy, the mysteriousness of his distance'.[31]

There is a clear enough sense in which God's otherness is compromised on this picture, for He loses 'the mysteriousness of his distance', and becomes 'part of the world that revolves around man'. He loses the mysteriousness of His distance because we are said to be capable of adopting His perspective, and He becomes part of the world that revolves around man in the sense that man exchanges roles with God, turning God into just one more item to be measured alongside everything else. He is reduced to a God for us, and the idea that there is the greatest conceivable contrast between man and God is lost. This contrast is lost, but there is a sense in which such a position strives to maintain the intimate connection between man and God. After all, man aspires to the position of ultimate measure, and he claims to have the measure of God. It should be clear, however, that this connection is secured only at the cost of compromising God's reality and of inflating man's reality beyond all

---

[30] 'Overcoming Onto-theology', p. 12. The quote from Heidegger comes from 'The Age of the World Picture', in *The Question Concerning Technology and Other Essays*, trans. William Lovitt (New York: Harper and Row, 1977), p. 134. The idea that man contends in this way for the posi-tion of God is eminently understandable if we accept with Sartre that 'man fundamentally is the desire to be God' (*Being and Nothingness: An Essay on Phenomenological Ontology*, trans. Hazel Barnes (London: Routledge, 1958), p. 566). Sartre takes this claim to be equivalent to the claim that 'to be man means to reach towards God'. Hence: 'To be man means to reach toward being God. Or if you prefer, man fundamentally is the desire to be God.' It is one of the tasks of this book to challenge this equivalence.

[31] 'Overcoming Onto-theology', p. 12. The Heidegger quote comes from 'The Question Concerning Technology', in *The Question Concerning Technology and Other Essays*, p. 26.

reasonable proportion, for God is not a thing to be measured without remainder and man is not the ultimate measure.

5.5 FURTHER CLARIFICATION OF THE OFFENDING APPROACH AND SOME CULPRITS

We have a conception of God as source which compromises His otherness and isolates us from Him. God becomes a means for satisfying our desire to know it all—a desire whose satisfaction demands that we occupy the perspective of this source. Such a position severs our connection with God because He cannot be exploited to this theoretical end. He cannot be so exploited because there is the greatest conceivable contrast between man and God, and man can neither assume the perspective of God nor treat Him as an object to be used in this manner. This much is clear enough, but it raises some important questions. First, does anybody in the history of philosophy and theology really think of God in these terms? Second, how does it relate to the theoretical approach to God which was criticized in the previous chapter? Third, where does it leave naturalism?

The question of who the position can be pinned upon is important given the reservations I have expressed about identifying an appropriate God of philosophy, and I shall argue that the offending line of thought is best appreciated in the context of our overall naturalistic themes. We can begin to get a sense of this more general issue by considering how the position is to be related to the theoretical approach discussed in the previous chapter. The context of the discussion there was the question of how we are to comprehend the concept of the supernatural, the target being the kind of position which identifies the supernatural with God and locates Him in an inaccessible, incommunicable beyond. We are left with a divine person behind the scenes who starts everything up to retreat into the background, and the supernatural becomes a spooky and ultimately unintelligible addition to a world—the natural world—which can be understood perfectly well in its absence.

This position involves a conception of God as source, for the emphasis is upon His role in getting things started. He is the source of things in this sense, but it is implied that His work is terminated at this point—He retreats into an inaccessible beyond to leave things to their own devices. We are therefore cut off from this source to become 'worldly' creatures in Heidegger's sense of that term. So there is no possibility of being inwardly transformed by God, and we can relate to Him, if at all, only by exploiting the naturalistic resources to which we are confined on this way of thinking. For example, we can endeavour to prove His existence, doing so perhaps by reflecting upon the observed order of the world we inhabit—the world which has been left to its own devices.

Equally, however, and this is important given the antinomy which has been set up between God and nature, we might employ our theoretical resources to demonstrate that the natural world is self-sustaining, and that reference to a theistic source is both redundant and needlessly problematic. In such a scenario, this source becomes 'other' in the pejorative sense and we quickly fall back on the world which is left once this worrisome ontological addition has been put to rest. That is to say, we move from dualism to pantheism in Rahner's sense of those terms.

This dialectical transition is going to provide the link between the theoretical approach to God at issue here and that which is operative when we treat Him as a means to the end of knowing it all. On the face of it, however, the two approaches are very different, for in the latter scenario we have no interest in proving God's existence or speculating about His nature. Rather, our interest in Him is purely instrumental—it is aimed at God only in so far as He can be put to the service of our theoretical aims. Second, and consequently, there is a sense in which this second position is shorn of any explicitly deistic dimension. For the source of reality is no longer a divine person behind the scenes. Rather, He is at our disposal and that in terms of which the whole of things is to be understood. So the antinomy between God and nature/man is broken at one level. At another level, however, it is simply reinforced, for God is not at our disposal, and man, being a part of the world, cannot take His place. We are led to suppose, however, that man's aspirations in this context will lead inexorably towards atheism—that in this case too we shall be compelled to fall back on the world which remains once this ontological addition has been eliminated. As Michael J. Buckley has put it, we have the glory of god in conflict with the glory of nature or human nature, an alienation which, he claims, 'will eventually be resolved in favour of the natural and the human. Any implicit, unspoken enmity between god and creation will issue in atheism.'[32]

We have two theoretical approaches to God both of which view Him as the source of reality and both of which lead fairly quickly to atheism. On the first approach we take a theoretical interest in the nature and existence of this source, but theory leads us to question its metaphysical and epistemological credentials, and it becomes a worrisome and superfluous addition to our ontology. Nature does not require reference to a theistic source, it sustains itself. The assumption here is that a theistic source is bound to be a separable something else, a further addition to the household of all reality—a household which can get along perfectly well in its absence. So our theorizing resources are put to the task of eliminating this something else, and God becomes part of the world that revolves around man—a part of the world we can do without. Theory looms large in the second approach to God, and it threatens likewise

---

[32] *At the Origins of Modern Atheism* (Yale: Yale University Press, 1987), pp. 348, 363.

to eliminate Him from the equation. In this case, however, our initial focus is not a separable something else which is subsequently discarded in favour of the natural world. Rather, our focus is already the natural world, God being the means for explaining it in the most ultimate and all-inclusive terms. So this position operates with a conception of reality as a God-sustained whole, but His position is usurped by man as our theoretical pretensions lead us to suppose that these explanatory terms are available to us. Working under this presupposition, we might then turn our theoretical aspirations to the task of explaining the whole of things and come to the conclusion that a theistic explanatory source was never a serious contender in the first place. After all, we are capable of getting the measure of things, we do not need God to assist us in this task, and He served, at best, as a placeholder for an explanation we are now in a position to give. On this way of thinking, God is on a level with the gods of pre-scientific superstition.

The reference to science is significant, for one obvious way of furnishing the details of this story is by reference to the explanatory resources which come with the advent of modern science. Modern science has allowed us to get the measure of many things, and to do so without making appeal to the 'occult' forces which ruled the day when the gods were on the scene. So our explanatory pretensions are met to this degree at least, but the difficulty arises when we are tempted to conclude that science provides the measure of everything, and that by exploiting its resources we can, as Heidegger puts it, give the measure and draw up the guidelines for everything that is. If we accept also that this conceit can be glossed in theistic terms—that it involves man's desire to usurp the position of God—then we have a possible answer to the question of who thinks of God in the relevant onto-theological terms. It is the scientific naturalist.

It may seem odd to describe the scientific naturalist as an onto-theologian, and to accuse him of using God as a means to his own theoretical ends, for he has already banished God from the equation. The description gains credence, however, once it is remembered that we are concerned with an approach to God which was never a serious contender for theology, that its primary aim is to secure man's status as ultimate explainer, and that man's aspirations in this context lead inexorably to atheism. They lead to atheism when motivated by scientism, for scientism generates a conception of God which turns Him into just the kind of spooky entity that such a position is designed to eradicate. After all, God cannot be comprehended by science, and science has the measure of everything.

So the scientific naturalist counts as an onto-theologian in this sense, as does any philosopher or theologian who contends for the position of ultimate explainer. The theologian seems far removed from the scientific naturalist, and one might suppose that it is built into his starting-point that the position of ultimate explainer must remain the exclusive preserve of God. In this respect it is difficult to make sense of the idea that such a figure could be an onto-theologian in the sense at issue here. Likewise for any philosopher who retains a modicum of epistemic humility. I have suggested, however, that there is a way of approaching God which involves a similar theoretical bias but which takes as its focus His nature and existence. We have been led to suppose that the relevant offenders are not confined to card-carrying atheists, but that their treatment precipitates such a move by turning Him into a spooky and ultimately dispensable addition to our ontology.

These thinkers are dualists in Rahner's sense of that term, but who exactly are they? Some of them will be scientific naturalists who are out to expose the errors of such thinking, doing so, for example, by demonstrating the futility of all proofs of God's existence, and identifying the needless metaphysical conundrums which are generated if we add Him to our ontology. There will also be those who have seen beyond the errors of scientific naturalism, but who continue to view God in the relevant dualistic terms and favour an atheistic response. Our expansive naturalist falls into this category. It is misleading at one level to describe his approach to God as theoretical, for he has absolutely no theoretical interest in the question of God. At another level, however, the description is exactly right, for although his dismissal of God is not scientistically motivated, it *is* theoretically motivated: we can explain what needs to be explained without this worrisome ontological addition. The assumption again is that God is just one more item within the larger household of all reality, and that this eliminative move leaves everything important in its place. Are we to conclude that the expansive naturalist is claiming to have the measure of everything? That he is an onto-theologian in the sense previously defined? In one obvious sense he is not, for he resists scientific naturalism, is anxious to explain things on their own terms, and acknowledges a dimension of reality whose worth is not a mere function of its capacity to satisfy. He also stops short of banishing God from our ontology. He stops short of doing this, but he does remove any trace of God from the natural world. Is he claiming to have the measure of nature? He would no doubt resist this charge, but there is a sense in which he has done so by assuming that it cannot be understood in God-involving terms. He can also be said to have taken the measure of God. He does so by relegating Him to a second, supernatural realm.[33] Again, God becomes other in the offending dualistic sense, and we are led to fall back on the natural world, albeit a world whose limits have been expanded beyond scientistic parameters. We have, if you like, a form of pantheism which is moving ever nearer to its theistic counterpart as the dualistic framework begins to unravel.

---

[33] Compare Lash: 'Agnosticism, and certain kinds of atheism, are forms of idolatry inasmuch as they suppose themselves to have identified the "nature" of God, a nature which proscribes all mention of him' ('Considering the Trinity', *Modern Theology*, vol. 2, no. 3 (April 1986), p. 193.

What of those theorizers of God who are not atheists but who encourage such a position by accepting a similar dualistic framework? Who are *they*? Rahner refers to the naïve theist in this context, Mascall talks of the theologian who ends up disowning the concept of the supernatural, and Heidegger implicates the philosophers. Mascall accuses Robinson of disowning the concept of the supernatural, but I have suggested that he is seeking its vindication, doing so by resisting the offending dualistic framework which forces God behind the scenes. Robinson himself implies that the framework is endemic to traditional Christian theology,[34] and is taken to task by those who object that his so-called discoveries and amendments are already firmly entrenched within the tradition.[35] It cannot be ruled out that Heidegger's discoveries invite a similar criticism, although his philosophical god is to be found in the treatment of the aforementioned naturalists.

Buckley implicates the theologian in this dialectic, arguing that the offending dualistic framework arises when the question of God becomes a philosophical question rather than a religious or theological one, and it is assumed that philosophy can proceed in abstraction from any common religious tradition and the experiences it involves.[36] The tradition with which he is concerned is the Judaeo-Christian one, and according to the offending position 'there are no specifically religious resources upon which theology might reflect'. Rather, the theologian must 'apply to the philosophers for philosophic information'.[37] The information in question is to be found within the natural world—a world which can be understood in abstraction from God—and the strongest evidence for God becomes the design within nature. It is in this way that nature comes to constitute the evidence for the existence of God, and philosophy is the discipline by which this evidence is analysed.[38] The theologian is transformed into a natural theologian, and such a figure has no need of sacred doctrine.[39] He is 'convinced or informed about god "from the outside" '.[40] The upshot is that 'impersonal nature eventually moved through its theological denials to reassert itself as dynamic with the predicates once reserved for god, "eternal" and "infinite" '.[41] That is to say, we move from dualism to pantheism—a pantheism

---

[34] See, for example, *Honest to God* (London: SCM Press, 1963), ch. 2 'The End of Theism?'.

[35] As Hugo Meynell puts it: 'what purports to be contemporary discovery in theology, in fact, turns out to be medieval metaphysics, summarily expressed and insufficiently worked out' (*The New Theology and Modern Theologians* (London: Sheed and Ward, 1967), p. 8. See also the contributions to *The Honest to God Debate*, ed. John A.T. Robinson and David L. Edwards (London: SCM Press, 1963). See in particular the reviews by C.S. Lewis, and E.L. Mascall; 'Concerning Theism', by David Jenkins; 'God and the Theologians', by Alasdair MacIntyre.

[36] *At the Origins of Modern Atheism*, p. 341.

[37] *At the Origins of Modern Atheism*, p. 342. The quote comes from Étienne Gilson's *Elements of Christian Philosophy* (New York: Doubleday, 1960), p. 33.

[38] *At the Origins of Modern Atheism*, p. 345.

[39] *At the Origins of Modern Atheism*, p. 343.

[40] *At the Origins of Modern Atheism*, p. 346.

[41] *At the Origins of Modern Atheism*, p. 359.

which, like the expansive naturalist version noted above, is veering ever close to incorporating the vital missing ingredient.[42]

It will be a task of the final chapter to unpack these claims about philosophy and theology, but the dialectic is familiar enough, and Buckley identifies various offenders in the theological tradition running from the seventeenth-century Jesuit Leonard Lessius of Louvain through to Descartes, Newton, Clarke, and Malebranche. He avoids oversimplification, acknowledges that there are dissenters, and has no issue with the project of natural theology per se. The point is simply that 'the god defined in religion cannot be affirmed or supported adequately over time without the unique reality of religion . . . *God* is not a neutral term'.[43] He claims also that:

> The dynamism of the human mind inevitably moves toward a transcendence that makes sense out of that which does not explain or justify itself. A doctrine of god can arise within such an inquiry when the namelessly transcendent is approached as its asymptotic horizon, or as the never-comprehended 'lure of transcendence', or as that which essentially is, giving context and intelligibility to everything else encountered and understood but remaining endlessly other. God has emerged again and again in the history of wisdom as the direction toward which wonder progresses. It is neither deluded nor simpleminded to discover with Augustine that everything within human scope, especially the human person, points beyond itself.[44]

5.6 CONCLUSION

We are returned to Rahner's conception of God as the ultimate measure which cannot be measured and a conception of His otherness which promises to transcend the dualistic terms at issue when He is located in an inaccessible realm. It is implied that we are no longer cut loose from God, but that we can relate to Him—and appreciate His radical otherness—only by moving beyond the naturalistic framework which is an inevitable by-product of this dualism. This framework is in place when we see God as the product of a problematic inference from the materials which are available to us at the level of (non God-involving) nature. It is operative also when we are compelled to move in an atheistic direction on the seemingly indisputable ground that the natural world contains no traces of the divine, and can, in any case, be

---

[42] See Bilgrami's 'The Wider Significance of Naturalism: A Genealogical Essay', in *Naturalism and Normativity*, ed.Mario De Caro and David Macarthur (New York: Columbia University Press, 2010) for a fascinating discussion of pantheism and its relevance to secular expansive naturalism.

[43] *At the Origins of Modern Atheism*, pp. 360–361.

[44] *At the Origins of Modern Atheism*, p. 362.

explained without this unnecessary theistic shuffle. In one important sense these conclusions are exactly right, for God is not a part of nature, and there is a sense in which nature can be understood as a self-sustaining whole. As we have seen, however, the idea that God is not a part of nature does nothing to undermine the thought that He is its source. Nor does it rule out the possibility that these terms are intimately connected. Likewise, the idea that nature is a self-sustaining whole is compatible with the idea that it has a theistic source, although we must be wary of conceiving of this source as a separable something else lest we revert to the kind of pantheism with which Rahner takes issue.

Expansive naturalism poses a challenge to the idea that pantheism is bound to assume a crude scientistic form.[45] To be sure, it is not a pantheism which involves seeing God in all things, but it does involve seeing nature as evaluatively enchanted—a nature which can move us to engagement with it on *its terms* rather than simply on ours.[46] So the expansive naturalist gives due weight to the moral, and provides a challenge to the assumption that values must be comprehended scientifically on pain of being intolerably odd. In this respect the offending dualistic framework is dislodged at the level of value, but it reasserts itself in a theistic context with the claim that God could only ever be a spooky *something else*. I have suggested already that we must take seriously the possibility of taking the expansive exercise in a theistic direction.

Where does this leave the relation between evaluative enchantment and divine enchantment? We know already that, for the scientific naturalist, these modes of enchantment form a joint package in the sense that they stand in equal need of rejection, and *can* be rejected whilst leaving everything else in its place. At least, this is so on the assumption that evaluative enchantment is comprehended in the required non-scientific terms. However, there need be no implication that they are connected in any deeper sense, for the point could simply be that the relevant

---

[45] Robinson cites the following extract from Paul Tillich in the context of discussing this issue: 'The Phrase *deus sive natura,* used by people like Scotus Erigena and Spinoza, does not say that God is identical with nature but that he is identical with *natura naturans,* the creative nature, the creative ground of all natural objects. In modern naturalism the religious quality of these affirmations has almost disappeared, especially amongst philosophising scientists who understand nature in terms of materialism and mechanism' (*Honest to God,* p. 16). The Tillich quotation comes from his *Systematic Theology: Existence and the Christ,* vol. II (Chicago: University of Chicago Press, 1975), p. 7.

[46] This is how Bilgrami describes the position in the context of relating it to the pantheism/deism debate which took place in Enlightenment thinking. One of the fundamental points he makes is that it is quite misguided to suppose that there was just one Enlightenment: 'For the dissenters, God and nature were not separable as in the official metaphysical picture that was growing around the new science, and John Toland, for instance, to take just one example among the active dissenting voices, openly wrote in terms he proclaimed to be "pantheistic"... The dissenters thought of the *world* not as brute but as *suffused with value.* That they happened to think that the source of value was divine may not be the deepest source of interest for us today' ('The Wider Significance of Naturalism', p. 39).

items belong to the inventory of those tempted by cosmic excess, that there are other such items, and that they can be added or subtracted in a piecemeal fashion. Now if our rejection of scientism is articulated with this picture in mind, then the idea will be that once we grant a place within nature to value, then there are good prospects for introducing other items which resist scientific treatment. The expansive naturalist calls a halt to the expansive exercise as far as God is concerned, and at one level his resistance makes perfect sense given that God is not a part of the natural world. If we accept, however, that the alternative 'supernaturalist' approach—God as a non-natural something else—is equally unsatisfactory, then we must consider what follows on a proper understanding of the idea that God is the source of nature. One obvious consequence is that God can no longer be treated as just one more item to be added to the inventory of the expansive naturalist. So He does not form a joint package with value in this sense, and could do so only on pain of being a member of the larger household of reality. Rather, He forms a joint package with value in the sense that He is its source as well as being the source of everything else.

The expansive naturalist will continue to protest, and if he does so on the ground that there is nothing in nature to warrant such a conclusion then he is in good company with the sensible theologian who insists upon God's necessary absence from the world. As noted, however, the point of this claim is to remind us that God is not a part of the world, it does not exclude the possibility of our standing in an intimate relation with Him, and we have been led to suppose that this relationship is fudged if God's otherness is compromised in the ways we have considered. How then is this relationship to be understood? We have been told that God can inwardly transform us, that our natural being is perfected in this manner, and that we are elevated hereby into His life. These claims would be absurd to our expansive naturalist. However, they become less obviously so if we substitute 'goodness' for 'God', and recall what the expansive naturalist wishes to say about our relation to value. The reference to value is fundamental for our purposes, for it is a commonplace of the biblical and theological tradition that we relate to God by being moral. Indeed, we shall see that Levinas goes so far as to claim that this is the *only* way of relating to God,[47] and that anything more has the effect of compromising both God's reality and our humanity.

If it is granted that we relate to God in moral terms then the gap between secular expansive naturalism and its theistic counterpart is narrowed considerably. If we grant also that this is the *only* way of relating to God, then the positions may be thought to merge into one, albeit in a manner which has the

---

[47] There is a clear biblical precedent for such a view: 'If anyone says, "I love God" and hates his brother, he is a liar; for can he who does not love his brother, whom he has seen, love God, whom he has not seen?' (1 John 4:20).

potential for squeezing God out of the equation again. It is in the context of these points that we can appreciate the following remarks of Rahner:

> The tendency today to talk not about God, but about one's neighbour, to preach not about the love of God, but about the love of neighbour, and to use not the term 'God', but 'world' and 'responsibility for the world'—we can see that this tendency has an absolutely solid foundation. However, going to the extreme of banishing God and of being radically silent about him is and remains false and does violence to the true nature of Christianity.
>
> But what is correct about all of these statements is the plain fact that we do not know God by himself as one individual object amongst others, but only as the term of transcendence...the term of this transcendence is mystery.[48]

---

[48] *Foundations of Christian Faith*, pp. 64–65.

6

God and Value

6.1 INTRODUCTION

God is wholly other with respect to man and nature, but these terms are intimately connected. This is the position we are seeking to comprehend, and my aim here is to shed further light upon the issue by trading upon the conclusions we have drawn about our relation to value. More specifically, the claim to be examined is that we relate to God by relating to value. We have pre-empted a potential objection to this approach, namely, that by focusing upon our relation to value we are in danger of banishing God from the equation. To this we might add that an adequate conception of the relation between God and nature requires reference not simply to *our* relation to God but also to God's relation to us, and more generally, to the world of which we are a part. The implication here is that the envisaged approach is doubly flawed: it fails to accommodate our relation to God, and it fails to accommodate God's relation to us.

The idea that we relate to God by relating to value does not lead inevitably to atheism, and we shall find Levinas insisting that it is exactly what is needed if we are to *avoid* such a position. Why? Because it promises to accommodate God's radical otherness, guaranteeing above all that, as Rahner puts it, we do not know Him as one individual object amongst others. If this is so, then, *pace* Rahner, the approach in question is precisely *not* a way of banishing God and of being radically silent about Him.[1] Second, however, it is not ruled out that there are other ways of relating to God, and that relating to value is just one of several such ways. Such a position will be manna to those who suspect that our relation to value is not properly God-involving, although it would be incumbent upon them to clarify what a properly God-involving relation amounts to, and to respond to Levinas's worry that we shall exceed these moral terms only at the cost of retreating into atheism.

---

[1] Rahner does not think that an ethical approach to God involves knowing Him as one object amongst others. However, he worries that the approach is in danger of banishing God from the equation in a different sense. I return to this point towards the end of the chapter.

It is equally important that we accommodate God's relation to us, but what does this mean? And why should it be thought that a focus upon our relation to value is bound to fall short in this regard? One possible worry is that the latter focus puts all the emphasis upon the human side of the relation. If we believe also that evaluative thinking is a mere reflection of our selfish interests, then the idea that our relation to value could have anything to do with God is doomed from the start. I have questioned this conception of value, and granted with the expansive naturalist that there are values which impose normative constraints upon us—constraints which, in a moral context at least, pose a challenge to the idea that they are bound to be 'human all too human' in the offending egoistic sense. So a focus upon our relation to value need not be limiting in *this* respect. But to repeat our previous worry, why suppose that this relation has anything to do with God? The expansive naturalist will insist that our relation to value is exactly what it seems, and that there is no justification for supposing either that God relates to us in a moral context or that we relate to God. An adequate response to this worry demands an account of what it could mean to introduce God in either of these ways, and we shall see that there are approaches which undermine our capacity to be moral. Levinas, by contrast, will insist that relating to value is both necessary and sufficient for relating to God, and offers a version of this position which promises to sidestep the relevant difficulties whilst accommodating the insights of expansive naturalism. I shall return to Levinas in due course. First though, we need to dispense with some of the more problematic conceptions of the relation between ourselves, value, and God.

6.2 GOD AND VALUE: SOME PROBLEMATIC MODELS

One such position—familiar from our previous discussion—is that God functions as a cosmic coercive force who guarantees unwavering obedience to the requirements of morality. He does so either by forcing us into submission in spite of ourselves or by rewarding and punishing conformity and disobedience to the relevant requirements. So we relate to God by relating to value in the sense that we relate to this cosmic coercive force. The idea that God is a cosmic coercive force threatens to undermine His status as a person, but we can incorporate this dimension by adding that moral requirements are determined by God's desires—we are made to do what He wants us to do. A further familiar extension of the position—one of the horns of the so-called Euthyphro dilemma—is that there is no guarantee that these desires are properly moral. That is to say, it remains open that the relevant requirements are produced with an indifferent toss of a coin or that they are the dictates of a tyrant whose only motive is to advance his own selfish ends. On this latter picture, God becomes an infinitely more powerful version of the gods, and we are forced into submission either because we fear punishment or foresee future rewards, or because we are compelled by a force beyond our control. The first two options grant us a modicum of choice, albeit one which is guided by prudential considerations; the third option, by contrast, takes the matter out of our hands—we just act, or, more accurately, we are moved. Either way, there is no sense to be made of the idea that we could be motivated to be moral.

This picture provides a hopeless interpretation of what it could mean to say that we relate to God by relating to value, for God is neither an omnipotent egoist nor an indifferent coin tosser, and *we* can be motivated to be moral. We could correct the offending conception of God by allowing that, being essentially good, He desires only what is good and right. This allows us to fill the normative gap which remains when value is constructed from the motivational tendencies of an immoral or amoral being. Thus understood, the will of God becomes the embodiment of what is good and right. Of course, there is no question of what a perfectly good being *ought* to do, so it would be misguided to say that the desires of such a being are normatively constrained. As Wiggins has put it in the context of discussing a different but related position—moral *requirement* is not even a question.[2] Moral requirement is not a question, but there is a question about how such a picture can shed any light upon the problem of how beings like ourselves who are not perfectly good in this sense could be motivated to be moral. It is familiar from Chapter 2 that there has been a tendency to turn the trick by reintroducing the remaining elements of the offending picture. That is to say that God remains a cosmic coercive force who compromises *our* capacity to be moral by exerting a necessary effect upon the will.[3] He does so, according to this particular version, by taking the choice out of our own hands—we are moved in spite of ourselves.

---

[2] The context is Kant's moral theory, and, in particular, his idea that we participate in the noumenal realm: 'when we consider the question of our interest in the moral law on the level of the noumenal, moral *requirement* is not even a question…There is no question of what noumenal beings "ought" to do' (D. Wiggins, 'Categorical Requirements: Kant and Hume on the Idea of Duty', in *Virtues and Reasons: Philippa Foot and Moral Theory*, ed. Rosalind Hursthouse, Gavin Lawrence, and Warren Quinn (Oxford: Clarendon Press 1995), p. 322). And Kant: 'Thus categorical imperatives are possible because the idea of freedom makes me a member of an intelligible world. Consequently, if I were a member of only that world, all my actions would always be in accordance with the autonomy of the will' (*Foundations of the Metaphysic of Morals*, trans. L.J. Beck (Indianapolis: Liberal Arts Press/Bobs Merrill, 1959), p. 454.

[3] Wiggins gives a Kantian gloss to this worry in the context of considering whether we could explain the possibility of moral motivation with reference to the Kantian idea that we exist at both the phenomenal and the noumenal level at once: 'But how, we may wonder, can the way in which a purely noumenal being *would* behave give rational reasons to one in our not purely noumenal state of being and intimate to him or her the idea of a requirement that is, *qua* normative and *qua* moral requirement, perfectly alien to a noumenal being' ('Categorical Requirements', p. 322).

We are returned to the kind of position our naturalists are so anxious to avoid. Moral values have become cosmic, they are severed from our motivational tendencies, but a divine coercive force bends our will in the required direction to guarantee instant acquiescence.[4] The position is to be rejected, but where does it leave the question of whether we relate to God by relating to value? The naturalist will say that a theistic framework leads to a distorted conception of value and of our relation to it, and that God must be rejected; the theist can respond that God has been distorted, and that it remains open that He can be part of the picture. Clearly, we must reject the idea that God has anything to do with the matter in the ways already described. So the naturalist and the theist are on firm and common territory to this degree at least. However, we may wonder whether the difficulty is solved simply by knocking God out of the equation and insisting that our focus should be on our relation to value. For there is ample scope for reintroducing the offending picture in a non-theistic guise, doing so by transposing the relevant coercive forces onto values themselves so that *they* exert the required necessary effect upon our wills.

This much suggests that the real issue is that of how we are to comprehend our relation to value, and whether we can accommodate our capacity to be motivated by the requirements they impose. A theistic framework has the potential to fudge this relation, when, for example, God is introduced in the guise of an external manipulator. However, this conception of God is not mandatory, and if the sensible theologian is to be believed, it must be rejected. If it is also the case that our relation to value admits of a similar distortion in a non-theistic context, then the possibility emerges that God has become a rather convenient scapegoat which has the effect of concealing the real difficulty at hand. The difficulty is clear enough as far as our naturalists are concerned, for their target is any position which severs morality from our motivational capacities. Railton takes as his prototype the idea that moral principles are to be grounded in the will or character of a deity, and McDowell implicates the kind of 'rampant' platonism which locates moral requirements in an 'alien' realm to which we could never respond as human beings. So morality must be brought back down to earth, and we know already that, for Railton, this means working from within social scientific parameters. Anything more, we are led to believe, is just one more concession to the offending coercive forces. McDowell and Wiggins object to this restriction on the ground that it is in equal danger of compromising our capacity to be moral. For it confines us to naturalistic materials which leave us with an impoverished conception of value, and a framework which forces the unwarranted conclusion that anything more is bound

---

[4] It is with this position in mind that we can appreciate Bernard Williams's point that an appeal to God in morality can end up adding the wrong sort of thing (*Morality: An Introduction to Ethics* (Cambridge: Cambridge University Press, 1972) p. 79).

to return us to the aforementioned cosmic excesses. The further claim is that there is a way of bringing morality back down to earth which exceeds these scientific parameters, and which relates it to our motivational capacities whilst preserving the required normative element. It is in this way that we arrive at a plausible synthesis of the normative and the empirical.

6.3 INTRODUCING LEVINAS

Where does this leave the idea that we relate to God by relating to value? If the position can be made good then it must accommodate our capacity to be moral. So we must reject the idea that God *forces* us to be moral, either by exerting a necessary effect upon our wills or by appealing to our egoistic tendencies. God cannot be part of the picture in this sense, and according to the proposal to be considered there is an important sense in which He must be removed entirely. This for the reason that the God to whom we relate by relating to value is wholly other with respect to man and nature. It remains to be seen whether the position can be classified under a theistic heading, and, if so, whether it could be remotely appealing to our expansive naturalist.

It is familiar from the previous chapter that, for Levinas, an acknowledgement of God's absence from the world shows that we have moved beyond the false and infantile gods of superstition. As he puts it, 'the adult's God is revealed precisely through the void of the child's heaven'.[5] Reference to the child's heaven is significant here, for Levinas is concerned not simply with the tendency to suppose that God is a being amongst beings, but also with the idea that He exists as a consoling father figure whose role is to satisfy our desires and reassure us that everything will be OK. He objects that this 'inhabitant' of the child's heaven has nothing to do with God, and that the 'consolation of divine presence' it promises has the effect of casting humanity in the role of a helpless child who turns to God in the way that one might turn to a parent.[6] We are led to suppose that a god of this kind will never live up to our expectations—prayers will go unanswered, consolation will give way to frustration, and frustration will give way to atheism.[7] God does not give me what I want, therefore He does not exist.

Such a god has something in common with the gods, for he is a 'demon' or 'strange magician' who can give us what we want.[8] He can be said also to fill a need we have to see the world as sensible and complete—a sensible and

---

[5] 'Loving the Torah More Than God', in *Difficult Freedom: Essays on Judaism*, trans. Seán Hand (Baltimore: Johns Hopkins University Press, 1990), p. 143.

[6] We shall see in the next chapter that Levinas takes the offending conception of God to be intrinsic to Christianity.

[7] 'Loving the Torah More Than God', p. 143.

[8] 'Loving the Torah More Than God', p. 143.

complete world being one in which things go according to my plan. So the focus again is upon what is good for me, and the god in question complies in this respect by dishing out rewards from on high. He also inflicts punishment and pardons sins.[9] The gods inflict punishment, but they do so according to whim and mood. Furthermore, there is no room for the idea that punishment could be the result of an act whose wrongness is not a mere function of the fact that it happens to conflict with the desires of the gods, nor that it could be justified on grounds which involve reference to something beyond the satisfaction it affords the punisher. Likewise, any sins which are pardoned according to this picture are those which involve contravening the desires of the gods, there being no place for the idea that there are things which ought not to be done regardless of how they stand with respect to such desires.

Levinas is anxious to accommodate a conception of value which exceeds these parameters. His position is shorn of any reference to the gods' desires, whether these gods be the volatile denizens of the pre-scientific world or the more user-friendly being he associates with the child's heaven, and takes as its focus the desires of human beings. He allows that some of our desires are for things for ourselves and our own satisfactions, classifies them as needs, and claims that they stem from a determinate lack in the subject which is filled by consuming or 'assimilating' an object that satisfies the desire: 'in need I can sink my teeth into the real and satisfy myself in assimilating the other'.[10] The terminology has a distinctly pejorative tone, but the picture is not entirely negative. After all, we are said to 'thriv(e) on our needs', and are 'happy' for them. Need is therefore 'a happy dependence', happiness is 'the satisfaction of all needs',[11] and the search for such happiness is that by which the self begins to establish itself as such. It is 'the egoism of life ... the very pulsation of the I',[12] or as Adriaan Peperzak puts it, the 'spontaneous egoism' of animal life.[13]

The reference to animal life suggests a concession to first nature in McDowell's sense of that term, and Levinas is concerned—in part at least—with the biological needs which structure human existence.[14] He agrees with McDowell that a proper account of humanity must give due weight to our animality,[15] and that our concern for the relevant 'things and needs' is, as he

---

[9] 'Loving the Torah More Than God', p. 143.

[10] *Totality and Infinity*, trans. Alphonso Lingis (Pittsburgh: Duquesne University Press, 1969), p. 117.

[11] *Totality and Infinity*, pp. 114–115.

[12] *Totality and Infinity*, pp. 113–114.

[13] Adriaan Peperzak, 'A Key to Totality and Infinity', in *To the Other: An Introduction to the Philosophy of Emmanuel Levinas* (West Lafayette: Purdue University Press, 1993), p. 137.

[14] See Michael Morgan, *Discovering Levinas* (Cambridge: Cambridge University Press, 2007), pp. 167–169 for a helpful discussion of Levinas's relation to McDowell in this context.

[15] Hence: 'I do not exist as a spirit...My being doubles with a having; I am encumbered by myself. And this is material existence. Consequently, materiality does not express the contingent fall of the spirit into the tomb or prison of a body' (*Time and the Other*, trans. Richard A. Cohen (Pittsburgh, Pennsylvania: Duquesne University Press, 1987), p. 56).

puts it, no mere frivolous preoccupation.[16] The focus upon things and needs also concedes something to Bilgrami's social scientist, for we have a picture in which human beings seek to satisfy their desires, and where things provide opportunities for such satisfaction and are valued for that reason alone. Levinas is happy to grant the significance of such satisfactions in the context of a proper human life. However—and it is at this stage that we can begin to appreciate the pejorative tones which accompany his claims in this context— he grants with Heidegger[17] that there is more to value than this, and accepts with our expansive naturalist that there is a source of value which comes to us from without. He accepts likewise that we are responsive to this external source, and that this responsiveness is fundamental to our humanity. His further claim is that it involves a kind of desire which is irreducible to that at issue when we are driven by purely egoistic considerations. Such desire is said to be situated 'beyond satisfaction and non-satisfaction' and it is described as 'metaphysical'.[18]

'Metaphysics' is a term of art for Levinas. He does not use it in his later work *Otherwise than Being*, perhaps in order to dispel any impression that he is restoring the kind of metaphysics attacked by Heidegger.[19] Metaphysics in the offending sense involves the kind of 'human mastery of the real' which was described in the previous chapter under the title of 'onto-theology', and Levinas seeks likewise to avoid a framework which gives expression to this humanistic conceit, doing so on the ground that it fails to accommodate a dimension of reality which resists such treatment. It also incorporates any position which involves the postulation of a further realm of being lying beyond anything to which we could intelligibly relate. It is familiar from previous chapters that a realm of this kind quickly becomes a worrisome and seemingly dispensable addition to our ontology, and that the framework may be equally demeaning of the reality it seeks to comprehend by this means.

Metaphysics in the sense embraced by Levinas has no truck with 'worlds behind the scenes',[20] and it promises to give due weight to a dimension of reality

---

[16] *Time and the Other*, p. 59. Levinas is here criticizing Heidegger's tendency to suppose that a concern for things and needs is a fall—'a flight before the uttermost finality that these needs themselves imply, an inconsequence, a nontruth, inevitable to be sure, but bearing the mark of the inferior and the reprehensible'. See Michael Purcell for a helpful discussion of this criticism (*Levinas and Theology* (Cambridge: Cambridge University Press, 2006), pp. 82–84).

[17] It should be clear from the previous footnote that Levinas takes issue with certain aspects of Heidegger's position. For a helpful discussion of their relation see Adriaan Peperzak's 'A Commentary on "Philosophy and the Idea of the Infinite"', in *To the Other: An Introduction to the Philosophy of Emmanuel Levinas* (West Lafayette: Purdue University Press, 1993) ; Michael Purcell's *Levinas and Theology*, pp. 78–80; and Merold Westphal's 'Divine Excess: The God Who Comes After', in *Overcoming Onto-theology: Toward a Postmodern Christian Faith* (New York: Fordham University Press, 2001).

[18] *Totality and Infinity*, p. 179.

[19] See Peperzak, 'Beyond Being', in *To the Other*, p. 211, and Westphal, 'Divine Excess', p. 261.

[20] *Otherwise Than Being or Beyond Essence*, trans. Alphonso Lingis (Dordecht: Kluwer, 1991), p. 8. In the final paragraph of this work Levinas tells us that it 'does not seek to restore any ruined

which eludes our theoretical aspirations. Thus, we are told that it involves that which is 'other than' and 'exterior' to the subject,[21] but also that which is superior and above.[22] Such characterizations suggest a possible concession to the cosmic excesses our naturalists are so anxious to avoid, although Levinas's rejection of any world behind the scenes puts paid to one version of that complaint. In any case, we know by now that the relevant terminology admits of various interpretations, that its usage does not spell inevitable philosophical disaster, and that it can serve as an antidote to problematic forms of reductionism. To return to an example which is going to suit Levinas's purposes, values can be said to be 'other than' and 'superior' to the subject in the sense that they provide a normative constraint upon our desires, our desires being responses to the callings of these values.[23] The claim is familiar from our expansive naturalist, and we shall find Levinas running a similar line which he articulates with reference to a notion of goodness inspired by Plato.[24] Metaphysics, we are told, is oriented towards a good 'beyond being', and it is made abundantly clear that this is no invitation to ascend to some second, supernatural realm.[25]

So values can be described as metaphysical to this degree at least, and desire counts as such to the extent that it is directed towards that which is 'other' and 'superior' in the relevant sense. This is part of what Levinas is getting at when he tells us that metaphysical desire 'tends toward something else entirely, toward the *absolutely other*'.[26] However, it is clearly not the whole story, for he is seeking to defend a version of the claim that we relate to God by relating to value. The implication here is that he is doing something more than simply making a plea for the irreducibility of value, and that his conception of the metaphysical—that which is *absolutely other*—carries theistic import. In one obvious sense then, he is exceeding the limits imposed by our expansive naturalist, and precisely *is* in danger of conceding to the aforementioned cosmic excesses. In another less obvious sense he is doing no such thing.

We can begin to appreciate this latter point by looking more closely at Levinas's conception of our relation to value. We have been told already that it

---

concept', and he refers with relief to 'the death of a certain god inhabiting the world behind the scenes' (p. 185).

[21] *Totality and Infinity*, p. 292.

[22] See *Totality and Infinity*, pp. 34–35, 200.

[23] See Akeel Bilgrami, 'The Wider Significance of Naturalism: A Genealogical Essay', in *Naturalism and Normativity*, ed. Mario De Caro and David Macarthur (New York: Columbia University Press, 2010), p. 27.

[24] See *Totality and Infinity*, pp. 34, 38, 218.

[25] As Levinas puts it, 'The other with which the metaphysician is in relationship and *which he recognizes as other* is not simply in another locality; this "other" recalls Plato's Ideas which, according to Aristotle's formula, are not in a site' (*Totality and Infinity*, p. 38). Notice that Levinas is rejecting any suggestion that Plato is a supernaturalist in the pejorative sense assumed by our scientific naturalist. So he concedes to the wisdom of Plato, and would appear to be in sympathy with McDowell's interpretation thereof (see chapter 3, footnote 23).

[26] *Totality and Infinity*, p. 33.

involves a kind of desire which is to be distinguished from that at issue when we are seeking our own satisfactions and that it tends towards the *absolutely other*. This makes it sound as if we are being led in the direction of an 'alien' realm of being which could have no bearing upon our moral practices, and that his expressed antipathy to such a move is empty. It becomes clear, however, that this is not the case, and that the focus is unambiguously located at the level of the moral relations in which we stand to other human beings. The human other, we are told, exists 'outside of the hunger one satisfies, the thirst one quenches, and the senses one allays',[27] and when I relate to her in moral terms 'I *am no longer able to have* power'.[28] I am able to have power in the sense that I *can* treat her as a mere means to my own satisfactions, or refrain from doing so simply because 'conquest is beyond my too weak powers'.[29] We are led to suppose, however, that a moral relationship has the effect of calling into question and silencing such egoistic impulses.[30] It is in this sense that I am no longer able to have power, and it is in this sense, we are told, that there is established 'a relationship not with a very great resistance but with the absolute Other, with the resistance of what has no resistance, with ethical resistance'.[31]

The idea that we are concerned with a relationship with the absolute Other returns us to the claim that this Other serves as the object of metaphysical desire, and I have noted already that the position is intended to have theistic import. So there is a question to be asked about the relation between this absolute Other, the human other, and God. At this stage we can note that Levinas is clearly rejecting any suggestion that it functions as a coercive force. As he puts it, it is not a matter of relating to 'a very great resistance' which subdues our egoistic tendencies by dint of force. Rather, it is a matter of relating to a resistance which is 'ethical'. We are to suppose then that ethical resistance is precisely not coercive—that it takes away my (egoistic) power without compromising my capacity to be moral. Levinas spells this out further by distinguishing between the situation in which my resistance to murder comes from something which blocks my will—something 'real' whose impact upon me involves no awareness on my part that murder is wrong—and that in which such awareness is registered and acknowledged. In the latter context my freedom 'renounces its

---

[27] 'Philosophy and the Idea of the Infinite', in Adriaan Peperzak, *To the Other: An Introduction to the Philosophy of Emmanuel Levinas* (West Lafayette: Purdue University Press, 1993), p. 114.

[28] 'Philosophy and the Idea of the Infinite', p. 110.

[29] 'Philosophy and the Idea of the Infinite', p. 110.

[30] Compare McDowell: 'If a situation in which virtue imposes a requirement is genuinely conceived as such, according to this view, then considerations that, in the absence of the requirement, would have constituted reasons for acting otherwise are silenced altogether—not overridden—by the requirement' ('Are Moral Requirements Hypothetical Imperatives?', in *Mind, Value, and Reality* (Cambridge, Mass.: Harvard University Press, 1998), p. 90).

[31] 'Philosophy and the Idea of the Infinite', p. 110.

imperialism proper to the ego', and I 'have access to an exterior being, to what one absolutely can neither take in nor possess'.[32]

This suggests that the exterior being to whom we relate in a moral context is a human being, and that she is 'exterior' in the sense that she belongs to a dimension of reality which takes us beyond the powers at issue when we seek egoistic conquest or find our wills blocked by a superior albeit analogous force. So we become receptive to this dimension in such a context, and Levinas refers to it as a 'dimension of the ideal'. The use of the term 'ideal' involves a further concession to Plato,[33] and serves to capture the sense in which we have ascended to a realm which is properly moral. So the distinction between ideal and real corresponds to that which has been drawn between the ethical and the real, the real being confined to the aforementioned powers and conquests. The further claim is that this ideal dimension emanates from the other's 'gaze'—her gaze 'come(s) to me from a dimension of the ideal'.[34]

6.4 SELF AND OTHER

Levinas's focus upon the gaze of the other captures the significance he accords to the face-to-face moral encounter. 'We know this relation', he tells us, 'only in the measure we effect it; this is what is distinctive about it. Alterity is possible only starting from *me*'.[35] The claims are reminiscent of what the expansive naturalist says when he warns against the possibility of conducting an investigation of ethical life and thought which leaves behind the moral point of view. The offending approach is said to proceed 'sideways-on' and 'from the outside', and the difficulty is that the relevant facts cannot be accessed in this manner. They must be approached from the perspective of one who is already caught up in such life and thought, this being the only way in which we can arrive at a proper understanding of our subject-matter. This is surely part of what Levinas is getting at when he tells us that alterity is possible only starting from *me*.[36]

Levinas has this much in common with our expansive naturalist, but the emphasis he places upon the relation between self and other might be thought to

---

[32] 'Philosophy and the Idea of the Infinite', p. 111.

[33] See 'Philosophy and the Idea of the Infinite', p. 90.

[34] 'Philosophy and the Idea of the Infinite', p. 111. There are two important claims here: first, the gaze of the other must come from the dimension of the ideal if it is to deliver moral knowledge; second, this knowledge can be imparted only via the other's gaze. My focus here is upon the second claim.

[35] *Totality and Infinity*, p. 40.

[36] Compare Peperzak: 'I must remain in the position that places me before the surprising Other and not surpass the relation in which I am caught—for instance, by reflecting or talking about it from a higher, nonengaged, and universal standpoint' ('A Key to Totality and Infinity', p. 135).

suggest a rather significant difference in their respective approaches. After all, it is our relation to *value* which provides the primary focus of the expansive naturalist.[37] The complaint threatens to undermine the idea—central to the argument of this chapter—that Levinas is concerned with our relation to value, and it would have a point if he were found to be ignoring this relation or if the expansive naturalist had nothing to say about our moral relations with others. We have seen, however, that many of the values which figure in the expansive naturalist's position are embodied in our moral relations with others, and it is for this reason that we can say without difficulty that persons impose normative constraints upon us. It is not ruled out that there are other ways of relating to value, and it is arguably a deficiency of Levinas's approach that he plays down the significance of such relations.[38] However, he *is* concerned with our relation to value—the values which impose their demands in the face-to-face encounter and whose pursuit orients the subject towards the realm of metaphysics proper.

The idea that Levinas is challenging the kind of detached approach which forms the target of the expansive naturalist's argument is borne out by what he says about our tendency to 'totalize' the relationship between self and other.[39] Simon Critchley describes the tendency as follows:

> When I totalize, I conceive of the relation to the other from some imagined point that would be outside of it and I turn myself into a theoretical spectator on the social world of which I am really part, and in which I am an agent.[40]

So the offending approach is theoretical and spectatorial, and Levinas takes it to be operative at a more general level when we strive to get the measure of things in the manner of Heidegger's onto-theologian. In such a context we treat the world as a whole as a totality, and end up compromising that which eludes such treatment. As Levinas puts it, 'the objective totality (does) not fill out the true measure of being'.[41] The expansive naturalist would say that the social scientist 'totalizes' our relations to others, and the complaint likewise is that he has failed to capture what is at issue in a properly moral context.

---

[37] See Hilary Putnam, 'Levinas and Judaism', *The Cambridge Companion to Levinas*, ed. Simon Critchley and Robert Bernasconi (Cambridge: Cambridge University Press, 2002), p. 54 for a version of this worry.

[38] Peter Atterton criticizes Levinas on this score in his 'Face-to-Face with the Other Animal?', in *Levinas and Buber: Dialogue and Difference*, ed. Peter Atterton, Matthew Calarco, and Maurice Friedman (Pittsburgh, Pennsylvania: Duquesne University Press, 2004), pp. 262–281. See also Michael Morgan who makes the point that, for Levinas, it is our responsibility to the other person which shapes all that we are and do. As he puts it, 'the self is engaged by the other person first and foremost, and it is this engagement that shapes our sense of obligation and the norms or values that occur in daily life as features of our selfhood' (*Discovering Levinas* (Cambridge: Cambridge University Press, 2007), pp. 170–171).

[39] *Totality and Infinity*, pp. 35–40.

[40] *The Cambridge Companion to Levinas*, ed. Simon Critchley and Robert Bernasconi (Cambridge: Cambridge University Press, 2002), p. 13.

[41] *Totality and Infinity*, p. 22.

It is no part of the expansive naturalist's position that we must reject the social dimension of ethical life and thought, and Levinas agrees that it must be accommodated. As he puts it, 'metaphysics is enacted where the social relation is enacted—in our relations with men',[42] it is the 'whole of humanity' which concerns me—'the poor one, the stranger, presents himself as an equal',[43] we answer 'for everything and everyone'.[44] He claims also that this social dimension is already implicit in any concrete face-to-face encounter—'The third party looks at me in the eyes of the Other...the epiphany of the face *qua* face opens humanity'.[45] So Levinas's focus upon the face-to-face encounter is intended to be compatible with this social dimension, but he believes—with our expansive naturalist—that the position is fudged if tackled in the aforementioned theoretical terms. It is fudged because these terms leave us at a fundamental remove from the context in which one self responds morally to another, and it is no longer possible to accommodate the kind of 'human fraternity' or 'kinship of men' which is expressed at this level of interaction and implied by the very idea of humanity.[46]

We are returned to Wiggins's idea that we should aspire to live with others on terms which are worthy of them, and that the envisaged solidarity is of human beings *qua* human. Wiggins's stress on the human blocks any suggestion that the relevant beings participate in a noumenal realm behind the scenes, and it should be clear from what has been said that Levinas seeks likewise to avoid such undertakings. It serves also to take us beyond the conception of humanity which is operative at the level of social science—a conception which, for Wiggins, fails to capture the irreducibly moral dimension which is presupposed in such solidarity and which marks us out as *properly* human. Levinas can be understood to be making a similar point, and it is in this context that we can appreciate his complaint that the offending theoretical framework, to the extent that it involves abstracting from the context of concrete moral relations, confines us to a realm of faceless beings whose interactions are bound to fall short of capturing the kind of human solidarity which is expressed, and only

---

[42] *Totality and Infinity*, p. 78.

[43] *Totality and Infinity*, p. 213.

[44] *Otherwise Than Being*, p. 114. One could protest that Levinas is demanding too much of us here, and that this model of impartiality takes us beyond anything with which the expansive naturalist would be comfortable. Indeed, the position would seem more appropriate to a form of utilitarianism. Levinas himself remains ambivalent about the extent of this 'utopian' vision, and is prepared to acknowledge some limitations. He claims, for example, 'my responsibility for all can and has to manifest itself also in limiting itself. The ego can, in the name of this unlimited responsibility, be called on to concern itself also with itself' (*Otherwise Than Being*, p. 128). See Hilary Putnam ('Levinas and Judaism', p. 57) for some Aristotelian worries about Levinas's position. Michael Morgan responds to some of these worries in his *Discovering Levinas*, pp. 289–299: 'Ethics does not eliminate or seek to eliminate the rest of human life; it does, however, seek to place it in its context of the good, as our determinative and unavoidable concern.'

[45] *Totality and Infinity*, p. 213.

[46] *Totality and Infinity*, pp. 214–215.

expressed, in such a context.[47] We are returned to Wiggins's worry that such materials will never get us to the idea of moral obligation, and that there is nothing herein we could fully recognize as the proper object of all our striving.

6.5 MORAL OBLIGATION AND INFINITY

The idea of moral obligation is fundamental to Levinas's conception of the face-to-face encounter between self and other. We have been told already that our egoistic impulses are silenced in such a context, that we are called upon to be morally responsive, and that this call comes from the other's gaze. This is spelled out further with the claim that she delivers a moral summons which is revealed in 'the sensible appearance of (her) face'.[48] This is the ethical resistance to which we have already referred; it is said to involve an 'infinity' that paralyses my powers—'infinity presents itself as a face in the ethical resistance that paralyses my powers';[49] and the face, thus understood, 'opens the primordial discourse whose first word is obligation'.[50] It calls my freedom to responsibility,[51] and 'invites me to a relation incommensurate with a power exercised'.[52]

Levinas's conception of infinity provides a further placeholder for the dimension of reality which is revealed at the level of metaphysics; it carries a theistic import which is familiar from our previous discussion; and I shall be returning to the question of how it is to be interpreted. For present purposes we can note the continued allegiance to the claim that this dimension is revealed in the face of the other. The further claim is that this face is a source of normativity—a moral summons is revealed in its sensible appearance and I am called upon to be responsible for the other. In saying this, Levinas can be understood to be providing a version of the normative/empirical synthesis which, for our naturalists, is a condition of satisfaction for any plausible moral philosophy. According to this version, normative demands come to us from the world we inhabit. More specifically, they come from the faces we perceive in concrete encounters with others, when, for example, we experience

---

[47] Levinas describes the offending position as one according to which society becomes 'a genus that unites like individuals'. He concedes that 'there does indeed exist a human race as a biological genus, and the common function men may exercise in the world as a totality permits the applying to them of a common concept', but denies that this adds up to the 'kinship of men' which is operative at the level of morality (*Totality and Infinity*, pp. 213–214). See also 'The I and the Totality', in *Entre Nous*, trans. Michael B. Smith and Barbara Harshav (London: Continuum Press, 2006), for further versions of the offending position.

[48] *Totality and Infinity*, pp. 196–198.
[49] *Totality and Infinity*, p. 199.
[50] *Totality and Infinity*, p. 201.
[51] *Totality and Infinity*, p. 203.
[52] *Totality and Infinity*, p. 198.

their suffering and dependency and become responsive to their needs.[53] These encounters point equally in the direction of those to whom we are not so immediately related—in this respect it is allowed that we can detect obligations from a distance—and we are responsive to the relevant demands by virtue of our human capacity to be moral. So the human connection is secured, there is a concession to the irreducibly social dimension of morality, and we have a position which grants us the right to say, with Railton, that moral values and imperatives are grounded 'in nothing more transcendental than facts about man and his environment',[54] albeit in a manner which concedes nothing to his reductive aspirations.

The expansive naturalist conceives of the moral as a domain of *rational* requirements, and our capacity to respond to them is a rational capacity which stems from our human nature. So we are rational beings in this sense, and it is here that Wiggins takes on board the idea that we should aspire to live with others on terms which are worthy of them, giving it a Kantian gloss which lends emphasis to this idea of rationality: we should aspire to live with rational beings on terms which are worthy of them. He suggests also that reason itself is immanent in the practices of those who are united in this respect. At one level Levinas stands opposed to this line of thought, objecting that an 'I' which is identified with reason loses its 'ipseity'.[55] 'What could a being entirely rational speak of with another entirely rational being?' he asks. 'How could numerous reasons be distinguished? How could the Kantian kingdom of ends be possible, had not the rational beings that compose it retained, as the principle of individuation, their exigency for happiness, miraculously saved from the shipwreck of sensible nature?' The worry here is that the notion of a rational being fails to capture what it is to be a human being, and that rational beings are compelled to participate in just the kind of noumenal realm that Wiggins is so anxious to reject—a realm which stands apart from the natural world to encompass beings who are similarly non-natural.

Wiggins agrees with Levinas that human beings cannot be rational in this sense, and defends a conception of practical reason which reinstates the

---

[53] Morgan argues that there is an important difference between Levinas and McDowell in this context, namely, that 'the moral perception that McDowell identifies is, in the end, much more epistemic than it is for Levinas, for whom the seeing of the face is not so much a cognitive act as it is an awareness of the other's need and a responsiveness to it, all at once, a reaching out to help that is an understanding of the other's need and a grasp of a responsibility that is an act in behalf of the other' (*Discovering Levinas*, pp. 253–255). It is unclear to me that the difference is as striking as Morgan suggests, for, as will become clear below, Levinas is happy enough to allow that our response to the other is cognitive in one important sense of that term.

[54] 'Moral Realism', *The Philosophical Review*, vol. 95, no. 2 (April 1986), p. 201.

[55] Levinas argues that the 'I' likewise loses its 'ipseity' when viewed in the aforementioned theoretical terms. This much is clear from what has been said about the 'faceless' beings to which we are confined at the level of social theory. See also *Totality and Infinity*, 'The I of Enjoyment is Neither Biological Nor Sociological', pp. 120–121. Clearly, he is in agreement with our expansive naturalist that the offending positions are two sides of a single coin.

required human element. Levinas can be understood to be making a similar move, albeit in a manner which gives equal weight to his theistic interests. Reason in the relevant sense has been rescued from any Kantian noumenal realm and is to be distinguished also from that which is operative when we are in business of theorizing in a non-moral context.[56] We are told that it is founded in the relation with the other, and that this ethical relation has a rational character.[57] So we are concerned with a conception of rationality which finds expression in the face-to-face ethical encounter with the other, and can agree with Wiggins that reason is immanent in the practices which involve such encounters. We can surely say also that the beings who are thus related—human beings—are rational.[58] They are rational in the sense that they are capable of acknowledging the requirements of morality.

This much situates Levinas in the camp of our expansive naturalist, but as noted already, his conception of reason has a further theistic import which transports us into the aforementioned metaphysical territory. Hence:

> To think is to have the idea of infinity, or to be taught. Rational thought refers to this teaching, and it involves 'knowledge' of a new structure. We seek to fix it as a relation with the face and to show the ethical essence of this relation. The face is the evidence that makes evidence possible—like the divine veracity that sustains Cartesian rationalism.[59]

And:

> The infinite is not the object of a contemplation, that is, is not proportionate to the thought that thinks it. The idea of the infinite is a thought which at every moment *thinks more than it thinks*. A thought that thinks more than it thinks is Desire. Desire 'measures' the infinity of the infinite.[60]

We are returned to the claim that infinity—the dimension of reality to which metaphysics is oriented—is revealed in the face of the other. It is by virtue of

---

[56] *Totality and Infinity*, p. 208. Levinas is working with a narrow conception of theory in this context, and it will become clear that he is not ruling out the possibility of there being a broader conception thereof which is more appropriate to the case of morality, and, indeed, God.

[57] *Totality and Infinity*, p. 203.

[58] This interpretation might be thought to compromise Levinas's claim that the ethical relation is asymmetric. The point of this claim is to capture the idea that ethics must proceed from the context of a concrete encounter in which I see myself as obligated before the other. This involves an irreducibly first-personal recognition of my responsibility. So there is an asymmetry between self and other to this degree at least, but it is no part of Levinas's position that subsequent theorizing cannot lead to the realization that others are similarly obligated. Crucially, however, this theorizing must proceed from a standpoint which recognizes the individuality of these others—an individuality which grants me the right to say that they are similar to me in the required moral respect, and which distinguishes the relevant theorizing from that which is at issue when they are reduced to faceless beings who, as Levinas would put it, have 'lost their ipseity'. We are not rational beings together in *this* sense! The points are familiar from our expansive naturalist.

[59] *Totality and Infinity*, p. 204.

[60] 'Philosophy and the Idea of the Infinite', p. 113.

this encounter that we acquire the idea of infinity, and the face in this context is said to perform a similar function to the God which sustains Cartesian rationalism. The further claim is that the thinking at issue here is irreducible to the contemplation of some object, for infinity (or the infinite) cannot be grasped in this manner. Rather, we are concerned with a thought which can never get the measure of its object, and a thought in this sense is said to be Desire. The implication in all of this is that we relate to God by standing in moral relations with others, and that this relation is both cognitive and desire-involving.

6.6 THE INTERHUMAN RELATION AND GOD

Levinas claims that 'there can be no "knowledge" of God separated from the relationship with men',[61] and that '[e]verything that cannot be reduced to an interhuman relation represents not the superior form but the forever primitive form of religion'.[62] The relation in question is moral, and the claim seems to be that our relation to God is *reducible* to our (moral) relation to man. Is this not a form of atheism? Levinas would respond that the reductionism at issue here is not a matter of knocking God out of the equation in favour of something else—the human other and our moral relation to her. Rather, it is a matter of removing a false god and a faulty conception of our relation to Him in order to make way for a proper revelation thereof.[63] So the interhuman relation, as Levinas conceives of it, is irreducibly God-involving. What could this mean?

We are told that to know God is to know what is to be done.[64] The focus here is upon the morally acting subject, and the knowledge in question 'comes to us like a commandment'. We are to '[b]e merciful like Him',[65] and it is in this way that 'the moral relation reunites both self-consciousness and consciousness of

----

[61] *Totality and Infinity*, p. 78. See also: 'It is our relations with men...that give to theological concepts the sole signification they admit of...Without the significance they draw from ethics, theological concepts remain empty and formal frameworks' (*Totality and Infinity*, p. 79); 'We have been reproached for ignoring theology; and we do not contest the necessary of a recovery, at least, the necessity of choosing an opportunity for a recovery of these themes. We think, however, that theological recuperation comes after the glimpse of holiness, which is primary' (*Of God Who Comes to Mind*, trans. Bettina Bergo (Stanford: Stanford University Press, 1998), p. ix). The holiness to which Levinas refers here is that which is revealed in the context of a moral encounter.

[62] *Totality and Infinity*, p. 79.

[63] Railton would no doubt provide an analogous defence of his own preferred brand of reductionism.

[64] 'A Religion for Adults', in *Difficult Freedom: Essays on Judaism*, trans. Seán Hand (Baltimore: Johns Hopkins University Press, 1990) p. 17.

[65] It should be clear from what has been said that the quality of this mercy is not remotely strained; after all, God is no manipulator, and could be so only at the cost of losing His transcendence. As Levinas puts it, 'The God of heaven is accessible, without losing any of His transcendence but without denying freedom to the believer' ('A Religion for Adults', p. 18).

God'.[66] So the consciousness in question involves an awareness of what we are commanded to do and a motivation to act accordingly: 'everything I know of God and everything I can hear of His word and reasonably say to Him must find an ethical expression'.[67]

So the interhuman relation is God-involving in the sense that it relates the subject to God. She does what is to be done—she does good—and in doing so can be said to give expression to God's Word. The context for action is the subject's relation to other subjects, and we are told that the human other 'is indispensable for my relation with God'—'[t]he dimension of the divine opens forth from the human face'.[68] This latter claim recalls the idea that the gaze of the other comes to me from the dimension of the ideal, this dimension is given an explicitly theistic gloss, and we are returned to the question of the relation between this human other and God. God is not reducible to the human other, for this would be to turn Him into a being amongst beings. Levinas denies also that the other plays any kind of mediating role. So she is not an incarnation of God,[69] nor does she serve as a *means* for gaining access to Him—as if her face were 'an appearance or sign of some reality...of a hidden God who would impose the neighbour on me'.[70] Such a picture would turn God into an entity behind the scenes, it would encourage a theorizing about God and the human other which detracts the subject from the moral work to be done if God is to be 'known',[71] and it would take responsibility out of her hands. These points are fundamental, for Levinas is stressing above all that the human other provides the only context by means of which the subject can relate to God, and that she relates to Him not by deducing His existence from the materials which confront her in such a situation, nor by succumbing to a force beyond her control, but rather, by doing the required moral work.[72] So the human other is related to God in the sense that she relates me to God, and this latter relationship is

---

[66] 'A Religion for Adults', p. 17.
[67] 'A Religion for Adults', p. 17.
[68] *Totality and Infinity*, p. 78.
[69] *Totality and Infinity*, p. 79.
[70] *Otherwise Than Being*, pp. 93–94.
[71] As Levinas puts it, we 'open the dangerous way in which the pious thought, or one concerned with order, hastily deduces the existence of God' (*Otherwise Than Being*, p. 93).
[72] In his later writings Levinas introduces the concept of a trace to spell out the relation between the human other and God. As he puts it, the face 'is a trace', and, as such, 'does not signify an indeterminate phenomenon' (*Otherwise Than Being*, p. 94). The face 'proceeds from the absolutely Absent', but its relationship 'does not indicate, does not reveal, this Absent; and yet the Absent has a meaning in the face' ('Meaning and Sense', in *Basic Philosophical Writings*, ed. Adriaan T. Peperzak, Simon Critchley, and Robert Bernasconi (Bloomington: Indiana University Press, 1996), p. 60). Morgan spells out the thought as follows: 'The face is not a thing or an appearance of a thing, the Absent is not an entity, and the relationship is not one of signifying, referring, pointing, revealing, or presenting, in one direction, nor is it one of explaining, justifying, or demonstrating, in the other. For the Absent is no "world behind our world" ('Meaning and Sense', p. 60). Levinas uses the word "trace" for this relationship; "the beyond from which the face comes signifies as a trace"...This *beyond* is neither I nor you. It is there, in the third

enacted when, and only when, I attend to her in the required moral terms. Anything more would be to compromise both God's otherness and the possibility of relating to Him. Hence:

> The infinite is not 'in front of me'; it is I who express it, but I do so precisely in giving a sign of the giving of signs, of the 'for the other' in which I am dis-interested: here I am [*me voici*]. A marvellous accusative: here I am under your gaze, obliged to you, your servant. In the name of God.[73]

God is no longer 'in front of me' as an object of a contemplation, and we have been told that this thought which 'thinks more than it thinks' is desire. The claim then is that our relation to God is desire-involving—we have a desire for God. The desire in question is metaphysical, and we know already that such desire has an irreducibly moral dimension which sets it apart from the motivational tendencies at issue when we are seeking our own satisfactions. It follows that a desire for God has nothing to do with wanting things for ourselves, and Levinas would insist that a being who complied in this respect would be a god of superstition, or, indeed, of onto-theology. So we fail to relate to *God* when we treat Him as a supreme satisfier, and we can relate to Him only by standing in moral relations to others. In one obvious sense then, a desire for God is a desire for goodness, and a desire for goodness has nothing to do with wanting goods. It is a desire to be moral. Levinas claims also that it involves 'an aspiration that the Desirable animates; it originates from its "object"; it is revelation'.[74]

The idea that the desire for goodness involves an aspiration that the desirable animates is reminiscent of the claim that values have 'to be pursuedness' built into them, and our expansive naturalist would be happy to allow that they 'animate' our moral responses in this respect. So values are desirable in this respect, and this is obviously a large part of Levinas's story given the significance he attaches to morality. However, it is not the whole story, and he adds the required theistic gloss by returning us to Descartes's claim that the idea of God originates from its object.[75] Crucially, however, it is a Descartes who has

---

person: something distant, separate, always so…The divine is only present in the face; it is never present in itself, and it is the *obliging character* of the face that is this trace of divinity…When we speak of encountering God or of God revealing Himself to me, this is an expression of my desire to respond to the other person with kindness and generosity, my sense of being called by the other and being obligated to her. Indeed, doing the latter is the only way one can experience the former. One cannot know God or encounter God directly; all religious experience is ethical action' (*Discovering Levinas*, pp. 189–190). See also Morgan, *Discovering Levinas*, pp. 183–198, and Jill Robbins, 'Tracing Responsibility in Levinas's Ethical Thought', in *Ethics as First Philosophy: The Significance of Emmanuel Levinas for Philosophy, Literature and Religion*, ed. Adriaan Peperzak (London: Routledge, 1995), pp. 173–183.

[73] 'God and Philosophy', in *Of God Who Comes to Mind*, p. 75.
[74] *Totality and Infinity*, p. 62.
[75] *Totality and Infinity*, p. 49.

assimilated the wisdom of Levinas. The upshot, familiar from above, is that it is our *desire* for God which is said to originate from its object. This desire is awakened in me by the presence of the human other, it motivates me to be moral, and this provides the setting for a true revelation of God: to know God is to know what is to be done.

6.7 INTERLUDE

There are further important details to be unpacked in all of this, but let us pause for a moment and summarize the general picture. God is wholly other with respect to man and nature, but we can relate to Him. He is wholly other in the sense that He is neither a part of the world nor an inhabitant behind the scenes. He does not intervene as an external manipulator, and eludes all attempts to be adequately grasped in thought.[76] So He does not push us around, nor can we push Him around by making Him comply with our demands, including, of course, the demand to conform to our conceptual specifications. Such connections would fall short of the kind of God/man relation at issue, for, to return to Mascall's terminology, they rule out the possibility of there being any 'real self-communication of God to man, any real elevation of man into the life of God'. If there were such connections, there would be no self-communication of God to man because we are either pushed around in spite of ourselves or isolated from Him by our own theoretical presumptions. For similar reasons there could be no real elevation of man into the life of God. The terms of the relation remain mutually exclusive.

For Levinas, the self-communication of God to man occurs at the level of moral consciousness. Such consciousness involves a desire for God which originates from its object and is awakened and sustained in our moral relations with others. These relations give expression to our knowledge of what is to be done, and this constitutes the only possible knowledge we can have of God. There is nothing remotely manipulative in any of this, for the relevant demands are not alien presences which impinge upon a resistant humanity, dictating to us from beyond our human attitudes and capacities. On the contrary, they are freely acknowledged and embraced from a first-personal agentive point of view, and give us reasons—our reasons—for acting accordingly.[77] The picture is familiar from our expansive naturalist, and Levinas can agree likewise that the relevant reasons supply the shape of our practical intellect.

---

[76] Levinas makes it sound as if the very attempt to theorize about God is both misguided and bound to misfire. We shall see eventually that he is prepared to temper the force of this claim.

[77] Bilgrami stresses the importance of accommodating these features of our response to value in his 'The Wider Significance of Naturalism', pp. 32–33.

He claims also that we are elevated hereby into the life of God. Given his particular way of understanding this elevation, it can be related without difficulty to the expansive naturalist's version of this claim. According to this version, we are concerned with the elevation which occurs when we become receptive to value—an added richness is brought to the world we inhabit and we are elevated into the life of goodness. It is Levinas's contention that we exceed this version only at the cost of undermining the theistic framework it is his purpose to defend. His further crucial claim is that it supplies the ingredients for mounting such a defence.

6.8 THE RETURN OF THE EXPANSIVE NATURALIST

How should the expansive naturalist respond? Clearly, he is not being invited to accept a God who is going to compromise what he wishes to say about our relation to value, for Levinas's God is out of the picture in the crucial respects, and it is for this reason that the positions are so close. Nevertheless, the theistic underpinning remains fundamental, for in relating to value we are said to relate to God. The expansive naturalist could continue to insist that God is too weird to be part of our ontology, that there is no philosophically defensible account of how we could relate to Him, and that He is irrelevant to the question of our relation to value. The difficulty, however, is that Levinas's position—in one respect at least—is no different from that of the expansive naturalist, for his account of our relation to God proceeds via our relation to value, and his conception of this latter relation corresponds in large measure to that of the expansive naturalist. The expansive naturalist could respond that it is unclear what extra work God does which values don't already do, and that the reference to God is dispensable for this reason. However, such a response presupposes that the position is unworthy of consideration, and that the question of value has already been closed. Against this latter claim we can note that the expansive naturalist's position is itself the target of an analogous criticism as far as the scientific naturalist is concerned. For according to the scientific naturalist, the expansive naturalist's values are too weird to be part of our ontology, there is no philosophically defensible account of how we could relate to them, and they are irrelevant to the question of our relation to value.

It is familiar that the expansive naturalist has a response to the scientific naturalist's charge which grants him the right to reinstate the relevant values, or, at least, to demonstrate that they do not pose the envisaged threat. We must consider then whether a version of this response stands to be exploited by Levinas in the context of defending his own preferred position. The expansive naturalist will object that the two cases are very different, and that his challenge to the scientific naturalist's position is justified on several grounds. First, the position involves an unwarranted commitment to scientism; second, it is doubtful that it captures all that needs to be said about value and our relation to it; third, we can fill the required explanatory gap by espousing expansive naturalism; and finally, the position involves no concession to anything remotely problematic, unless of course we continue to insist that science is the measure of reality. By contrast, although Levinas's position discourages any commitment to scientism and captures much of what needs to be said about value and our relation to it, it does involve reference to something inherently problematic, namely, God. At this stage we can remind the expansive naturalist that *his* position is similarly culpable from the point of view of the scientific naturalist, and that the scientific naturalist will insist that his own preferred alternative can fulfil the required explanatory aims. So the scientific naturalist sees no explanatory gap in his own position, although if Wiggins is to be believed it can be rendered satisfactory only with an implicit concession to the opposing anti-scientistic viewpoint. If this is so, then the scientific naturalist can no longer accuse his opponent of introducing a further realm of being which is irrelevant to the matter at hand. The relevant realm turns out to be exactly what is needed if we are to relate to value in the first place.

Could we defend Levinas's introduction of God along analogous lines? In order to do so we would have to show that the position captures what needs to be said about value and our relation to it, that its rejection is on a par with the scientific naturalist's rejection of expansive naturalism, and that the expansive naturalist's objections can be overcome. Levinas promises to sidestep the relevant objections, for his God does not undermine our capacity to be moral by intervening as a coercive force, nor does He hover beyond the realm in which our moral responses are enacted as an irrelevant and unknowable presence. On the contrary, God is central to the question of our relation to value, and His centrality in this respect serves to explain how we relate to Him—we relate to Him by standing in moral relations to others. Levinas agrees with the expansive naturalist that our moral responses are to be distinguished from those which belong to our merely animal nature, and that they are part and parcel of our humanity. He insists, however, that they involve a desire for God, that this desire has its source in God, and that in responding thus we give expression to His Word.

It follows from this that we are a source of value in the world, for we create goodness by performing good acts. The expansive naturalist grants this much, and he denies that, in realizing value in this way, we create the requirements they impose. Thus, the relevant acts are good not simply because we do them or because we want to do them. Rather, they are good and desirable in themselves, and we desire to do them for this reason. Levinas agrees with the expansive naturalist on this score. So he can accept with Wiggins that we desire x because we think x good. He can accept likewise that x is good because x is such that we desire it, and can agree with Wiggins that the point of this second claim is to allow that such desiring by human beings is part of what is required for there to be such a thing as the perspective from which the goodness of *x* is there to be perceived. Wiggins insists that such desiring is just a *part* of what is required in this context, for he is concerned to establish the right *general* basis of effect which must be operative if our valuations are to have the required motivational force, allowing that the ingredients to which we must appeal may be more complex. As he puts it, we are concerned with 'desire etc.'.[78] He denies therefore that an explanation of someone's acting thus and so necessarily depends upon the explainer attributing to the agent *the desire to act so*. He claims also that when we do make such an attribution, the desire in question will be 'consequential upon the operation in its actual context of the moral sentiments'.[79] The relevant sentiments are that by virtue of which the agent becomes responsive to the relevant values, and it is precisely for this reason that he forms a desire to promote them: he desires *x* because he thinks *x* good. This desire is intrinsically moral, and, as such, compels us to question the assumption that the appetitive and the cognitive are, as McDowell puts it, 'distinct existences'.[80] The desire which figures in Levinas's account is intrinsically moral in this sense, and he grants its irreducibly cognitive dimension. He insists, however, that it involves a desire for God, that this desire is at the basis of our moral responses, and that it is animated by God. So God makes it possible for us to realize value in the world by animating our desire to do so. For the expansive naturalist, by contrast, it is our humanity which grounds this capacity, for we have a second nature by virtue of which we are responsive to the relevant requirements. Levinas can say this too, for he takes the desire for God to be intrinsic to our humanity. The expansive naturalist would deny this of course.

We have a distinction between values realized and values as requirements. It is granted on both sides that we can realize value in the world, and that this capacity is fundamental to our humanity. Levinas, insists, however, that it has

---

[78] 'Moral Cognitivism, Moral Relativism, and Motivating Moral Beliefs', *Proceedings of the Aristotelian Society*, New Series, vol. 91 (1990–1991), p. 83.

[79] 'Moral Cognitivism, Moral Relativism, and Motivating Moral Beliefs', p. 83.

[80] 'Are Moral Requirements Hypothetical Imperatives?', p. 83. McDowell argues that this assumption involves a commitment to the idea that the world is motivationally inert and that it provides the proper and only province of cognition. If we accept this, he continues, we are bound to insist that desire must function as an independent component in the explanation of why an agent acts in the relevant way. Why? Because cognition, taken in itself, could not explain an agent's motivation to act. Rather, there must be a desire which 'combines with that conception of the facts to make the action attractive to its possessor' (p. 82). McDowell, by contrast, rejects the assumption that the world is motivationally inert. Hence: 'The idea of the world as motivationally inert is not an independent hard datum. It is simply the metaphysical counterpart of the thesis that states of will and cognitive states are distinct existences, which is exactly what is in question' (p. 83).

its source in God. Both sides deny that we are the source of the requirements which the relevant values impose. So values as requirements have an external source according to both pictures, and it is agreed likewise that they have their source in the world—the value-involving world to which we respond in a moral context. Levinas takes as his focus the values which are embodied in the interhuman relation. He adds, however, that God is the ultimate source of the relevant requirements, albeit a source which is no coercive power, and to which we relate only by doing good in the required sense. So he can agree with the expansive naturalist that I am required to help the person before me because she is in need, and would insist that any further theistic justification—for example, that God commands me to do so—would be one thought too many.[81] He would insist also that the very demand for such a justification involves abstracting from the concrete encounter which serves as the site of genuine Revelation to a level of theorizing which turns God into just one more being behind the scenes.[82]

We have two positions which say very similar things about value and our relation to it, the difference being that one of them spells it out in God-involving terms. The relevant terms leave intact our moral capacities, they make God central to their existence and execution, and we are faced with the question of whether the expansive naturalist should concede to this theistic framework. It can look as if he is being asked to swallow a camel. However, he has done so already from the point of view of the scientific naturalist, and I have suggested that we could lend support to this theistic move if it could be shown that its rejection is comparable to the scientific naturalist's rejection of expansive naturalism. The scientific naturalist rejects this position on the ground that

[81] See Morgan, *Discovering Levinas*, p. 180. Would it be one thought too many to say that I am morally required to help this person? Clearly not. What of the idea that Goodness commands me in this context? This formulation brings us closer to a theistic position, but I would contend that the claim remains perfectly acceptable. I contend also that this version brings us as close as we can get to Levinas's position, for the crucial thing is to deny that God provides any kind of *external* justification for morality. Levinas is right to reject such a picture, and I believe that we can acccept this negative constraint from within a theistic framework, and that this model offers the best prospects for vindicating such a framework. See Erik J. Wielenberg's 'In Defense of Non-Natural, Non-Theistic Moral Realism', *Faith and Philosophy*, vol. 26, no. 1 (Jan 2009), for some compelling—and to my mind decisive—criticisms of the offending 'externalist' conception of God's role in theistic moral realism. Wielenberg is led to defend a non-theistic form of moral realism which has much in common with the view of my expansive naturalist. It will become clear from what I go on to say that I have great sympathy for his position, but would contend that it admits of a (sensible) theistic gloss. To put it another way, the idea that God provides an 'external' source for morality is no better than the idea that social science can provide the required external source. The two positions are just two sides of the same problematic coin.

[82] As Morgan puts it: 'Levinas wants us to realize what theoretical thinking and reason—"representation and thematization"—do to the face, how they can lead us astray by asking the wrong questions and by giving us the wrong idea of what the face means...The way to respond to the face authentically is with responsibility, not by thinking, deducing a divine commander or a first cause' (*Discovering Levinas*, p. 184).

it brings insuperable philosophical difficulties—difficulties which, I have suggested, are products of an underlying commitment to scientism. The expansive naturalist retorts that scientism is an ideological prejudice, and that once it is rejected the values he espouses no longer pose the envisaged threat. The expansive naturalist's opposition to Levinas's position is not motivated by a commitment to scientism, for he has already exposed and rejected this particular prejudice. However, he does assume that his own preferred framework has the monopoly on the question of value, and that this framework must remain resolutely secular. The claim is in order on the assumption that God could only ever be a spooky something else which is irrelevant to the issue at hand or which has the potential to fudge it. However, this assumption is a by-product of the aforementioned secularist commitments and can be used to justify them only at the cost of begging the central question at issue. The case of Levinas compels us to reconsider these commitments, and to do so from within a framework which concedes in important respects to that of the expansive naturalist. If the present line of argument is correct, then we forsake this possibility at the risk of compromising the very spirit of the expansive naturalist's approach. For according to this approach we are to reject dogmatism in favour of open-mindedness and remain ever alert to the imposition of frameworks which distort the phenomena we are seeking to comprehend. It remains open then that secular expansive naturalism involves an ideological prejudice, and that it is no better than the scientific naturalist position it purports to upstage.

6.9 WHITHER NOW?

This much suggests that the expansive naturalist *could* concede to Levinas, and that it may be in his philosophical interests to take the position seriously. However, it remains unclear whether he ought to make this concession, and I have suggested that this move could be defended if it could be shown that it makes for a more satisfactory conception of value and our relation to it. The expansive naturalist purports to vindicate his own preferred alternative along these lines by arguing that it accommodates the required synthesis of the normative and the empirical. In this respect it is said to improve upon scientific naturalism (which threatens to eliminate the normative) and theistic or Kantian ethics (which leave these terms in not so splendid isolation). Levinas cannot be accused on this latter score, for the values in his picture are embodied in the world and we are capable of acknowledging the demands they impose upon us. He insists, however, that God is their ultimate source and that God is the source also of our responses to them. The implication here is that the normative/empirical relation collapses at both ends if the theistic underpinning is removed.

If this is right, then the expansive naturalist should concede to Levinas. But how is the matter to be decided? It would be easy enough to adjudicate if there were an obvious explanatory gap in the expansive naturalist's position, but he appears to satisfy the required aims. Given that this is so, he can surely take any argument which could be produced in favour of a theistic position and turn it on its head. Take, for example, the claim that objective moral values do not exist in a non-theistic world.[83] The claim has a point if a non-theistic world is the world as comprehended by science,[84] but the expansive naturalist resists this identification and offers a framework which grants us the right to reinstate the relevant values without any need for God. Likewise he will deny that there is any need to trace their normative force to a divine origin. Rather, the source of normativity is to be found in the values themselves, these values are part of a non-theistic world, and the demands they impose upon us have a categorical action-guiding force which we appreciate by virtue of being morally receptive beings. So his position purports to take us all the way to the idea of obligation, and he would no doubt insist that the real problems arise when this idea is given a further theistic gloss.

The word 'further' here is telling, for it is easy to think that the envisaged theistic gloss is a matter of adding something to the equation which is either irrelevant to the matter at hand or in danger of bringing an undermining effect—as if the addition of God is just a variant upon the kind of proposal which involves reducing (or, in this case, inflating) morality to something else entirely. There are theistic positions to be accused on this score, yet Levinas himself is surely innocent. He accepts with the expansive naturalist that the world we inhabit provides an adequate source of normativity. He would accept also that this world is non-theistic if this is simply a way of lending emphasis to the fact that it contains no intervening God who either forces us to be moral or encourages us to pass the buck with the promise that, come what may, everything will be alright. Nevertheless, he insists that in responding to others in the required moral terms we are drawn closer to God, and that it is our destiny to be so drawn. On this position then, theism is given an expansive naturalist

[83] An argument along these lines is advanced by Paul Copan in his 'The Moral Argument', in *The Rationality of Theism*, ed. Paul Copan and Paul K. Moser (London: Routledge, 2003), pp. 149–174. Related arguments have been formulated by others. For example—and this is surely perfect grist for the atheist's mill—William Lane Craig tells us that 'On the atheistic view, there's nothing really *wrong* with your raping someone', *God? A Debate Between a Christian and an Atheist* (Oxford: Oxford University Press, 2004), p. 18. Elsewhere he tells us that human life in a godless universe is 'not qualitatively different from that of a dog', and that man becomes 'a freak of nature…a lump of slime that evolved into rationality', *Reasonable Faith* (Wheaton, IL: Crossway Books, 1994), pp. 62–63. Wielenberg discusses these claims in his 'In Defense of Non-Natural, Non-Theistic Moral Realism', pp. 34–35, and I am grateful to him for bringing such views to my attention.

[84] Copan assumes this identification, taking as his paradigm a form of naturalistic moral realism according to which moral facts are 'natural and social scientific'. He claims further that '[w]hat makes moral claims true are naturalistic features, which are themselves "posits, or

gloss. We could say equally, however, that expansive naturalism has become theistic, albeit with the essential caveat that this theistic dimension is no longer to be viewed as the addition of a further something else which can be accepted or rejected whilst leaving morality in its place. On the contrary, it is that without which morality—as comprehended by the expansive naturalist—would cease to be. If this is right, then the attempt to accommodate morality without God becomes the attempt to comprehend morality without morality.

We have reached a similar stalemate to the one we reached in the context of considering whether Railton's scientific naturalist should concede to the expansive naturalist. For in this case too, we seemed to be faced with two alternatives which are barely discernible at one level, but which, as far as our disputants are concerned, are a world apart (quite literally speaking). So, for example, we have the expansive scientific naturalist objecting that the expansive naturalist's values have no place in our ontology, to which the expansive naturalist responds that they can be removed only at the cost of leaving us with an impoverished and ultimately unsustainable conception of morality. Likewise, we now have the expansive naturalist telling us that God is not required for morality, to which Levinas will respond that His removal has a similar undermining effect to that which occurs when the scientific naturalist retreats from an expansive naturalist conception of value.

Wiggins criticizes the expansive scientific naturalist's position on two grounds: first, it is doubtful that it gets us all the way to the idea of moral obligation; second, it is unclear that it identifies anything we could fully recognize as the proper object of all our striving. We know already that, for Levinas, the proper object of all our striving is God, and that this striving is expressed—and only expressed—in our moral relations with others. So morality draws us closer to God, and God is the proper object of all our striving. But why say this? Why isn't it enough to say that morality draws us closer to goodness, and that this is the proper object of all our striving? After all, it is surely more compelling to suppose that goodness is something we could *fully recognize* as such, God being rather conspicuous by His absence. Of course, this is precisely what Levinas is saying, for it is no part of his position that a striving towards God could diverge from this moral goal, and he agrees that God is absent from the world in one obvious sense. He insists, however, that this striving has its origin in God and that it relates us to God.

The idea that God is the proper object of our moral striving promises to guarantee that morality is to be taken seriously without reservation, and in this respect deflates the worry expressed by Railton when he concedes that it is a possible objection to his own approach that it doesn't make morality serious

composites of posits, of empirical science" ' ('The Moral Argument', pp. 152–153. The quotation comes from Michael Smith's 'Moral Realism', in *The Blackwell Guide to Ethical Theory*, ed. Hugh LaFollette (Malden, MA: Blackwell Publishers, 2000), p. 23.

enough. How does it do this? It does so by guaranteeing that, as Levinas puts it, 'we are not duped by morality'.[85] We are not duped by morality because morality relates us to God, God is the source of all that is good, and it is our destiny to be drawn in His direction. The expansive naturalist will protest that morality is to be taken seriously without reservation on his view. He will add that any suggestion to the contrary stems from the unjustified assumption that it must be grounded in God, and that there is equal if not greater incentive to see goodness as the proper object of all our striving in a non-theistic world. After all, this is as good as it gets, the matter lies in our hands, and any suggestion that we are not up to the task stems from a conception of human nature this position is designed to undermine.

Levinas would second such protests, and we shall see in the following chapter that they form the basis for his rejection of the Christian God—a God who, from his point of view, precisely does take the relevant moral matters out of our human hands. But where does this leave the question of adjudicating between Levinas and the expansive naturalist? It should be clear that there is no question of providing any kind of proof either way. It will always be open to the expansive naturalist to turn the argument to his own particular advantage, and, of course, for Levinas to return the favour. With these points in mind I want to consider a final court of appeal which comes from John Cottingham. Cottingham argues that a theistic framework offers us hope. The naturalist will, of course, object to the very idea that we are in need of hope. Doesn't this suggest that there is something lacking in what we already have? Isn't the move just a product of the offending theistic framework? And how could such an appeal be anything more than wishful thinking on the part of those who have mislocated the proper object of all our striving? The points are well taken, but the hope Cottingham has in mind is rather more interesting than this, not least because it resonates—in part at least—with what the expansive naturalist wishes to say. The hope is that:

> [t]he 'cave' of our human world (to use Plato's image) is not utterly sealed and closed, but that our flickering moral intimations reflect the ultimate source of all goodness.

By choosing to act morally, he continues:

> We conform to an intelligible, rational pattern, the pattern that a being of surpassing love and benevolence intended for us. Believing this may be partly a matter of faith, but it may also reflect a more coherent and compelling conception of the nature of goodness than anything else that is on offer.[86]

---

[85] Hence, the opening words of the preface of *Totality and Infinity*: 'Everyone will agree that it is of the highest importance to know whether we are not duped by morality' (p. 21).

[86] *Why Believe?* (London: Continuum, 2009), pp. 47–48.

The idea that our human world is not utterly sealed and closed is fundamental to the expansive naturalist's position, and he would reject any suggestion that it involves wishful thinking. We know also that he is anxious to exploit the wisdom of Plato in this context. Levinas has similar aspirations and offers a picture in which we are open to God by virtue of being moral. On both positions we can be said to conform in this manner to an intelligible rational pattern, and Levinas would accept that it is one that God intended for us. We are not compelled to accept this theistic gloss. Nor do we have to accept that it makes for a more coherent and compelling conception of the nature of goodness. The expansive naturalist provides an obvious case in point here, and he is a significant one. He is significant precisely because he goes so far in this direction, allowing us a glimpse beyond the cave which, in one respect, takes us all the way to Levinas's God—the object of all our striving. What do we lose on this position? Perhaps we lose nothing at all. If this is so, then we can conclude either that the expansive naturalist is a closet theist or that Levinas has banished God.

It would come as no surprise to the scientific naturalist that the expansive naturalist is a closet theist, for it was always his belief that the position smacks of unwarranted cosmic excess. We have challenged this complaint, and likewise the idea that a move in the direction of God must invite a similar charge. So the threat is lifted in either context, and it remains open that in relating to value we relate to God. The alternative is to suppose that we do not, and that Levinas is not, after all, talking about God. Such a conclusion may be motivated by atheistic presuppositions and we are free to take or leave them. Equally, however, it may stem from the kind of worry expressed by Rahner when he complains of the tendency today to talk not about God, but about one's neighbour, and to use not the term 'God', but 'world' and 'responsibility for the world'. We are encouraged to suppose that this amounts to a banishing of God and a way of being radically silent about Him, and that we can bring God back into the equation only by transcending such a position. This much promises to lend weight to the conclusion that Levinas has, after all, banished God, and that expansive naturalism can be returned without further ado to its professed secular boundaries. However, it would be a distortion of Levinas's position, for he clearly takes himself to be operating within a framework which is irreducibly God-involving, and would insist that the threat of atheism comes, rather, when we look for a more *direct* way of relating to or talking about God. So he agrees with Bernard Williams that God adds *nothing* to morality. He would insist, however, that this is not an atheistic position, and that, on the contrary, it provides the only way of bringing God into the equation. Anything more would be an addition of the wrong kind of thing, for it would compromise the possibility of our being moral, ruling out the possibility of our relating to God.

If this is right, then the expansive naturalist's framework is already God-involving, and anything more would be just one more concession to the false gods of superstition and onto-theology. Where does this leave Rahner's misgivings? One option is to say that we do relate to God by relating to value, that this way of relating is by no means second best, but that the position, taken in itself, makes for an impoverished conception both of God's reality and of our relation to Him. This is the position I shall seek to defend, and it suggests that we *can* go further than Levinas. However, the claim is not that we must ascend to a different, non-moral level if we are to be really talking about God rather than about something else, for this would suggest that there is a more direct way of relating to God, and we would be in danger of compromising his radical otherness. It would suggest also that we can better relate to Him by ignoring the needs of others. Rather, the claim is that talk of God involves talking about value but that it is not reducible to such talk. In effect then, I am suggesting an expansion which is horizontal rather than vertical, and doing something akin to what the expansive naturalist does when he insists that our descriptions of nature exceed those of the scientific naturalist. That is to say, just as there is more to nature than what the scientific naturalist can comprehend, so, too, there is more to God than what can be comprehended at the level of morality. Of course, there is more to God than what can be comprehended at any level, and we can deny this point only at the cost of compromising His radical otherness. The point, however, is to allow for other ways of relating to a radically other God, and other ways in which He might be revealed to us.

I shall argue in the following chapter that a theistic expansion along these lines takes us to the God of Christianity, and that Levinas's objections to this move can be challenged. So the relation between Levinas and the Christian theologian is comparable to that which exists between the expansive naturalist and Levinas, and, just as we can say that the expansive naturalist misunderstands God, so, too, we can say that Levinas misunderstands the Christian God. This will return us to the question of whether the envisaged move brings any significant gains, and the answer will likewise be familiar, for we shall reach another stalemate, albeit with a sense that something important has been brought to the equation—something which Levinas may or may not be in a position to acknowledge. The expansive naturalist will remain in the background, and some of what I say will help to dispel the force of the worries he would express in this context. However, the dialectic will be played out for the most part between Levinas and the Christian theologian, and it will be the task of the final chapter to spell out the remaining details of this threefold relationship.

7

The God of Christianity

7.1 INTRODUCTION

We relate to God by relating to value. I have argued that the position can be defended, that it is compatible with an expansive naturalist framework, but that it remains open that there are other ways of relating to God, and other ways in which God can relate to us and to the world of which we are a part. Levinas takes such a move to be a fast track to primitive religion. As he puts it, 'Everything that cannot be reduced to an interhuman relation represents not the superior form but the forever primitive form of religion.'[1] Primitive religion in this context incorporates positions which hold court with the magic-making gods to whom we appeal when we want things for ourselves, and Levinas takes the offending picture to be reasserted when such beings are shunted out in favour of an all-powerful God who works His magic from on high to offer the consolation of divine presence to a needy humanity. He will implicate the Christian God in this context, objecting that He compromises our capacity to be moral. The implication here is that the Christian God is not God properly so called.

Levinas holds that religion remains primitive if it exceeds his own preferred parameters, yet these parameters would be as primitive as it gets from the point of view of our naturalists, and they would deny that we require reference to God in order to comprehend our capacity to be moral. They would deny also that He is required in any theoretical context, doing so on the ground that the natural world can be comprehended adequately and more satisfactorily in His absence. The familiar assumption here is that God could only ever be a separable *something else* which has no bearing upon the question of nature. This question is to be tackled in exclusively scientific terms as far as our scientific naturalist is concerned, and anything else—whether it be God or the values espoused by the expansive naturalist—becomes an unnecessary cosmic excess. The expansive naturalist challenges this framework in one important respect

---

[1] *Totality and Infinity*, trans. Alphonso Lingis (Pittsburgh: Duquesne University Press, 1969), p. 79.

with his evaluatively enchanted conception of nature. He insists, however, that the enchantment in question must remain partial, and that it contains no trace of God. The assumption again is that God is irrelevant to the matter at hand.

I have questioned this assumption as far as the matter of morality is concerned, and allowed that the expansive naturalist's position admits of a theistic gloss. In one respect this adds nothing to what the expansive naturalist is already saying. At another level, however, it changes everything, for his evaluatively enchanted world is now traceable to a divine source. This much grants us the right to talk about a *divinely* enchanted world, but there is a question of how far we are permitted to go in this direction. Are we compelled to accept a version of the expansive naturalist's claim that this enchantment must remain partial? And if we go further than this, are we not in danger of reawakening the superstitions which, for the naturalist, are an unwelcome and inevitable by-product of a theistic framework?

The worry loses some of its force once we remember that accusations of this kind can be ideologically motivated, and it is familiar that the expansive naturalist vindicates his own preferred brand of enchantment by showing that it is scientifically and philosophically respectable. Levinas agrees that superstition is a perennial temptation for the theist, and believes that we succumb in this regard if we exceed his own preferred terms of theistic engagement. So his world remains partially enchanted in one obvious respect, and total enchantment becomes the province of any position which violates the required strictures by introducing a god who does more than to implant in us a desire to follow His way. The mark is overstepped with a god who satisfies our theoretical needs, and the point is well taken if intended to guard against the idea that we could ever know all about God. It remains open, however, that there is a way of theorizing about Him which respects the relevant constraints. It is in the context of considering such a possibility that we might recall Lash's claim that any viable approach to the question of God must be made, at least metaphorically, 'on one's knees'.[2]

One gets on one's knees for various reasons, and Levinas would reject any suggestion that God is at our behest in such a context—rightly so, if this is just a way of guaranteeing that the term-making is not unfairly loaded towards the all too human end. The onto-theologian tries to force God into this role at a theoretical level, but he is hardly on his knees, this gesture being more appropriate to a god who has the potential to dish out gifts or to induce the wonderstruck attitude favoured by Heidegger. Levinas would protest that a giver of

---

[2] It will be remembered that Levinas seems prepared to concede in this direction. Hence: 'We have been reproached for ignoring theology; and we do not contest the necessity of a recovery, at least, the necessity of choosing an opportunity for a recovery of these themes. We think, however, that theological recuperation comes after the glimpse of holiness, which is primary' (*Of God Who Comes to Mind*, trans. Bettina Bergo (Stanford: Stanford University Press, 1998), p. ix).

gifts belongs to the domain of primitive religion, and that such a conception of God is demeaning of His reality, and, indeed, of our humanity. He would add that wonderstruck individuals are not best placed to relate to God.

There are gifts and gifts, and we must hesitate before concluding that God cannot be a giver in this sense. Levinas concedes this point in one obvious respect, for His God gives something of fundamental importance to humanity, albeit nothing on a level with rain for crops or consolation for woes. Likewise, we might question the assumption that wonder is beyond the theistic pale. To be sure we can be awestruck before something less than God, and we may mistake such things for God.[3] However, this does not show that the attitude lacks theistic import, and there are two good reasons for resisting this conclusion. First, it may be that something akin to such an attitude is exactly what is needed if our theoretical aspirations towards God are to have a chance of meeting their mark (Lash's point); second, we open up the possibility of there being a non-theoretical way of relating to God which exceeds Levinas's preferred moral parameters and offers a possible route to vindicating Rahner's claim that there is a love of God which is irreducible to that of one's neighbour.

7.2 NATURE, GOD, AND SCIENCE

Modern science has moved us away from the idea that the gods do the work of nature—that they are magic-makers in this sense—and it is familiar from Chapter 1 that God is the magic-maker par excellence as far as the naturalist is concerned. He is 'an agent or force that somehow stands outside the familiar natural world and whose doings cannot be understood as part of it,'[4] He 'preternaturally interferes with the natural course of events', and remains 'in principle unaccountable by science, ineliminable from our ontology, and contradictory to scientific knowledge'.[5] The idea that God is in principle unaccountable by science is precisely what is to be expected given that He is not a part of the world, and to reject Him on this ground would be to commit to scientism. So He is irreducible to the natural causes within the world to which

---

[3] Compare Lash: 'To act religiously is to give God *God's* due. Acting virtuously, for Aquinas, is always a bit like walking a tightrope, taking care not to fall off on either side. Fall off on one side, and you fall into the vice of superstition, which is the vice of treating some creature as God—idolatry, magic, fortune-telling are amongst the examples he lists. The superstitious person suffers from too much religion, treating all manner of things as God' ('The Impossibility of Atheism', in *Theology for Pilgrims* (London: Darton, Longman and Todd, 2008), p. 28).

[4] Barry Stroud, 'The Charm of Naturalism', in *Naturalism in Question*, ed. Mario De Caro and David Macarthur (Cambridge, Mass.: Harvard University Press, 2004), p. 23.

[5] Mario De Caro and Alberto Voltolini, 'Is Liberal Naturalism Possible', in *Naturalism and Normativity*, ed. Mario De Caro and David Macarthur (New York: Columbia University Press, 2010), pp. 71–75.

we rightly appeal at the level of scientific explanation. Nor, however, does He lie *beyond* the world as an agent or force behind the scenes with the magical power to interfere with the normal run of things and to push them around to His own preferred ends. It is familiar from Chapters 4 and 5 that God is neither outside nor inside the world in these senses. Rather, He is its ontological source and, as such, both radically distinct from the world whilst also being intimately connected to it.

According to this position, the world is dependent on God for its existence, and God is, as Brian Davies puts it, 'present to his creatures as their sustainer or preserver. He is "omnipresent" and "ubiquitous".'[6] So we have parted company with the deistic picture according to which God can intervene, if at all, only from the outside as a clockmaker intervenes to modify the workings of the clock he has put in motion, and have adopted an alternative in which divine action is all-pervasive. It is easy to think that this picture rules out the possibility that anything other than God could do its own thing—a problem which is at least partially solved on the assumption that God's action is limited to the occasional interventionist shove. The implication here is that God's omnipresence in the world is going to leave things causally inert, and that our only hope now is to grant those things their own special power of intervention—to interrupt the theistic workings of a world which unfolds inexorably according to the law of God. We are left with a rather interesting but no less problematic variant upon the original deistic picture.

God's omnipresence in the world is intended to be compatible with the idea that things—including, of course, things like ourselves—can do their own thing, and could undermine this possibility only on the assumption that He functions as a competitor cause in this context. However, the position is intended to call into question this assumption, not least because a competitor cause would not be omnipresent. On the contrary, it would be exactly as it says—a competitor cause amongst other possible causes, and we would live 'under a regime of endlessly repeated miracles'.[7] How then is the position to be understood if not in terms of this either/or framework? First, it is allowed that

---

[6] 'Miracles', *New Blackfriars*, vol. 73, issue 857 (2007), p. 104.

[7] As Fergus Kerr puts it in his *After Aquinas: Versions of Thomism* (Oxford: Blackwell Publishers Ltd, 2002), p. 45. I am leaving on one side the vexed question of miracles except to say that the picture according to which they involve special interventions from an absent God cannot be right. How could God intervene with what he is already irreducibly involved with? This does not, however, rule out the idea that God could act in unique ways and not only through universal laws and patterns. For more on all of this see John McDade, 'Some Thoughts on "Miracles"'(unpublished); Brian Davies, 'Miracles'; Rowan Williams, *God's Advocates: Christian Thinkers in Conversation*, ed. Rupert Shortt (London: Darton, Longman and Todd Ltd, 2005), pp. 7–9; Terence Nichols, *The Sacred Cosmos: Christian Faith and the Challenge of Naturalism* (Oregon: Brazos Press, 2003), ch. 8. McDade makes the daring suggestion that the Incarnation is not a miracle. Robinson makes a similar claim in his *Exploration Into God*, (London: SCM Press, 1967), p. 105.

there are natural causes in the world, and that they are susceptible to scientific investigation and explanation. So things are left to their own devices to this degree at least, but they are understood to be created and sustained by God. It follows that the knowledge imparted by science is knowledge of the workings of a created order which is sustained in this manner, and precisely because God does not function as a competitor cause, this theistic underpinning does nothing to undermine the findings of science, nor does it add anything to it *qua* science. We can deny therefore that the position is, as our naturalist puts it, 'contradictory to scientific knowledge'.

So what difference does God make? In an important sense He makes no difference at all, but in another sense—and this is familiar from an analogous point that was made in our discussion of value—He changes everything. He does so because He is the source of things, He sustains them in existence, and is the condition of there being creaturely agency at all.[8] So the naturalist is quite right to say that God is ineliminable from our ontology on this way of thinking. He will insist, however, that the theist is wrong about this, and that things can be explained perfectly adequately on their own terms. The assumption again is that the two positions are mutually exclusive: either we explain things on their own terms or on God's terms, *tertium non datur*.

We are returned to the question of where God fits into the equation once this either/or framework has been abandoned. The alternative—the only alternative if we are to be talking about God rather than a god, and about things rather than ciphers—is to say that God does everything in a manner which allows, and indeed, requires things to do their own thing.[9] This is the mere form of a solution which demands further—however faltering—elucidation. However, it will cut no ice with our naturalist who will insist that the position is both unintelligible and unnecessary. It is unnecessary because we can explain things without this theistic detour. It is unintelligible because we have no understanding of how such double agency could work. Both objections beg the central questions at issue. The idea that the position is unnecessary assumes that the naturalist has the monopoly on explanation, and that such

---

[8] See John McDade, 'Creation and Salvation: Green Faith and Christian Themes', *The Month* (November 1990), p. 9. McDade cites Kathryn Tanner in this context: 'Non-divine being must be talked about as always and in every respect *constituted by*, and therefore *nothing apart from*, an immediate relation with the founding agency of God...created being becomes what it is and this all the more fully, not by way of separation and neutrality from God, but within the intimacy of a relationship to divinity as its total ground' (*God and Creation in Christian Theology* (Oxford: Blackwell Press, 1988), pp. 84–85).

[9] See Fergus Kerr, *After Aquinas*, pp. 45–46. Kerr brings Aquinas's doctrine of double agency into the equation: 'Without arguing or developing any explanatory theory, [Aquinas] merely notes that there is nothing to stop us from thinking that the same effect is produced by a lower agent and by God—thus by both immediately—though in different ways.' Kerr concedes that there is no question of providing an adequate explanation in this context. We are left with a mystery which we can take or leave and 'Thomas has nothing more basic to offer than these observations.'

explanations exclude the envisaged theistic underpinning; that it is unintelligible means simply that it is unintelligible by the lights of the naturalist, and that this conclusion is sufficient to undermine its cogency. The theist would insist that there is a fundamental distinction to be drawn between unintelligibility and mystery, that it is a scientistic prejudice to suppose that mystery stands always to be eliminated, and that we shall insist upon this move at the cost of excluding the dimension of reality it is his purpose to reveal.

It is no part of my argument that God's omnipresence in the world can be demonstrated, nor that we could ever fully comprehend what it means. All that I have sought to show is that the position is compatible with the findings of science, and that it can be neither demonstrated nor excluded by science for God lies beyond the scope of such investigation. His omnipresence in the world rules out the idea that He functions as a competitor cause, so He makes no difference in *this* sense, and does not therefore 'interfere with the natural course of events'. He does, however, stand outside the natural world in one obvious sense, for He is not a part of it, and remains radically other. Being radically other he can never be totally comprehended, but His doings precisely can be understood as part of the natural world because He is omnipresent in all things, albeit in a manner we can never properly understand. So our inquiries must terminate inevitably and appropriately at the level of mystery—the mystery which, for Rahner, is the proper term of transcendence. However, the position is not unintelligible. On the contrary, the idea that God does everything in a manner which allows, and indeed, requires things to do their own thing—this 'form' of a solution to our predicament—is precisely what is to be expected on the assumption that He is wholly other in the required sense. For, being wholly other, He is neither within the world nor beyond it. So He cannot be distinguished from the world as a separate or rival cause, nor can He be conceived as a spatially distinct being. As Brad S. Gregory has put it, God, if real, 'would be wholly present to everything in the natural world precisely and only *because* He would be altogether *inconceivable* in spatial categories. Divine transcendence would thus be not the opposite but the *correlate* of divine immanence'[10]—God and the world do not add up to two.[11]

---

[10] Gregory adds: 'So too, God in this sort of view would be neither temporally prior to nor a cosmic observer of sequential events as they unfold, as if an extraordinarily remote cause of the Big Bang some fourteen or fifteen billion years ago were merely an updating of Voltaire's deistic watchmaker. Rather, God could be fully present to all events and at every moment of time precisely and only *because* he would be altogether *inconceivable* in temporal categories. Divine eternity would then be not the opposite but the *correlate* of divine providence' ('No Room for God? History, Science, Metaphysics, and the Study of Religion', *History and Theory*, vol. 47 (December 2008), p. 503). The paper as a whole is a *tour de force*, and provides a wonderful antidote to scientism. It is to be found in expanded form in Gregory's recent—and equally impressive—book, *The Unintended Reformation: How a Religious Revolution Secularized Society* (Cambridge, Mass.: Harvard University Press, 2012).

[11] Compare Janet Soskice: 'God's omnipresence doesn't mean that God is nowhere, but everywhere—nearer to you than anything can be. Two "things" can only be so near—but God is

7.3 NATURE, SUPERNATURE, AND DIVINE TELEOLOGY

We are returned to the position which was introduced in Chapter 4 in the context of discussing the relation between the supernatural and the natural. The supernatural is that dimension of reality which involves God and His action, while the natural incorporates things which are 'sustained by the forces of nature'. There is the greatest conceivable contrast between these terms, but they also stand in the most intimate connection—a connection which is lost when the supernatural defines the divine in separation from the natural. God ceases to be 'the most real thing in the world', the natural world is conceived in isolation from God, and His action is reduced to the external manipulation of a competitor cause. The way is paved towards atheism, and nature becomes a self-sustaining whole which has no need of God. The alternative is to reject this conception of the relation between God and nature so as to allow that nature is irreducibly open to His communicative action.

The idea that nature is irreducibly open to God's communicative action is just another way of saying that He is omnipresent. As Fergus Kerr puts it, the supernatural dimension is preserved 'in the midst of immanent-everyday realities' rather than being exiled to leave these realities in (non God-involving) possession.[12] So we avoid any implication that the supernatural is an extrinsic addition to the world—a mere 'supernature'[13] which can be removed whilst leaving everything in its place. On the contrary, it is a fundamental dimension thereof—a dimension which, according to our previous discussion, serves to fulfil and to perfect it. Talk of fulfilment and perfection takes us some distance from what has been said so far in this chapter about God's communicative action in the world, for the focus has been upon His role as creator and sustainer of things. By contrast, such talk was relevant to our previous discussion, for we were concerned with the relation between God and man, and with the way in which we can be inwardly transformed by God in a manner that leads to our fulfilment or perfection.

---

not a thing. The non-thingness of God means, as Augustine says, that God can be nearer to me than I am to my own self' ('Philosophical Theology', in *God's Advocates: Christian Thinkers in Conversation*, Rupert Shortt (London: Darton, Longman, and Todd, 2005), pp. 32–33).

[12] *Immortal Longings: Versions of Transcending Humanity* (London: SPCK, 1997), p. 168.

[13] Compare Henri De Lubac: 'The supernatural, deprived of its organic links with nature, tended to be understood by some as a mere "super-nature", a "double" of nature. Furthermore, after such a complete separation what misgivings could the supernatural cause to naturalism? For the latter no longer found it at any point in its path, and could shut itself up in a corresponding isolation, with the added advantage that it claimed to be complete' (*Catholicism: Christ and the Common Destiny of Man* (London: Burns and Oates, 1950), p. 313, cited in Kerr, *Immortal Longings*, p. 168).

It is fundamental to this picture that God's communicative action is understood in the context of its overall teleological aim which is to turn human nature towards its end in God. The picture gives a sense to Cottingham's idea that we conform to an intelligible pattern which God intended for us, and it challenges the deistic assumption that the question of God is to be focused exclusively upon His role in getting things started—an assumption which is already undermined with the claim that His action remains all-pervasive.[14] It suggests also that there is something misguided about a doctrine of creation which places all the emphasis upon what happens at the beginning, as if 'God is more present, more real, more active *then*, in those first milliseconds, than at any other point in time'.[15] On the alternative way of thinking, by contrast, this doctrine concerns the condition of the whole natural order as it is sustained by God's action.[16] The further claim is that creation, thus understood, has an irreducibly teleological aspect—an aspect which can be understood—in part at least—in terms of man's God-given movement towards God.

Talk of man's God-given movement towards God offends the expansive naturalist, but his position contains the seeds for it. Man's onward 'movement' can be interpreted to mean that he is a striving or desiring being, and the expansive naturalist can accept this much. He can allow also that this movement has a teleological orientation, his version being that it is a movement towards goodness which goodness itself calls forth. However, the expansive naturalist would reject any theistic gloss on this movement. By contrast, Levinas accepts such a gloss, but insists that we relate to God only by standing in moral relations to others. So we have a God-given movement towards God, but this movement is comprehended in terms which would be acceptable to the expansive naturalist. It remains to be seen whether we can go further than this, and I have hinted already that a Christian framework may offer such a resource. It is to this position that I now turn.

[14] See John McDade, 'Creation and Salvation: Green Faith and Christian Themes', p. 434.
[15] McDade, 'Creation and Salvation: Green Faith and Christian Themes', p. 434. McDade implicates Stephen Hawking in this context.
[16] Compare McCabe: 'I hope it will be evident that creation is here being used in a quite different sense from the way it is used by people who seek to discover the origin of the universe (was it a big bang or a lot of little pops or whatever). Whatever processes took place in remote periods of time is course in itself a fascinating topic but it is irrelevant to the question of creation in the sense that makes us speak of God. When we have concluded that God created the world, there still remains the scientific question to ask about what kind of world it is and was and how, if ever, it began. It is probably unnecessary to say that the proposition that the universe is made by God and that everything that is, is begun and sustained in existence by God, does not entail that the universe has only existed for a finite time. There may be reasons for thinking that the universe is finite in time and space but the fact that its existence depends on God is not one of them' ('Creation', in *God Matters* (London: Continuum Press, 1987), pp. 8–9).

7.4 THE TRINITY AND GOD AS LOVE

The God of Christianity is said to be irreducibly triune.[17] It has been claimed also that this conception of God puts to rest any suggestion that He is a separable something else which has no bearing upon the question of nature (and of human nature), and that, as such, it offers a coherent and persuasive alternative to atheism.[18] Others have argued that a triune God is the ultimate camel to swallow, and cannot be taken seriously.[19] Some of these critics are atheists who treat the relevant difficulties as further proof that a theistic framework is beyond the pale, albeit without any real sense of what they are rejecting. However, there are also theists who take the theoretical difficulties of the doctrine of the Trinity to be compounded by its practical irrelevance, although it is not always clear whether this is intended to undermine the very idea of a triune God.

John Wren-Lewis encapsulates the putative sins of the doctrine of the Trinity: 'It appears to many people to be a puzzle and a paradox invented by theologians to make life difficult for ordinary folk.'[20] We are to suppose then that it is theoretically problematic, that the problems it creates are unnecessary, and that it is of no practical relevance to life—at least, not to the lives of those who have no time for such conundrums. The theoretical objection is expressed more recently by Gerald O'Collins who tells us that '[f]inding the trinitarian mystery irretrievable and even intolerable, some opt for "one God" and jettison "three persons" '.[21] The implication here—hardly more palatable—is that the one God we might prefer to opt for is *not* irretrievably mysterious.

The practical objection is summed up by Kant:

> The doctrine of the Trinity, taken literally, has *no practical relevance at all*, even if
> we think we understand it; and it is even more clearly irrelevant if we realize that

---

[17] See, for example, John McDade, 'Creation and Salvation' (unpublished); James P. Mackey, *The Christian Experience of God as Trinity* (London: SCM Press, 1983); Walter Kasper, *The God of Jesus Christ* (London: Continuum, 2012, new edition); Rowan Williams, 'The Deflections of Desire: Negative Theology in Trinitarian Discourse', in *Silence and the Word: Negative Theology and Incarnation*, ed. Oliver Davies and Denys Turner (Cambridge: Cambridge University Press, 2002), pp. 115–135; Frans Jozef Van Beeck 'Trinitarian Theology as Participation', in *The Trinity*, ed. Stephen Davies, Daniel Kendall, and Gerald O'Collins (Oxford: Oxford University Press, 1999), pp. 295–328; Gerald O'Collins, 'The Holy Trinity: The State of the Questions', in *The Trinity*, pp. 1–28.

[18] See Michael Paul Gallagher's article 'Show the Atheists the Trinity' in *The Tablet* (24 Jan 1998). For a longer version of this thought see Walter Kasper's *The God of Jesus Christ* (London: Continuum, 2012).

[19] Gerald O'Collins provides a good summary of the relevant objections in his 'The Holy Trinity: The State of the Questions'.

[20] 'Modern Philosophy and the Doctrine of the Trinity', *The Philosophical Quarterly*, vol. 5, no. 20 (July 1955), p. 214.

[21] 'The Holy Trinity: The State of the Questions', p. 1.

it transcends all our concepts. Whether we are to worship three or ten persons in the Deity makes no difference.[22]

This objection at least involves a preparedness to acknowledge the irretrievable mystery of God, and there is no suggestion that a triune God is to be rejected in favour of a more user-friendly version. Rather, the claim is that our failure to comprehend the doctrine has no practical impact upon our capacity to relate to God in an attitude of worship. At least, it has no such impact when this doctrine is *taken literally*.[23]

It is unclear how we are to interpret the force of this concession, but we are to suppose that our worshipful encounter with God is to be given priority, and that this encounter is not compromised by any theoretical incapacity on our part to comprehend His nature.

Thus far, we have two responses to the God of Christianity: *either* He is an unknowable and unintelligible *x or* we have the perfect antidote to this way of thinking about God. The worries which have been expressed about the Trinity can encourage the first attitude, and are welcomed by those who are looking for further proof that theism is untenable. By contrast, those who are more sympathetic to theism will take the relevant difficulties to be inevitable given that we are concerned with *God*. However, they would deny that they are sufficient to rule out the possibility of any relationship between God and man, and we have been encouraged to suppose that a Christian position is well placed to satisfy this aim.

In the Christian tradition the Trinity is associated with love or 'charity', especially in the person of the Holy Spirit.[24] We are familiar enough with Levinas's take on the God/man relation, but how does it relate to the Christian conception thereof? Wren-Lewis implies that Christianity and Levinas's position are rather similar. He says that Christianity involves a rejection of the idea that God relates to us as an omnipotent and coercive controller,[25] and that this way of thinking about God is based on analogy with a picture we have of ourselves as controllers and users of things.[26] The limitations of this picture are familiar

---

[22] Gerald O'Collins considers this objection in his 'The Holy Trinity: The State of the Questions', pp. 1–2. The quote is taken from Kant's *Conflict of the Faculties* in *Religion and Rational Theology*, trans. A.W. Wood and G. di Giovanni, *The Cambridge Edition of the Works of Immanuel Kant* (Cambridge: Cambridge University Press, 1996), p. 264.

[23] A telling comparison can be made here with Gregory of Nyssa's view that number cannot strictly apply to God. As Sarah Coakley sums up the position: 'we cannot "add up" the numbers in the Trinity in the *same* way as we count heads at the gathering of humans' ('"Persons" in the "Social" Doctrine of the Trinity', in *Powers and Submissions: Spirituality, Philosophy and Gender* (Oxford: Blackwell Publishing Ltd, 2002), p. 121).

[24] See St Augustine, *The Trinity*, trans. E. Hill (New York: New York City Press, 1990), Book XV, pp. 27–37.

[25] 'Modern Philosophy and the Doctrine of the Trinity', p. 217. See also Sarah Coakley, 'Kenōsis and Subversion', in *Powers and Submissions*, pp. 3–39.

[26] 'Modern Philosophy and the Doctrine of the Trinity', p. 218.

from our previous discussion, and Wren-Lewis recommends likewise that we lend emphasis to a quite different way of thinking about ourselves, namely, that which is at issue when we engage with a level of value which is not a mere function of its capacity to satisfy our needs and interests. Like Levinas, he focuses upon interhuman relations, especially those in which we open ourselves 'in sympathy and enter into relationships of love with [our] fellows'.[27] He claims also that this focus reveals what is really at issue when we talk about God, for God is 'precisely That which is between man and man in personal relationship'. More specifically, he claims that the word 'God' refers to a sort of relationship rather than to a sort of individual, the relationship in question being that of love.[28]

This might be taken as amounting to atheism, reducing God to a relationship within the world. Nor is it clear what the identification of God with love commits us to. The claim that God is love has a clear enough biblical and theological precedent.[29] However, the notion of love is hardly unambiguous, and even if we restrict it to love in a moral context (assuming that we know what *this* love amounts to) we are still left with the question of how, if at all, God enters the equation. It is at this stage that our atheist will turn the tables to his own advantage and insist that what we should really be saying is that *love* is God.[30] On this way of thinking, love is a relationship within the world which can be comprehended in wholly human terms—it is 'between man and man' in *this* sense—and any residual reference to God merely expresses its value to our humanity: it is the best thing in the world, it has the highest value etc.

Matters are more complex, of course, and Levinas offers a version of this position which has irreducible theistic import. On this way of thinking, the notion of love is given a moral gloss, and God is 'That which is between man and man in personal relationship' in the sense that we relate to Him by standing in moral relations to others. Levinas's further claim is that this is the only way we can relate to God. Does it follow that the word 'God' refers to a relationship rather than an individual? At one level this is precisely what Levinas is saying, although he would insist that his focus upon the interhuman relation is not to be interpreted as a positive claim about God's nature. Rather, it serves as a prohibition to all such claims, and a reminder that our knowledge of God must remain irreducibly practical: to know God is to know what is to be done.

The Christian theologian is hardly claiming to have the complete measure of God, and he can agree with Levinas that the conception of God as love has

---

[27] 'Modern Philosophy and the Doctrine of the Trinity', p. 219.

[28] 'Modern Philosophy and the Doctrine of the Trinity', p. 220.

[29] See 1 John 4.8 and 16. Werner G. Jeanrond provides a helpful historical survey and critical discussion of this way of thinking about God in his *A Theology of Love* (London: T&T Clark, 2010).

[30] Feuerbach insists upon this formulation in his *The Essence of Christianity*, trans. George Eliot (New York, Dover Publications, 2008/1881), p. 217.

practical significance. This much is implicit in the claim that God is 'That which is between man and man in personal relationship'. However, the idea that the word 'God' refers to a relationship rather than an individual *is* intended to be a positive claim about God Himself, and it raises the following questions. First, what does it mean? Second, what does it add to what Levinas is already saying? Third, should we concede in its direction? The denial that God is an individual can make it sound as if He has been banished from the picture, but one of the points here is to distinguish God from any kind of thing—whether it be something within the world or a further something beyond it. Rather, the claim is that God's Being is irreducibly relational—He just *is* relationship. Lash offers a preliminary gloss upon the line of thought when considering whether the word 'God' is a noun or a verb:

> Whereas, where creatures are concerned, it is always possible to distinguish between their identity and their activity, between who they are and what they do, no such distinction is applicable to God. The holy mystery of God simply *is* the giving, the uttering, the breathing that God is said to be and do. And, for those unreconstructed souls who prefer the language of scholastic metaphysics to the imagery of Scripture, what else are we saying when we say that God is *actus purus*, 'pure act', if not that, in Him, the distinction between 'is' and 'does' has no application?[31]

This poses a challenge to the idea that a relational conception of God is not a conception of God properly so called, and the stress upon His holy mystery guards against any suggestion that we have at our disposal a handy conceptual definition of what is involved in being God.[32] So God's radical otherness is preserved in one obvious sense, and there is no implication that His relationality is reducible to any relationship within the world. The further claim is that there is one such relationship—namely, that of love—which can relate us to God and help us to understand what it might mean to talk about Him in relational terms.

7.5 LEVINAS ON THE INCARNATION

Walter Kasper offers a take upon the Christian interpretation of this meaning with the claim that 'God is love communicating himself.'[33] This means at least that God is a giver, or as Lash prefers to put it, that the holy mystery of God is the giving that He is said to be and do. The gods are givers in one obvious sense, but they give isolated goods, they do not give out of love, and love is in

---

[31] 'The Impossibility of Atheism', p. 23.
[32] See Rowan Williams, 'The Deflections of Desire', pp. 115–116.
[33] *The God of Jesus Christ*, p. xxiii.

any case something more than spasmodic or even sustained acts of distribution.[34] Likewise, the goods we receive from the gods are for personal gain, and they have no particular impact upon our being other than to cheer us up in the way that we might be cheered by winning the National Lottery.[35] God is not a giver of goods, and Levinas distinguishes his manner of giving by saying that He gives us His Word and animates our desire to express it. We do so by standing in moral relations to others. So Levinas's God can be said to be a giver of love in one obvious sense, for He makes it possible for us to love. However, the emphasis is placed exclusively upon the love we have for others, this love is expressed in moral terms, and God's love for us does not exceed these morality-giving parameters.

The Christian God is a giver of love, but this love involves His Incarnation in Jesus Christ. On the face of it then, we have a God who is more obviously present in the world, and one way of expressing this manner of revelation—a way which lends justice to the idea that Jesus is both fully divine and fully human[36]—is to say that Jesus is a God-man.[37] The gods can be described as such in one obvious respect, for they are modelled on men. Crucially, however, they are modelled on men who are motivated purely by egoistic considerations, and they can be said to be divine only in the sense that they have an unrivalled capacity to get what they want. It would be more appropriate then to describe them as men-gods, albeit with the caveat that they lack both genuine divinity and humanity.[38] At least, this is what we must say on the assumption that a

---

[34] See Max Scheler, *Ressentiment*, trans. Lewis B. Coser and William W. Holdheim (Wisconsin: Marquette University Press, 2003), p. 65 for a discussion of the kind of sustained giving which masquerades as love. He refers to it as 'altruism'.

[35] McCabe describes the National Lottery as a rather familiar god: 'As an example of worshipping a familiar minor god let me take the British National Lottery. Since the time at least of Pascal there has been a scientific account of the laws of probability, I don't want to go into details (mainly because I am incompetent) but it seems clear that if you want to increase the amount of spare cash you have without doing any work, your chances of doing so successfully by investing it in what look like reliable stock, or even just putting it on a deposit account in the bank, are, by a large factor, greater than if you buy a ticket or scratch card in the lottery. Yet a large number of people choose the lottery. The conclusion can only be that they regard it (probably without thinking of this) as supernatural, to some extent outside the order of nature. There is a mystique about the National Lottery and it has become part of the national religion, and also a lot of fun (but only for those with money to spare, as many who play the lottery have not)', ('The God of Truth', in *God Still Matters* (London: Continuum, 2002), p. 31).

[36] The point of reference here is the Council of Chalcedon in 451 AD: 'We teach...that one and the same Christ, the Son, the Lord, the Only-Begotten is to be recognized in two natures without mixture, without transformation, without division, without separation; the difference of the natures being in no way abrogated through the unification; the properties of each nature remaining, rather, preserved' (cited in Robert Sokolowski, *The God of Faith and Reason: Foundations of Christian Theology* (Washington, DC: The Catholic University of America Press, 1982), p. 35).

[37] The term 'God-man' is used by St Anselm in his *Cur Deus Homo*, Book II, ch. VI.

[38] See Levinas's 'A Man-God?', in *Entre Nous*, trans. Michael B. Smith and Barbara Harshav (London: Continuum Press, 2006), p. 47.

powerful egoist is not properly divine, and that its more limited counterpart falls short of being properly human.

The Christian God would appear to be the polar opposite of an egoist, for He gives Himself without remainder, and is revealed in the world as a man whose fate is to suffer and die at the hands of those who seek dominion. So we seem to have left behind any suggestion that God is a coercive controller of things, or that his business is to dish out goods which have no positive impact upon our humanity. On the contrary, we are concerned with a God who gives us love. Such at least, is the most obvious interpretation of the claim that we have a God of love who offers the gift of Himself.

Levinas rejects this interpretation of the Incarnation, and with it the idea that the Christian God is a God of love properly so called. As he sees it, this God—or 'god' as he would have it—is just one more coercive controller who compromises our capacity to be moral by pandering to our egoism. If this is right, then the Christian God has no role to play in motivating our love for others. On the contrary, He serves to guarantee that we remain enslaved within the circuit of egoism, incapable of giving expression to God's Word. We know already that, for Levinas, we express God's Word by assuming responsibility for the other, and it is in this context that we are told that 'the infinite is not "in front of me"; it is I who express it'. I express it by being the other's 'servant', 'in the name of God'.[39] So the focus is upon my status as a servant before the other, and in adopting this status I am said to give expression to God's Word. This suggests that Levinas is wanting to put *me* in the place of Jesus Christ; at least, this interpretation becomes compelling if we grant that Christ gives expression to God's Word, and that he assumes the status of a servant in this context.[40] We shall have reason to question the precise force of this description as it is applied by Levinas both to ourselves and to Christ. At this stage, however, we can note that he is rejecting any suggestion that God could or should manifest Himself in this manner on the ground that this would preclude my standing in a genuine relation to Him. Why should this be so? The answer seems to be that this would reduce God to a being who pardons the crimes we commit against others,[41] in which case our status as morally responsible beings would be undermined. Hence: 'No one, not even God, can substitute himself for the victim. The world in which pardon is all-powerful becomes inhuman.' [42]

The notion of substitution is central to Levinas's conception of moral responsibility, for we are told that 'responsibility is possible only as substitution for

---

[39] 'God and Philosophy', in *Of God Who Comes to Mind*, p. 75.

[40] Compare Philippians 2:7: '[he] emptied himself, taking the form of a servant, being made in the likeness of man, and in habit found as man'. I shall return to the question of how this form of kenosis is to be understood.

[41] 'A Religion for Adults', in *Difficult Freedom: Essays on Judaism*, translated by Seán Hand (Baltimore: Johns Hopkins University Press, 1990), p. 20.

[42] 'A Religion for Adults', p. 20.

the other'.[43] So he does not take issue with the idea of substitution per se, but insists that it is the moral subject who must substitute herself for the other, doing so by being responsible for everything that has to do with the other, even to the point of being responsible for her responsibility and for the persecutions she undergoes at her hands.[44] I noted in the previous chapter that Levinas tempers the force of this 'utopian' vision by granting that 'the ego can, in the name of this unlimited responsibility, be called on to concern itself also with itself'. The caveat is essential if Levinas is to be acquitted of recommending an ideal which threatens to be as compromising of our humanity as the egoistic position he is seeking to avoid. He takes untrammelled egoism to be inevitable if Jesus Christ is brought into the equation.

We have been told already that God cannot substitute himself for the victim, and that a world in which pardon is all-powerful becomes inhuman. We are to suppose then that Jesus functions as a substitute, but that he does so in a manner which compromises our role in this context—he is one substitute too many. What could this mean? The idea seems to be that Jesus becomes a substitute for humanity by assuming responsibility for our immoral behaviour and absolving us from the requirement to be moral. That is to say that he suffers and dies in order that we might be restored to God, and we have no role to play in this movement. The upshot, spelled out by Franz Josef Van Beeck in a discussion of Levinas's position, is that:

> the world is redeemed by a purely heavenly transaction between God and Jesus Christ—one that occurred without our involvement and from which we benefit without our assent.[45]

Van Beeck agrees that this model of salvation is 'humanly unacceptable' and 'unworthy of mature, responsible humanity', and makes explicit its problematic theological implications:

> A Jesus viewed as a substitute for humanity reveals a God who, like an omnipotent ruler who owes no one an explanation and who shows his power by being capricious, has decided, his anger appeased by the suffering and death of Christ, to impute his 'merits' to humanity free of charge. This makes the suffering and death of an innocent human being into a punishment for sin darkly and ominously willed by a mortally offended God, yet also, at the same time, into the saving

---

[43] *Otherwise Than Being or Beyond Essence*, trans. Alphonso Lingis (Dordecht: Kluwer, 1991), p. 182.

[44] See *Ethics and Infinity: Conversations with Philippe Nemo*, trans. Richard Cohen (Pittsburgh: Duquesne University Press, 1985), pp. 99–100. Levinas goes so far as to claim that I am responsible for the persecutions that I undergo. As Putnam adds, this is 'to the point of offering myself as substitute for the other—think of a concentration camp—to the point of martyrdom' ('Levinas and Judaism', *The Cambridge Companion to Levinas*, ed. Simon Critchley and Robert Bernasconi (Cambridge: Cambridge University Press, 2002), p. 56).

[45] 'God's Love and God's Law: The Incompleteness of Salvation', in *Loving the Torah More Than God?* (Chicago: Loyola University Press, 1989), pp. 76–77.

expedient, mysteriously effective for the salvation of the world, by an inscrutable divine design. Confusingly, the one God must in the same act be feared as the judge who, in cold blood, demands whatever he decides he wants in the way of satisfaction for human wickedness, and loved for being an endlessly indulgent, if totally capricious, parent.[46]

There is no God of love in this picture, for this god is hungry for power, he thrives on pain and suffering, and guarantees that his lust for such a spectacle will remain ever satisfied. He does so by offering a gift—a bloody sacrifice—which encourages just more of the same behaviour. We have, if you like, a god of violence communicating violence to his creatures, and guaranteeing that they remain locked within this mode of existence by holding out the promise of paradise—look unto me and you shall be saved.

Van Beeck objects that this interpretation is a travesty of Christianity, albeit one which has been accepted on occasion and encouraged by certain dubious historical developments within the tradition.[47] Jesus, he continues, was never intended to be a *substitute* for humanity. Rather, our reconciliation with God is accomplished by Jesus's *representing* humanity:

> Though sinless, he had voluntarily, out of love and compassion, shared and taken responsibility for the sinful human predicament, down to accepting a criminal's death *at the hands of sinful people*. In doing so, Jesus had abandoned himself completely to God, and God had accepted his self-offering and raised him to life. In this way the whole work of salvation was ultimately rooted in the love of God, whose son had taken on humanity, along with its inhumanity, in order to redirect it and renew it and bring it home to God.[48]

Crucially:

> This conception of Christ's saving work entails responsibilities for those who accept its benefits. Christ's suffering, death, and resurrection do not get anyone off the hook. No one can rest in the assurance of a salvation procured, at great expense to himself, by someone else…Someone who *represents* me does not *replace* me: I remain involved—there remains an active relationship of mutual responsiveness, which implies a continuing responsibility on my part. Someone who is my substitute, however, supplants me, displaces me, excludes me, makes me superfluous. In other words, whereas *representation invites participation*, substitution excludes it.[49]

To sum up Levinas's view: we relate to God only by standing in moral relations to others. This involves our giving expression to God's Word, to which

---

[46] 'God's Love and God's Law', p. 77.
[47] See 'God's Love and God's Law', pp. 70–78 for a helpful discussion of the relevant developments which, he claims, account for 'what Levinas sees as elements of injustice and immaturity in the Christian faith'.
[48] 'God's Love and God's Law', p. 75.
[49] 'God's Love and God's Law', p. 76.

Jesus would be an obstacle. A God who reveals Himself in the Christian manner is just one more omnipotent controller of things who wields His power
with a capricious system of rewards and punishments. Jesus is the loser and
we are the winners, but the prize comes at the cost of our humanity. Levinas's
solution is to knock Jesus from the equation so that *we* can take on the required
responsibility for humanity. Then, God is no longer a coercive controller, our
role as responsible beings is not sacrificed, and the reward is the regaining of
our humanity. In this sense we stand in an intimate relation to God.

Levinas is right to reject the conception of God as a coercive controller,
and we can agree that His Incarnation would be morally reprehensible if it
were, as he puts it, a cheap intervention of 'extrahuman factors' which operates
independently of any 'consciousness of good' on our part.[50] So Jesus cannot be
a substitute in this sense. According to Levinas's preferred alternative, we are
to become substitutes for Jesus, where this involves our assuming an analogous responsibility for others by functioning as *their* substitutes. The picture
runs no risk of compromising our humanity in the Christian manner, yet it
might be thought to generate this effect from the opposite direction. At least,
this conclusion becomes compelling if it is a requirement upon our satisfying the required aim that we exist purely for the sake of others and become
'nothing' to ourselves. Assuming that it is not humanly possibly to exist in
this self-sacrificing way, we are returned yet again to the picture of God as a
coercive controller, for we could meet this demand only by become ciphers for
God's love. As Werner Jeanrond says, in criticizing a similar interpretation of
Christianity:

> The loving subject must love without concern for him—or herself. Instead the
> subject is asked to surrender his or her subjectivity in love and in praise of love
> for God. The question is not only whether or not the self will get rid of any egois-
> tic or self-centred desires; rather the self is asked to get rid of all self in the act of
> loving. 'Through self-denial a human being gains the ability to be an instrument
> by inwardly making himself into nothing before God. Through self-sacrificing
> unselfishness he outwardly makes himself into nothing, an unworthy servant'. The
> human being 'is nothing'. Here total self-emptying (*kenosis*) is both the way and
> the goal of Christian love.[51]

The idea that we are ciphers for God's love in this sense seems a far cry from
Levinas's considered position, and it remains open that his talk of substitution
and self-sacrifice in this context admits of a less problematic interpretation.
I have argued that his interpretation of Christianity is wide of the mark, and

---

[50] See Levinas, 'A Religion for Adults', p. 20.
[51] *A Theology of Love*, pp. 111–112. Jeanrond is discussing Kierkegaard's position in this
context. For an atheist version of a similar position and criticism see Bernard Williams's
'integrity objection' to Utilitarianism in *Utilitarianism: For and Against*, with J.J.C. Smart
(Cambridge: Cambridge University Press, 1973), pp. 116–117.

that we must reject the assumption that it reduces us to pure egoists fated to remain enslaved to a similarly egoistic god who sacrifices Jesus for the hell of it. On the contrary, Jesus functions as a representative for humanity rather than a substitute. His status as representative is compatible with the idea that we have a fundamental role to play in this drama, so there is no suggestion that our humanity is compromised, nor that God functions as a coercive controller. Rather, He is a God of love, and His Incarnation has a similar effect to that which Levinas reserves for his own God, namely, to give us what is required if we are to relate to Him. We must therefore look more closely at the details of Christianity and see whether it adds anything of significance.

7.6 THE CHRISTIAN GOD OF LOVE

We have granted that God does not control things coercively. The stress upon *coercion* is important, for the point is not to deny that God controls things in a non-coercive way, and it is crucial to both Levinas and the Christian that God precisely *is* in control in this sense. This is what it means to talk of God's communicative action or of a God-given movement towards God. So we can—and indeed, must—accommodate the idea of divine power, but it is denied that this power is coercive—as it would be if God reduced things to the status of ciphers, victims, or slaves. We can therefore lay it down as a requirement upon a satisfactory interpretation of the Incarnation that God is not coercive. Likewise, we must deny that Jesus is a mere cipher for God's overall purpose—as he becomes on Levinas's interpretation—and we must deny also that it is our human fate to be so reduced. Rejecting the idea that God is a coercive controller rules out saying that He functions as a competitor cause, and we have stressed already that His radical otherness precludes this. It also prevents us from treating Him as a being amongst beings, and it follows from this that the Incarnation cannot reduce Him to such a being.

So there are no prospects for treating God as some kind of alien invader from without who lands on earth to become just one more part of it. Such treatment suggests that God Himself becomes a part of the world—that, as Robinson puts it, 'Jesus was really God almighty walking about on earth, dressed up as a man... God for a limited period taking part in a charade'.[52] This is theistically objectionable for it turns God into just one more being within the world. It also compromises Jesus's humanity, for he is swamped and eliminated by the presence of God to become a mere tool for His overall purpose.

---

[52] John Robinson, *Honest to God* (London: SCM Press, 1963), p. 42.

We are reminded of the difficulties we faced in explaining what it could mean to talk of God's presence to the world. There we seemed to be confined to one of two alternatives. *Either* we explain things on God's terms alone and exclude the sense in which they can do their own thing. *Or* we explain things on their own terms alone and exclude God from the equation. The idea of a God-man provides a stark illustration of this supposed impasse. *Either* Jesus just is God, and we are left with God minus the man, and precisely because God is neither a being amongst beings nor a competitor cause, we have also eliminated God as well as the man. *Or* Jesus is just a man, leaving the man minus God. Again, we have jettisoned the God-man, and if we remain within the offending framework, we can reinstate God only by reverting to the position which made this atheist response so compelling in the first place.

Such difficulties would be readily embraced by the atheist, as well as by the unitarian. They would object that the reference to God is both unintelligible and superfluous, and that Jesus is best viewed as a moral paradigm for humanity—a good man but not a God-man. Such a response would be compelling if the alternatives we have considered were exhaustive of the available options, but neither of them is adequate for comprehending the God-man, and a more fruitful direction is to be found by trading upon what has been said more generally about God's omnipresence. That is to say, the Incarnation is the supreme instantiation of God's omnipresence. So McDade:

> The conditions which make Incarnation possible are precisely the conditions operative in creation: the ontology of Incarnation is the ontology of creation. This is not a proof of the Incarnation—how could it be proved? But it is to say that in their operation, both Incarnation and creation are governed by principles which respect the transcendent character of the divine and the dependent status of the created order. God does not become part of anything and so it is a mistake to think that Christ is 'composed' of a divine part and a human part as though he were a hybrid amalgam, the product of a singular divine-human fusion. Only an ontology along these lines can prevent the category of Incarnation from being read either as a Zeus-like metamorphosis into creaturely shape, as a mixing in which the divine absorbs the creaturely, or as a masquerade in which the divine only seems to be connected to us.[53]

On this alternative, God and Jesus remain distinct, but not as two distinct beings or parts—they do not add up to two—and in such a way that Jesus can be said to be wholly human and wholly divine. We can allow then that there are two natures in Christ, and this is thinkable (albeit neither provable nor fully graspable) because we have here the supreme instantiation of God's omnipresence to the world—an omnipresence which entitles us to deny that divinity and humanity are inevitably incompatible, and to lend justice to the

---

[53] 'Creation and Salvation', pp. 11–12.

intimate connection between man and God which is so important to Levinas. In the Incarnation, however, this connection reaches its zenith, for Jesus is himself God's self-communication—he is God's Word made flesh, or as Robinson puts it, the 'complete expression, the word of God'.

The idea that a human being could give expression to God's Word is familiar from Levinas. I have suggested already that his stress upon self-sacrifice might risk eliminating man from the equation, and that there is an analogous way of thinking which lurks in some versions of Christianity, suggesting that we are to become mere channels for God's love—'unworthy servants' as Jeanrond puts it. It is significant then that Robinson claims that:

> It is in Jesus, and Jesus alone, that there is nothing of self to be seen, but solely the ulti-
> mate, unconditional love of God...Jesus, that is to say, reveals God by being utterly
> transparent to him, precisely as he is nothing 'in himself'.[54]

The claim that Jesus is nothing 'in himself' involves difficulties, however. Is self-lessness compatible with his humanity or, indeed, with his divinity? And where do *we* fit into the equation? We have abandoned the picture of God as a coercive controller, so our task is not the impossible one of explaining how Jesus could be said to retain a divine status as such a controller, nor how he could remain human in the face of a controlling and obliterating presence.[55] Divine power is non-coercive. Sarah Coakley describes this power as 'the subtle but enabling presence of a God who neither shouts nor forces, let alone 'obliterates',[56] claiming that what we have in Christ is the concurrence of 'non-bullying divine "power" with "self-effaced" humanity',[57] the 'unique intersection of vulnerable, "non-grasping" humanity and authentic divine power'.[58]

The denial that God's presence has an obliterating effect rules out the most obvious way of interpreting the notion of self-effaced humanity, and Coakley insists that it is not to be interpreted as a form of self-abnegation or slavery.[59] As she puts it, this 'rather special form of "vulnerability" is not an invitation to be battered'.[60] Rather, it involves being volitionally open to God's transformative effect. This transformative effect is the work of divine power properly so called—or God's Spirit[61]—and its presence goes hand in hand with relinquishing

---

[54] *Honest to God*, pp. 48–49.
[55] Sarah Coakley offers a helpful discussion of some of the moves which have been made by those who cling to the offending framework in her 'Kenōsis and Subversion'.
[56] 'Kenōsis and Subversion', p. 35.
[57] 'Kenōsis and Subversion', p. 31.
[58] 'Kenōsis and Subversion', p. 38.
[59] 'Kenōsis and Subversion', p. 36.
[60] 'Kenōsis and Subversion', p. 35.
[61] As James Dunn puts it: 'The Spirit is that power which operates on the *heart* of man—the "heart" being the centre of thought, feeling, and willing, the centre of personal consciousness...The Spirit is that power which transforms a man (or a woman) from the inside out' (*Jesus and The Spirit* (London: SCM, 1975), p. 201). Moser cites this passage in his *The Elusive God* (Cambridge: Cambridge University Press, 2008), and, like Coakley, identifies Spirit with

any desire to be a coercive controller—a 'batterer', a 'grasper', a 'snatcher'. The self-effacement at issue here is that which is operative when the relevant grasping tendencies have been silenced, and silenced to the extent that the self is transformed by the power of God. The concurrence of these two poles, divine power and self-effacement, is said to gain supreme expression in Christ, and it is in this sense that He can be described as God's Word made flesh. We are told also that He is a model of 'perfect humanity'.[62] It is fundamental to this picture that God's transformative power or spirit can work upon *our* humanity provided that we open ourselves in the required way. We do this by 'making space' for God to be God,[63] and this involves a 'yielding to divine power which is no worldly power', a form of 'self-effacement'.[64] The relinquishing of our powers in this egoistic sense paves the way to a more authentic form of empowerment which can make us more properly human as we 'expand' into God and become transformed in the process.[65] In this way we are said to enact or enter into the 'mind' which Christ himself instantiates.

The idea that we are to enter into the mind of Christ—or, as St Paul puts it, that we are 'in Christ' or 'in the Spirit'[66]—returns us to the question of the nature of the envisaged communion. We have already ruled out some of the more problematic interpretations of such a position, and Paul Moser suggests that we can sidestep the metaphysical puzzles by emphasizing St Paul's idea of 'being led' by the Spirit of God as it is manifested in Jesus. Moser then spells this out in terms which are mostly familiar from Coakley's discussion and partly familiar from Levinas: the Spirit of God is said to bring 'new noncoercive *power* to a receptive person', and is to be distinguished from any 'worldly power'; it involves appropriating 'the available motivational power of God's Spirit'; and it 'empowers us to love as God loves'.[67] The further claims are that 'apart from such empowerment, we would lapse into unloving, selfish ways and thereby violate any command to love unselfishly as God loves',[68] and that

---

'non-coercive power' (p. 146). It is in the context of such claims that we might appreciate Balthasar's claim that 'the Holy Spirit does not wish to be seen but to be a seeing eye of grace in us'. As McDade has pointed out to me, this is important because it exemplifies the way in which God cannot be objectified and cannot be an object for us. The scholastic principle that 'God is known only in His effects' means that knowledge of God is mediated through what God brings about rather than in an objectified manifestation. It should be clear from what has been said already that even in the 'objectified' Incarnation, God's otherness is not violated or diminished. Jesus conveys God's expression of Himself, but we do not have an adequate grasp of that.

[62] 'Kenōsis and Subversion', p. 30. Compare Lash who claims that Jesus is 'the only *complete* human there has been' ('The Impossibility of Atheism', p. 27).

[63] 'Kenōsis and Subversion', p. 34.

[64] 'Kenōsis and Subversion', p. 35.

[65] 'Kenōsis and Subversion', p. 36. Moser offers a similar account in ch. 3 of his *The Elusive God*.

[66] Romans 8:1, 9.

[67] *The Elusive God*, pp. 146–147.

[68] *The Elusive God*, p. 152.

this 'power of divine self-giving love... is perfectly manifested in Jesus as God's fully obedient Son'.[69]

7.7 THE CHRISTIAN SUPERMAN?

There are further questions to be asked about what it means to be empowered to love like God. However, it seems clear enough that we have been presented with a model of proper humanity which has nothing to do with self-abnegation, slavery, or unworthy servitude. Rather, it is a matter of rising above our egoistic tendencies—or, more weakly and plausibly—resisting their dominion. The picture is familiar from our expansive naturalist, and it captures at least part—perhaps even all—of what Levinas is getting at with his talk of self-sacrifice. The expansive naturalist grants a kind of 'self-effacement' which involves yielding to a non-coercive yet motivating power, and Levinas's notion of ethical resistance would suit his purposes. However, the expansive naturalist would deny that we are being elevated into the life of God, just as Levinas would deny that we are entering into the 'mind' of Christ.

So we have three positions which, terminology notwithstanding, have much in common, and the question of whether Levinas could or should concede to the Christian raises similar issues and difficulties to those raised by the question of whether the expansive naturalist could or should concede to Levinas. I have argued that the expansive naturalist could make this concession at no cost to his own position, but it was unclear whether he gained anything by making this move, if indeed he hadn't already made it. The problem there was pitched at the level of morality, and this level is relevant to Levinas's discussion of an Incarnate God, for he takes such a God to compromise our capacity to be moral. So his criticisms in this regard are analogous to the naturalist's more general criticisms of any form of theistic ethics, with the difference that, according to Levinas, an Incarnate God, rather than forcing us to be moral, relieves us of any need to bother in the first place. I have rejected this interpretation of Christianity on the ground that Christ was never intended to get us off the moral hook. As Beeck puts it, His saving work entails responsibilities for those who accept its benefits. If this is so, then Levinas is wrong to claim that an Incarnate God impedes morality, just as the expansive naturalist would be wrong to criticize Levinas's God on this score.

Talk of benefits and saving work suggests that we gain something significant by introducing Christ into the equation. But how are these gains to be understood? We are told by Beeck that Christ 'takes on our humanity, along with

---

[69] *The Elusive God*, pp. 146–147.

its inhumanity, in order to redirect it and renew it and bring it home to God'. This suggests that, without Christ, we remain imprisoned in our inhumanity, incapable of being moral and cut loose from God. Levinas, on the other hand, denies that Christ could be of any use, but that's because he sees him as a figure who remains in cahoots with a coercive controller, robbing us of what is required if we are to become properly human, i.e. if we are to stand in a proper relation to God. By contrast, the Christian takes Christ to be central to attaining this aim, albeit a Christ who is a far cry from Levinas's view of him, and whose transformative effects have more in common with those of Levinas's God.

This narrows the gap between the two positions. We can note also that although Levinas insists that God is 'hidden' and 'distant'—suggesting a further significant contrast with the more obviously present God of Christianity—he is perfectly happy to describe Him as a 'living God amongst us' who remains 'present and intimate' to the extent that we express His Word.[70] So Levinas has no issue with the notion of divine presence per se, and grants that it has a transformative effect on the subject. However, he denies that this transformative work could be the effect of an Incarnate God—understandably so, given that he has severed any possible connection between Christ and God. This leads him to reject the idea that the 'link between God and man' could be 'an emotional communion that takes place within the love of a God incarnate',[71] and he distinguishes such a communion from that which is operative when we give expression to God's Word by standing in moral relations to others. We are returned to the familiar claims that we can love God only by loving others, and that God's love for us is confined to His giving of His Word—'the harsh words of an exacting God', we are told; one who 'demand(s) the superhuman of man'.[72]

As Levinas sees it then, our love for an Incarnate God is not a love for God properly so called, and an Incarnate God's love for us is not the love of God—it is the fake love of a god who diverts us from the path of goodness. These conclusions are compelling if we accept Levinas's conception of Jesus Christ, for the putative emotional communion with God becomes an entirely self-centred affair which involves relating to someone who panders to our egoistic desires, and we are returned to the inhuman hell which, for Levinas, can be avoided only by giving ourselves to a non-Incarnate God, i.e. by giving ourselves to others. If, by contrast, we reject Levinas's interpretation and allow that our communion with Christ—as God's Word made flesh—has a similar transformative effect to that which Levinas reserves for a non-Incarnate God, then it remains

---

[70] 'Loving the Torah More Than God', in *Difficult Freedom: Essays on Judaism*, trans. Seán Hand (Baltimore: Johns Hopkins University Press, 1990), p. 144.

[71] 'Loving the Torah More Than God', p. 144.

[72] 'Loving the Torah More Than God', p. 145.

open that the required link between man and God precisely could be 'an emotional communion that takes place within the love of a God Incarnate'.

If this is right, then Levinas could concede to the Christian position at no cost to his own. But would he gain anything by doing so? The question is analogous to the question whether the expansive naturalist should concede to Levinas. To that question I suggested an affirmative answer, if only it could be shown that Levinas's position makes for a more satisfactory conception of value and of our relation to it. Levinas and the Christian agree that God is indispensable to this relation. We could therefore claim that Levinas should concede to Christianity if it could be shown that Christianity makes for a more satisfactory conception of God and of our relation to Him, and that this, in turn, has important implications for an understanding of morality and humanity.

Rahner would applaud such a move on the ground that Levinas's position is in danger of banishing God altogether, and it is in this context that he complains of the tendency 'to talk not about God, but about one's neighbour, to preach not about the love of God, but about the love of neighbour'. Rahner believes that a Christian framework can procure these advantages, and that we shall neglect them at the cost of embracing an impoverished conception of God and of our relation to Him. Alternatively, and more seriously, we shall retreat into atheism. Levinas agrees that it is not enough simply to talk about others and the importance of loving them in one obvious sense, for he comprehends such talk in irreducibly theistic terms. He can allow also that there is room within his framework for a love of God. Thus, he says of the 'superhuman' man who faces the challenge of God's 'excessive demands' that '[h]e will love Him in spite of all God's attempts to discourage such love'.[73] We know also that he takes the threat of atheism to come, rather, from Christianity, with its putative reduction of God-love to self-love.

God is on a different level from the objects with which we engage at any other level of reflection and speculation, and we must approach Him in a very different way. He is an object of wonder and worship, and we know already that Kant gives priority to such an attitude over the tendency to treat Him as a theoretical conundrum. But worshipping God involves loving Him, and we are faced again with the question of how this love is to be understood if not in exclusively moral terms. Love for God and love for others cannot be competitors. For this would mean that others get in the way of our loving God, and that we can best love Him by putting them on one side—a consequence which returns us to the kind of self-interested communion which Levinas is so anxious to avoid. It would suggest also that God is just one more part of reality—a

---

[73] 'Loving the Torah More Than God', p. 145. Compare also: 'The Justice rendered to the Other, my neighbour, gives me an unsurpassable proximity to God. It is as intimate as the prayer and liturgy which, without justice, are nothing' ('A Religion for Adults', p. 18).

part which, in this instant, competes for our affections at the cost of anyone and anything else.

How then is our love for God to be understood? It cannot detract from our love for others, nor must it imply that loving others is an inferior substitute for those who are incapable of loving God Himself. The idea that God is love fulfils both of these requirements. God is no longer just one more love to be added to our human loves with the potential to upstage them. Rather, He is love itself, and, as such, to be met 'between man and man in personal relationship'. This entitles us to say that loving God entails loving others, and to avoid any suggestion that this latter is less than the Real Thing. However, the focus upon love itself rather than any particular love does not lead inevitably either to morality or to God, let alone a God we could love. It takes us to something less than morality if we interpret it as an invitation to become inveterate seducers, although we should reserve the right to question whether this amounts to a genuine love of *love*.[74] It takes us to something less than God if we interpret love in non-God involving terms and treat the love of love as an expression of a commitment to morality. This would return us to the claim that *love* is God. It *seems* to take us to something less than a God we could love if we can love Him only by loving others, although Levinas would contest this conclusion.

So we love something less than God if we treat Him as just one more object to be loved, and a focus upon love itself can yield a similar result. It can yield such a result, but the position surely supplies the required ingredients in one obvious sense, for if God is love then how else could we love Him other than by loving love itself? This is true, but the further crucial claim is that we are loving God in this context, and that the content of such love exceeds the aforementioned moral parameters. The position is a non-starter if God is wholly absent from the world, and there is enough in Levinas to suggest that God's absence is precisely what is needed to safeguard His divinity. However, this is not Levinas's considered view, for His God is present enough for us to relate to Him, albeit only by our moral relations to others. Levinas will say that this is just what it is to love God, and that the mistake is to suppose that we need anything further. We *could* say this, but we could be excused for thinking that something important has been lost.

Levinas is in no doubt about what is missing, namely, the 'warm and almost tangible communion' he associates with a Christian framework and rejects in

---

[74] As an example of how such thinking can go awry the following quotation from a recent book by Troy Jollimore is irresistible: 'If God is permitted to love not one person but many, why should we, whose love is supposed to be an image of God's, not be granted similar permission?' The context makes it clear that the permission in question involves nonmonogamous sexual arrangements, a permission which is justified on the dubious ground that since 'different things make different people happy, making nonmonogamous sexual arrangements a possibility would seem likely to increase overall happiness' (*Love's Vision* (Princeton: Princeton University Press, 2011), p. 164).

favour of a 'difficult adoration' which 'demand(s) the superhuman of man'.[75] This latter picture is said to grant us the right to 'approach God and speak to Him without always being in His debt', and to 'love Him in spite of all God's attempts to discourage such love'—it is 'a personal relationship worthy of the name'.[76] The implication here is that what we gain from Christianity is a God who encourages our love, is easy to love, and who no longer demands that we be 'superhuman'.

These gains seem significant, but we are led to suppose that they sever our connection with God. However, the Christian will deny that his love of God is either egoistic or particularly easy. After all, it involves loving others, and this imposes demands upon us. But what are we to make of Levinas's claim that we are required to be superhuman? One thing this could mean is that we are required to live up to a standard which lies beyond our human capacities, and which could be met only to the extent that we cease to be human, doing so, perhaps, by becoming ciphers for God's love. God would indeed be guilty of discouraging our love on this picture, for it would be impossible to love Him in the required way. We must therefore reject the idea that we must be superhuman in *this* sense. On a more plausible interpretation, we are required to live up to a standard which is demanding of our humanity, but which can be met to the extent that we resist the temptation to exist as purely self-concerned beings. God can no longer be accused of discouraging our love according to this picture. After all, He is giving us a standard we can meet and our acceptance of it fulfils rather than obliterates our humanity. The standard can be met, but it is crucial to both Levinas and the Christian that God's input is required, that He motivates our love, albeit in a non-coercive way. Does this not mean that the standard is, after all, beyond our human capacities? Not in the sense that we can meet it only by ceasing to be human. For God's motivating power fulfils rather than obliterates our humanity—we become properly human in a way that would not be possible without God's transformative power. This surely counts as divine encouragement of a sort. But Levinas distinguishes it from the encouragement afforded by an Incarnate God.

An Incarnate God gives Himself in Jesus Christ. This seems a world apart from the showering of mere goods, and it also takes us beyond the harsh words of Levinas's more exacting God, although it is a harsh enough word in one obvious sense. What does it add to the equation? Contrary to Levinas, the Christian claims that Christ empowers us to love as God loves, Christ being the perfect human expression of this love. Christ's influence is not merely extrinsic, as it would be if he were simply a moral exemplar who could do nothing to help us change our ways. Rather, the claim is that the Spirit of God which works through Christ has a transformative effect upon us to the extent

---

[75] 'Loving the Torah More Than God', p. 145.
[76] 'Loving the Torah More Than God', p. 145.

that we allow it to 'enter our hearts'. It is in this sense that we are empowered to love like God.

This might suggest that we are empowered to sacrifice ourselves without remainder, transformed into the superhuman beings which lurk in Levinas's scheme of things. I have argued already that such self-surrender is too demanding of our humanity and risks reducing us to God's ciphers. The idea that Jesus was wholly human suggests a way of avoiding this difficulty, for we are shown that the ideal is, after all, humanly attainable. Perhaps it is humanly attainable for the few saints amongst us, but it would surely be too demanding for the ordinary decent human being, and there is no good reason for insisting that we should meet it. The Christian can respond that we are not required to abandon any remnant of self-concern. The point is, rather, that Christ can lead us away from a purely self-concerned existence. So we are empowered to love like God in the sense that we become capable of giving ourselves to others in the required moral sense and of respecting the requirements they impose upon us. This is a humanly attainable ideal, for Christ is no mere cipher to God's love, and the love He embodies serves to motivate us in this direction. However, it is compatible with this position that we retain an element of self-concern, for we are not, and are not required to be, God-men.

Levinas's demand that we exist purely for the sake of others suggests that he is committed to the first, austere, interpretation of the Christian position. Perhaps he could allow likewise that the ideal is humanly attainable by making appeal to the lives of the saints or perhaps his own life (assuming that he was a saint). As for the required motivation, he could fall back on the power of God's love and deny that we need a further mediator in Christ. He *could* make these moves, but we could object again that the position is too demanding of our humanity, and that there is no good reason for accepting it. Levinas gestures towards allowing a measure of self-concern, and he could insist again that Christ is dispensable. We ourselves testify to the fact that it is humanly possible to exist in the required way provided that we remain open to God's non-coercive influence. We can describe this as being 'in Christ' if we like, but such terminology serves more properly to capture the kind of intimate connection between God and man which is available to a non-Christian framework, and which can be accommodated without any further intermediary.

Levinas's position remains compelling if we accept his interpretation of this mediating factor. If we reject it, then we are returned to the question of whether we gain anything by moving towards Christianity. Christianity may or may not make it easier to accommodate our love for others, but there seems a clear enough sense in which it is better placed to accommodate our love for God, and, indeed, His love for us. After all, God is no longer totally inaccessible to us—He has 'made Himself visible: in Jesus we are able to see the

Father'.[77] Furthermore, we have been shown how far He is prepared to go for us, how much He loves us, the extent to which He identifies with us.[78] Levinas will respond that His God is hardly inaccessible, and that He goes so far as to refuse the easy route of Incarnation for the sake of our humanity. What better proof of God's love could there be? And how could we not love Him in return? The response is persuasive if we accept that the love of an Incarnate God is bound to be counterfeit. However, the Christian rejects this interpretation, and, with it, the idea that God's love for us could only ever involve issuing excessive demands. Rather, the claim is that God's Incarnation is a genuine expression of love, and this goes hand in hand with the idea that we can enjoy a loving communion with Him which is not just a matter of respecting the aforementioned demands. The further claim is that this brings a measure of warmth and consolation to the equation which is missing on the opposing picture. *Pace* Levinas, this is not a matter of succumbing to a 'suspect intoxication'[79] which severs our connection with God to rob us of our humanity and our morality. On the contrary, the envisaged communion is said to empower us to love others, and it does so precisely because it involves being in communion with a God who can both love and be loved. What are the reasons for resisting this move? That warmth and consolation have no role to play in love properly so called? That a God who gives us something more than the demand to give ourselves to others is not a loving God? That we are required to be superhuman? Levinas himself qualifies this latter claim, and the only justification he offers for the others is that they provide the only alternative to a position which leaves us cut loose from God and imprisoned in our egoism. The Christian position provides a challenge to this either/or framework, its insights are implicit in at least some of Levinas's claims, and it remains open that we shall forsake this middle ground at the cost of courting an alternative which is as damaging to our humanity and to God's reality as the one Levinas so unfairly associates with an Incarnate God.

7.8 CONCLUSION

The previous chapter left us with the following dilemma: Levinas and the expansive naturalist say very similar things about our relation to value, but Levinas sets it out from within a theistic framework. One option is to say that

---

[77] See Benedict xvi's *Deus Caritas Est,*, s. 17, <http://www.vatican.va/holy_father/benedict_xvi/encyclicals/documents/hf_ben-xvi_enc_20051225_deus-caritas-est_en.html>.

[78] See Moser, *The Elusive God*, p. 166.

[79] See 'Education and Prayer', in *Difficult Freedom*, p. 270.

he has banished God in all but name, but we could conclude equally that the expansive naturalist has introduced Him—minus the name. The first option would appeal to the expansive naturalist, but it is also motivated by the minimalism of Levinas's theism, and the need to say something more about God and our relation to Him if we are to prevent the position from collapsing back into atheism. The question then was whether we could go a bit further than Levinas, but not so far as to commit the opposite error of introducing a god who remains unworthy of the name. For, of course, it is the desire to avoid such an error which motivates Levinas's minimalism in the first place.

Enter the God of Christianity. A Christian framework promises to satisfy the required aim in one obvious sense, for its Incarnate God is no longer wholly absent from the world, and the prospects are opened up for relating to Him and talking about Him in a manner that exceeds Levinas's preferred parameters. Levinas objects that the Christian God is not God properly so called because He compromises our capacity to be moral, and given that we can relate to God only by standing in moral relations to others, it follows that, in relating to the Christian God, we are relating to something less than God. I have argued that Levinas's objections are misplaced, and that the Christian God plays a morally motivating role similar to that of Levinas's God. It appeared then that Levinas could concede in a Christian direction at no moral cost, and it remained open that the move could bring significant gains. Getting clear about these gains has been difficult, for many of the supposed differences between the positions dissolve upon analysis, and we are led to suppose that the Christian God has more in common with Levinas's preferred alternative than with the morally reprehensible figure he so rightly rejects. In this respect—and the move has its analogue in the case of the relation between Levinas and the expansive naturalist, and indeed, that between the expansive naturalist and the scientific naturalist—we ended up tracing a path from 'could concede' to 'should concede' to 'maybe has conceded already'.

Similarities notwithstanding, Levinas is not about to concede to the Incarnation. The refusal is understandable given his interpretation of what the Incarnation means and brings. However, it goes hand in hand with a reluctance to allow that the love of God could exceed the demand to give ourselves to others (the giving of His Word in this sense), and that our love for Him could be expressed other than by respecting this demand. This threatens to bring a more serious limitation to Levinas's position, for it seems to rule out the possibility of our standing in a loving relation to God—a possibility which, for Rahner, must be accommodated if the position is not to collapse back into its secular moral counterpart. Furthermore, there are two senses in which it might be thought to exclude this possibility. First, it threatens to compromise the idea that we could love *God* rather than simply loving others; second, it threatens also to compromise the idea that we could love God in the sense demanded by Levinas (i.e. by loving others). Levinas could insist that God has empowered us to this end, but his understanding of what is required in this context seems to take us some distance from what is required of an ordinary decent human being, and some distance from what it is to be properly human. The picture seems equally compromising of God's love for us.

Levinas would deny that his understanding of these loves is deficient, and I have hinted already at the justificatory moves he could make in this direction. We are free to conclude that his position remains problematic and that he should concede in the direction of Christianity. Alternatively, we may be persuaded that he has put to rest the relevant difficulties. This latter conclusion can be interpreted in several ways. First, we can say that we have two equally compelling but distinct conceptions of God and our relation to Him; second, that Levinas's position is preferable; third, that the positions have the potential to merge into one. The first option suggests, somewhat problematically, that there are two Gods to choose from, but it could equally be a concession to the impossibility of pinning down His nature once and for all. This would leave open the possibility of carrying out further reconciliatory work, or it could lead us to opt for one position over the other. I hope that I have said enough to suggest that the similarities are significant, that Levinas's interpretation of Christianity is unfair, but that he introduces important insights.

One such insight is to be found in the strictures he imposes upon our talk about God, and he would no doubt object to the positive claims which comprise Christian doctrine. Levinas is talking about God in one obvious sense. If he were not then there would be no question of distinguishing his position from that of the expansive naturalist. Of course, he tells us very little about what God is like, other than to say that He gives us His Word. So we have a God who stands in relation to us, and He stands in a relation of love, albeit a love which is tough by modern standards if not by human ones. The God of Christianity could hardly be accused of sentimentality, although there are those—Levinas included—who make the mistake of viewing it all in terms of sickly sweetness and light because it suits their purposes to do so. In any case, the Christian's talk of God bears some resemblance to what Levinas is saying, and 'theology' seems an appropriate label for their respective endeavours. It is in this context that we might recall Levinas's preparedness to concede to a kind of theology which 'comes after the glimpse of holiness'.[80] Yet another concession to suggest that not all of his claims are to be taken at face value, in this case, the claim that we can relate to God only by relating to value. We shall need to clarify what such theology could amount to.

---

[80] To repeat: 'We have been reproached for ignoring theology; and we do not contest the necessity of a recovery, at least, the necessity of choosing an opportunity for a recovery of these themes. We think, however, that theological recuperation comes after the glimpse of holiness, which is primary' (*Of God Who Comes to Mind*, p. ix).

Theology raises questions for believers, but what of its relation to the atheists? I have suggested already that the scientific naturalist is a theologian of sorts, albeit one who contends for the position of God and glimpses holiness only in his own scientific aspirations. The expansive naturalist puts to rest this particular god, but it is familiar that he has no time for either God or for talk of Him, even whilst endorsing a position which concedes so far in the required direction. Could he concede to the God of Christianity? The leap seems massive, but if we allow that he can and perhaps should concede to Levinas's God, and that Levinas can and perhaps should concede to the God of Christianity, then the gap is considerably narrowed. It seems a lot to ask, just as it seemed a lot to expect the scientific naturalist to expand *his* preferred boundaries. I hope that I have said enough to suggest that the position is not bound to be scientifically or philosophically disastrous, and that the expansive naturalist has already taken considerable steps in this direction. It remains to be seen whether the remaining step can be made good, and where it leaves the question of naturalism.

8

Expansive Naturalism III

8.1 GETTING OUR BEARINGS

We began with a picture which opposes the natural world to something super-natural. This something is either of fundamental significance to self and world or an unnecessary and problematic addition. We are encouraged to suppose that the latter response is the intellectually respectable one, the first being reserved for those who retain a preference for cosmic excess. So we are left with the natural world minus the supernatural something else. This raised the question of how the natural world is to be understood, and we were faced again with two alternatives: either the natural world is to be comprehended in exclusively scientific terms or it is not. The scientific naturalist opts for the first response on the ground that anything more returns us to the afore-mentioned cosmic excesses, but there are versions of his position which fail to accommodate all of the phenomena at issue when we direct our attention to the study of human beings, our initial focus being the phenomenon of value. The implication here is that the putative excesses may, after all, have a rightful place in our ontology, and hence, that we require reference to the supernatural.

The expansive scientific naturalist objects that this conclusion is premature, and that the supposed deficiencies of scientific naturalism can be rectified by broadening its parameters. The natural world can be adequately compre-hended in scientific terms, provided that these terms are expanded to incorp-orate the human sciences. This leaves us again with the natural world minus the supernatural something else, and the cosmic excesses are dropped once and for all. The expansive naturalist objects that *this* conclusion is premature, and that the position still seems to fall short of what is required if we are to have a satisfactory conception of value. He agrees with the scientific naturalist that we should be avoiding unnecessary and problematic cosmic excesses, but questions the assumption that the scientist has the monopoly on the natural world. He argues that once we reject this assumption, then it becomes possible to allow that there is more to nature than what the scientist comprehends, and that we can concede this something more without the risk of cosmic excess. He concludes that value can be accommodated thus.

The expansive naturalist takes us beyond the limits of scientific naturalism, but his position remains compatible with the findings of modern science, and he agrees that there are cosmic excesses to be avoided. It is in this context that he decries the superstitions which were operative when the magic-making gods were on the scene, distinguishing this brand of 'enchantment' from that which is operative in his own partially enchanted world. The scientific naturalist is in no doubt that belief in God counts as one such excess, and the expansive naturalist says enough to suggest that he has sympathy for this verdict. He denies, however, that such excesses await anyone who transcends the boundaries of science. So the question of the limits of nature is in dispute, and this led us to think more carefully about the naturalist's refusal to concede in a theistic direction. The idea remains a non-starter if God could only ever be a separable something else which stands opposed to nature and cannot be intelligibly related to it, but this assumption can be challenged in much the way that we can challenge the scientific naturalist's assumption that the values of the expansive naturalist must suffer a similar fate. We were led gradually towards an alternative which made our relation to God sound rather like the expansive naturalist's conception of our relation to value. That is to say that in both cases we are relating to something which serves to transform and to fulfil our natural human being—something which is precisely not an unnecessary and problematic something else. The difference with God, however, is that He remains radically distinct from anything within the world even whilst retaining the most intimate connection with it. In one sense then, the natural world stands opposed to something supernatural, but this something is not a mere addition to the world which can be rejected whilst leaving everything else in its place. Rather, it is that without which the natural world would cease to be and without which we would cease to be properly human.

Levinas lends emphasis to God's significance for our humanity, and his position promises to bring God and value into even closer proximity. However, it was tempting to conclude that God had been squeezed out of the picture again. The alternative was to reject this implication, in which case there were grounds for describing the expansive naturalist as a closet theist. Christianity offered the prospects for defending a more robust theism, although Levinas sees the move as just one more concession to atheism. From his point of view then, it is on a par with any other primitive religion, and he rejects it on this basis. He denies, however, that this is tantamount to a rejection of God, for we require reference to God if we are to have a satisfactory conception of morality and humanity. We challenged his moral objection to the God of Christianity, noting that the naturalist has a related and equally contestable objection to any form of theism. It was unclear whether Christianity brings any moral or theistic gains, but it remained open that it makes for a more satisfactory conception of God, and that this, in turn, has important implications for an understanding of morality, humanity, and nature.

This is the position we have reached, and I have already given a hint of some of the questions which remain. One question concerns the relation between Christianity and expansive naturalism. Could the expansive naturalist concede in this direction? And are there any good reasons for doing so? Our discussion of his relation to Levinas has gone some way towards addressing the question of whether he could or should move in the direction of God, and if we accept Levinas's conception of Christianity, then our question becomes that of whether he could or should revert to a primitive form of religion which severs our connection with value and God. It would be absurd to suppose that the expansive naturalist could or should concede to a position which severs our connection with value, and he would object that we risk this consequence if we bring God into the equation. Levinas's position offers the prospects for resisting this conclusion, and we have challenged his conception of the God of Christianity, granting that this God has more in common with his own preferred alternative than he is prepared to allow. It remains open then that the expansive naturalist could concede in this direction.

The step seems formidable for it brings commitments which seem to take us beyond the limits of anything the expansive naturalist could reasonably accept. In particular, it involves claims about the nature and action of God which transport us into the realm of theology. These claims are contentious enough even if we accept a theistic framework and Christian theologians are hardly in agreement about how the relevant doctrines are to be interpreted. We know already that Levinas refuses such a move, and he is on firm enough ground if the point is simply to warn against the kind of theology which leaves us with something less than God. We have noted also, however, that he seems prepared to concede to a theology which comes 'after the glimpse of holiness'—a concession which bears comparison with Lash's insistence that the question of God be approached 'on one's knees'.

These claims require elucidation, but we shall see that the conception of theology at which we arrive bears comparison with what the expansive naturalist wishes to say about our talk of value. We shall have to consider the relevant points of comparison, relate them to the similarities which have already been identified with respect to our relation to God and to value, and draw out some of the implications for an understanding of the relation between philosophy and theology. Are the relevant similarities merely structural, leaving us free to conclude that philosophy and theology are distinct disciplines with distinct subject-matters—that they add up to two in this sense? Yes, if our naturalists are to be believed, although they would be quick to dispense with the second discipline or relegate it to the realm of idle speculation. No, if the position to be defended can be made good, in which case we are left with the question of how this relation is to be comprehended, and what the implications are for an understanding of the approach which has led us in this direction.

8.2 THEOLOGY, PRAYER, AND TWO TYPES OF NATURAL THEOLOGY

The idea that we must approach the question of God 'on our knees' makes it sound as if theology is a form of prayer. It calls to mind Kant's claim that our worshipful attitude to God be given priority and Heidegger's preference for a God before whom we can fall to our knees in awe. Kant implies that this approach to God is to be embraced in preference to one which takes as its focus the theoretical conundrums surrounding God's nature, and Heidegger is anxious to reject the God of the philosophers, suggesting that the God before whom we can fall to our knees in awe is more properly divine.

This cannot mean that we must be literally on our knees if we are to relate to God. To be sure, we sometimes are on our knees literally when we relate to Him, when, for example, we engage in explicit acts of worship. However, we can worship God from other positions, and both Levinas and the Christian allow that we can relate to Him other than by engaging in explicit acts of worship, doing so, for example, by standing in moral relations to others. It remains open that such activity involves being on our knees in some other, perhaps non-literal, sense, and Lash implies that some such sense is at issue when we are doing theology, for he tells us that 'there is a *sense* in which' such theoretical work must be done 'at least metaphorically' on one's knees.[1] This raises the question of how this sense is to be understood, and I have noted already that it suggests that theology is a form of prayer. Saying this much is unhelpful as it stands, for there is no consensus upon the precise meaning of prayer.[2] Nor is it ruled out that we are concerned with some non-literal sense of *this* term.

According to one interpretation, prayer involves asking God for something or other. The idea that theology could be a form of prayer in this sense seems odd to say the least. However, it becomes less obviously so if we have in mind the kind of theology which involves putting God at our beck and call and recall the prayerful activity at issue when He is reduced to a distributor of goods. We could respond that there is more to prayer than such petition,[3] and that

---

[1] 'The Impossibility of Atheism', in *Theology for Pilgrims* (London: Darton, Longman and Todd, 2008), p. 28.

[2] Simon Tugwell offers a helpful discussion of the various meanings of prayer in his 'Prayer, Humpty Dumpty and Thomas Aquinas', in *Language, Meaning and God: Essays in Honour of Herbert McCabe OP* (Eugene, Oregon: WIPF & Stock, 2010), pp. 24–50.

[3] I am leaving open the possibility that petitionary prayer does not have to take an egoistic form. Simon Tugwell explores this possibility in his 'Prayer, Humpty Dumpty and Thomas Aquinas'.

it is best understood as the attitude in play when we '"make space" for God to be God' and open ourselves to His transformative power.[4] The idea that we are to 'make space' for God to be God grants us the right to respect what Heidegger describes as the mysteriousness of His distance, guaranteeing that He remains 'exalted and holy'. It also leads us from the temptation to place Him at our disposal. But what could it mean to describe theology as a form of prayer in this sense? It seems to bring it more in line with what Levinas is getting at when he grants a kind of theology which comes after the glimpse of holiness. Furthermore, it offers the prospects for explaining God on His own terms rather than simply on ours. It might be thought to imply also, however, that only a believer can talk properly about God.[5] At least, this is so if we accept that proper God talk demands openness to God, and that the non-believer remains closed in this respect.

The idea that only a believer can talk properly about God has a point as far as the theoretical endeavours of some atheists are concerned. After all, one is inclined to say that they just don't know what they're talking about. On the other hand, there are believers whose talk about God invites a similar criticism, and it is not ruled out that figures on either side could learn to talk more properly in this context. The question, of course, is how this feat is to be accomplished. The idea of an atheist theologian is hardly a contradiction in terms, and one could imagine such a figure being adept enough to defend his stance by challenging some of the arguments which purport to take us to God. Some such arguments will be bad, none of them will be conclusive, and if we accept with Mascall that they can persuade only those who already have an 'intuition of God and finite being together',[6] then the atheist is going to stick

---

[4] See Sarah Coakley, 'Kenōsis and Subversion', in *Powers and Submissions: Spirituality, Philosophy and Gender* (Oxford: Blackwell, 2002), p. 34. This rather broad understanding of prayer might be thought to empty the notion of any determinate content, and, assuming that we accept Levinas's conception of what it is to relate to God in the required sense, it implies that we pray by virtue of standing in moral relations to others. As Tugwell points out, this raises the question of whether I should also be expected to pray in any other sense ('Prayer, Humpty Dumpty and Thomas Aquinas', p. 26). We are faced here with similar difficulties to those which arose in the context of considering whether our love for God could exceed our love for others.

[5] Compare the theological point of departure which, for Paul Tillich, belongs to the 'onto-logical religious' type: 'their whole emphasis was on the immediacy of the knowledge of God...God is most truly present to the very soul and immediately knowable' ('The Two Types of the Philosophy of Religion', *Union Seminary Quarterly Review*, vol. 1, no. 4 (May 1946), p. 4). As John E. Smith puts it: 'For this way the religious consciousness is presupposed; there is no going outside the self and its awareness of itself in order to find a proper beginning for reflection. "Enter the inner chamber of thy mind" is the first and chief text, and the aim is to discover or, better recover the *presence* of God in the form of some ultimate such as truth immediately grasped' ('The Present Status of Natural Theology', *The Journal of Philosophy*, vol. 55, no. 22, (23 Oct. 1958), p. 928). Tillich describes this approach as platonist and contrasts it with the Aristotelian 'cosmological-scientific' approach which, we shall see, is operative in the conception of natural theology with which Buckley takes issue.

[6] *The Openness of Being: Natural Theology Today* (London: Darton, Longman, and Todd, 1971), p. 141.

to his guns. The implication here is that one can be convinced by such arguments only if one has already accepted their conclusion. So we now have two seemingly problematic claims: first, only a believer can talk properly about God; second, only a believer can be convinced by arguments for God's existence. This latter claim can likewise be contested, for although we can allow that there will be atheists who remain resistant to such arguments—and, of course, believers who retain a similar antipathy for the arguments of the atheist—we must surely grant that arguments from either direction can do more than simply reassure those who have already accepted their conclusions. This much should be clear from my endeavours to persuade the expansive naturalist that his own arguments can be exploited in a theistic direction.

The expansive naturalist can help us to make better sense of what we should be saying in this context, and we can begin to make the required link by recalling Buckley's reluctance to allow that the question of God be tackled in abstraction 'from any common religious tradition and the experiences it involves'. We are told that religion 'presupposes personal engagement as the permeating and fundamental relationship with God', and that it involves viewing God as a 'living presence'.[7] By contrast, the offending abstractive exercise turns the question of God into a purely philosophical question, and it involves being informed about God 'from the outside'.[8] Buckley implicates a certain kind of natural theologian in this context, telling us that such a figure is compelled to 'apply to the philosophers for philosophic information'.[9] This information is to be found in the natural world, it constitutes the putative evidence for God's existence, and we are encouraged to conclude that it does no such thing. We are to suppose then that we must be informed about God 'from the inside'. But what could this mean? Is it just another way of saying that we must assume the perspective of the believer? And if so, what becomes of the possibility of there being arguments which could open the way to faith?

The expansive naturalist has his own version of the 'internalist' position we are seeking to comprehend. According to this version, our theorizing about value must be 'engaged' and 'participative' in the sense that it leaves intact all the resources and commitments of the first-order thinking it seeks to interpret, and concerns itself with the 'full gamut of valuational considerations that actually weigh with real life moral agents'.[10] We must work from within in this sense, the justification being that this is the only way we shall be in a position to engage properly with our subject-matter. We are said to fail on this score when we tackle the question of value in exclusively scientific terms, and the

---

[7] *At the Origins of Modern Atheism* (Yale: Yale University Press, 1987), p. 348.

[8] *At the Origins of Modern Atheism*, p. 348.

[9] *At the Origins of Modern Atheism*, p. 342. The quote comes from Étienne Gilson's *Elements of Christian Philosophy* (New York: Doubleday, 1960), p. 33.

[10] David Wiggins, 'A Neglected Position?', in *Reality, Representation, and Projection*, ed. John Haldane and Crispin Wright (Oxford: Oxford University Press, 1993), p. 333.

expansive naturalist claims likewise that this involves an attempt to approach our subject-matter from without. It does so in the sense that it involves detaching from the concepts and commitments which give us the values we are seeking to comprehend. It is not ruled out that a scientific approach can cover some of the explanatory ground, but the expansive naturalist denies that it can take us all of the way, even whilst conceding that there are versions thereof which come close to eliminating the offending explanatory gap.

We then face the question of whether there are any good arguments in favour of an expansive naturalist approach to value. There are no prospects for satisfying this aim if we remain within the confines of scientific naturalism, for the scientific naturalist takes himself to have defined a satisfactory conception of value, objecting that anything more leads to unwarranted cosmic excess. As he sees it then, the expansive naturalist ends up postulating a further level of being which is irrelevant to the question of value and intolerably odd to boot. The expansive naturalist responds that scientific naturalism involves an unwarranted commitment to scientism, that this commitment generates the conclusion that an expansive naturalist position is metaphysically and epistemologically problematic, and that this position is better placed to capture all that needs to be said about value and our relation to it. In this way, we are encouraged to suppose that their respective aims are not so disparate after all, and that the scientific naturalist has every reason for taking seriously the envisaged position. This point gains credence once it is made clear that there is no question of denying the significance of scientific investigation, nor of courting an alternative which conflicts with its findings.

The case of God presents us likewise with two theoretical approaches— one 'from the inside' and one 'from without'. The details of the first approach remain vague—in particular, it is unclear which concepts and commitments must be operative here—but it seems to involve being receptive to God, or, more weakly, to presuppose reference to some common religious tradition and the experiences it involves—experiences in which God figures as a living presence. The second approach abstracts from such experiences, it is aligned with a kind of natural theology, and takes as its starting-point the evidence for God's existence which is to be found in the natural world. The implication here is that we should be wary of taking religious experience at face value, and ensure that our claims about God are empirically grounded if we are to avoid the kind of idle speculation which culminates in those familiar cosmic excesses. As F.R. Tennant has put it, we must be 'empirically-minded' theologians, 'letting the Actual world tell its own story' rather than silencing it 'while abstractive speculation...weaves a system of thought which may prove to conflict with the facts.'[11] We are encouraged to suppose that the putative

---

[11] *Philosophical Theology*, vol. II (Cambridge: Cambridge University Press, 1930), p. 78.

natural evidence falls short, and that there are good philosophical reasons for insisting upon this negative conclusion. After all, nature can be adequately comprehended in non-God-involving terms, and a move in the direction of God does no more than to introduce a *further* and highly problematic realm of being which explains precisely nothing.

This much suggests that the prospects for defending a theistic framework are bleak, for such arguments would have to come from natural theology, and the model we have been given of such an approach suggests that it cannot meet this aim. The predicament is similar to that we face when we try to argue for an expansive naturalist conception of value from the standpoint of scientific naturalism. The solution to this predicament in the case of value was to try to persuade the scientific naturalist that a move in the direction of expansive naturalism does not pose the envisaged threat, and that it promises a more satisfactory conception of value. This suggests that if we are going to argue for a theistic framework along analogous lines, then the natural theology we exploit in this context is going to have to involve considerations which could appeal to an atheist, and which do not proceed from a standpoint which blocks this possibility at the outset. The difference in this case, however, is that the relevant considerations cannot involve claiming that the framework makes for a more satisfactory conception of God, for the atheist has no desire to bring God into the equation. I have sought to satisfy this aim by taking as my opponent the expansive naturalist and arguing that a theistic framework does not pose the threat he foresees. In particular, I have questioned the assumption that a move in the direction of God involves the postulation of an intolerably odd level of being which is irrelevant to the question of value—and, more generally, that of nature—and suggested that his reluctance to concede in this direction may involve a version of the error he finds in the scientific naturalist's starting-point. I have claimed also that a willingness to take seriously a theistic framework retains the spirit of expansive naturalism, for it is built into this approach that we must challenge the impulse to close off avenues of enquiry by imposing frameworks we have no good reason to accept.

This argumentative strategy occupies a position between two problematic extremes. According to the first extreme, we argue for a theistic framework using resources and assumptions which preclude the possibility of meeting this aim. This would be like arguing for an expansive naturalist conception of value from a scientific naturalist standpoint, the analogue in a theistic context being an approach which presupposes that God could only ever be a problematic cosmic excess. According to the second extreme, we accept a theistic framework and make no attempt to argue for it—either you get it or you don't, and if you don't then there's nothing to be done about it. This would be like throwing expansive naturalism in the scientific naturalist's face and ignoring his protests to the contrary. The alternative is to argue for the position in a manner which precisely does have a chance of meeting the required aim, for it is a matter of challenging some of the considerations which suggest that the position is a non-starter, and bringing it more into line with the standpoint of the disputant.

Natural theology in this sense involves 'applying to the philosophers for philosophic information'. However, the philosopher in question has already set in motion the required line of argument, and the information we are given is that there is more to nature than what the scientist can comprehend. Are we being informed about God 'from the outside'? Buckley's natural theologian informs us about God 'from the outside' by abstracting from any experience of God, and taking as his starting-point the evidence for God's existence to be found in the natural world. We can applaud his wish to ensure that our claims about God are empirically grounded.[12] However, there is no immediate requirement that religious experience be excluded from the picture, for such experiences belong to natural beings in a natural world, and, as such, could surely constitute part of the evidence to which one could appeal in the context of defending a theistic framework. The natural theologian in question has been told by the philosopher that there is no good evidence for such a framework, the implication being that any putative evidence from religious experience is inadmissible, and that there is nothing else to which we could appeal. The evidence does indeed fall short if it is assumed that nature contains no trace of God, and this assumption is compelling if we accept the truth of scientism.[13] It will then be tempting to treat the term 'God' as a misleading and dispensable placeholder for whatever *scientifically* explains the relevant natural facts, which latter will be interpreted in a manner that lends credence to this framework. On this way of thinking, God is a hypothesis we can do without, the God question is really a scientific question, and theology is but an embarrassing and dispensable extension of science. As for those putatively religious experiences, they are simply the province of

---

[12] Compare an analogous requirement as it applies to the case of value.

[13] Natural theology in this sense can be aligned with the 'cosmological-scientific' approach to God as understood by Paul Tillich. As John E. Smith puts it: 'the point of departure for the cosmological-scientific type is...the *world* of limited things and processes as they are known both through ordinary experience and the precisely formulated knowledge of the natural sciences. This way of approach, often called the "way from Nature to God", begins the quest with a world of fact beyond the self, although this world is often said to include man as well' ('The *Present Status of Natural Theology', The Journal of Philosophy*, vol. 55, no. 22 (October 1958), p. 929). Smith cites F.R. Tennant's approach in his *Philosophical Theology* as exemplary in this context, for it 'starts with physical fact and presupposes the validity of science as a method and its picture of the world. "Natural theology", says Tennant, describing his own approach, "sets out from facts and inductions; its premises are as firmly established and as universally acknowledged as any of the stable generalizations of science"' (*Philosophical Theology*, vol II, p. 79). Smith raises the crucial question of whether Tennant's conception of experience is broad enough 'to permit consideration of the whole range of distinctly human experience made possible by the fact that man is a *subject* or whether man will be included only as one *object* beside others in virtue of the fact that the scientific knowledge with which we are bound to begin is incapable of regarding man in any other way' ('The Present Status of Natural Theology', pp. 929–930).

superstitious[14] minds—minds who have succumbed to a similar error to that which is operative when the magic-making gods were around. The fact that no religious adherent conceives of God in these scientific terms is left unexplained,[15] although his protests would cut no ice with the philosopher whose faith is scientism.

The expansive naturalist shares no such faith, but he denies that nature contains any trace of God. I have argued that his philosophical framework grants him the right to resist this negative conclusion. So it is appropriate to say that he is being informed about God 'from without' if this is taken to mean that the relevant philosophical information can be appreciated by a non-believer. Does it involve abstracting from any experience of God? In one obvious sense it does, for the natural world, as conceived by our expansive naturalist, involves no reference to God, and it is therefore denied that natural beings could engage with Him. In another sense, however, it does not, for the framework within which he is operating offers the resources for questioning these imposed strictures so as to allow that at least some of our experiences already carry theistic import. If this is right, then an empirically minded theologian is not forced into atheism, and his evidential domain—nature—is not irrevocably sealed from the 'supernature' of the so-called 'revealed' theologian. As Mascall puts it, they are not 'two apartments on adjacent floors, with a layer of soundproof packing between the natural ceiling below and the supernatural floor above'.[16]

8.3 ENGAGING WITH GOD AND TALKING ABOUT GOD

The considerations I have rehearsed presuppose a distinction between theology, philosophy, and science and offer various ways of understanding these terms and their respective relations. Buckley challenges the idea that the question of God is purely philosophical, he aligns this philosophical approach with a brand of natural theology, and takes it to operate in abstraction from any personal engagement with God. Natural theology in this sense takes the natural world as its point of departure, it treats God as an explanatory hypothesis to be confirmed or rejected by the available evidence, and we are encouraged to suppose that there are good reasons for its rejection. Buckley's objections to

---

[14] I shall be returning to the question of whether the notion of superstition admits of a less pejorative interpretation. My answer will be that it does, and hence, that being superstitious need not be as intellectually embarrassing as our naturalists tend to assume.

[15] See John Hutchison, 'The Uses of Natural Theology: An Essay in Redefinition', *The Journal of Philosophy*, vol. 55, no. 22 (23 Oct. 1958), p. 939.

[16] *The Openness of Being*, p. 151.

a philosophical approach to God bear comparison with the expansive naturalist's objections to a scientific approach to value. The scientific naturalist treats this question in purely scientific terms, and the expansive naturalist complains that such treatment cuts us loose from the very values we are seeking to comprehend. So this philosophical/natural theological approach to God is structurally equivalent to a scientific naturalist/natural philosophical approach to value, and the complaint in both cases is that we lose our grip upon our subject-matter.

Buckley's philosopher is unconcerned with the question of value,[17] but our expansive naturalist works likewise from within an atheistic framework and claims that this question has nothing to do with God. However, he denies that it is a purely scientific question and upholds a distinction between philosophy and science which maps onto Buckley's distinction between theology and philosophy. I have argued that there is a form of natural theology which poses a challenge to the expansive naturalist's atheism, and that he is in a position to appreciate this challenge given his philosophical starting-point. Natural theology in this sense involves approaching the question of God in philosophical terms, these terms are anti-scientistic, and they are exploited by the expansive naturalist in the context of defending his own preferred position against that of the scientific naturalist. So this philosophical/natural theological approach to God is no longer to be aligned with a scientific naturalist approach to value. However, it can be described as a brand of natural philosophy, and the hope is that it might persuade the expansive naturalist to take the God question seriously. This requires a spirit of open-mindedness on his part, and I have suggested already that this spirit underlies and motivates his philosophical approach to value. We might even say that it involves a preparedness to 'make space' for God to be God—to be open to Him to this degree at least—where this involves a willingness to question the kind of approach which excludes God from the picture by imposing a contestable model of His reality. The complaint is familiar from the case of value, and the expansive naturalist would object that the scientific naturalist makes no space for value to be value.

---

[17] It is not ruled out that a natural theologian of this type could make reference to our experience of value. Hence Smith on Tennant's approach: 'although it is claimed that man no less than the world forms part of the starting point for this kind of theology, there exists within it no tendency to allow man's religious dimension and experience to dictate the meaning of the theistic concepts. This is not to say that man is excluded altogether from the facts which determine the content of the divine idea, but Tennant is inclined rather to confine himself to the moral or esthetic aspects of human experience and to admit the religious only *after* his empirical theism has been established. In this regard religion may be said to be postponed or left out of the account until the constitutive idea of God has been elaborated; it is then introduced only as a means of enriching and enhancing a theistic idea which it had no hand in shaping. God appears primarily as the explanation of the world conceived as a certain type of teleological system, and theology stands not as a discipline coordinate with philosophy or the theory of being but rather as an extension of or extrapolation from science' ('The Present Status of Natural Theology', p. 932).

The criticism has a point as far as some brands of scientific naturalism are concerned, but our expansive scientific naturalist takes seriously the question of value, and would claim to be personally engaged with his subject-matter. He grants that it is a possible objection to his approach that it does not make morality serious enough, but worries that anything more serious would have the effect of severing morality from our human grasp—moral values become 'cosmic' and there are no prospects for engaging with anything like this. The expansive naturalist is happy to go cosmic if this is just a needlessly pejorative way of describing his anti-scientistic stance, and I have allowed that this might lead him to take seriously the question of God. However, he would deny that he is personally engaged with God, and certainly has no inclination to fall to his knees in awe or wonder—not before God at least. His denial is understandable if God is assumed to be cosmic in the aforementioned pejorative sense. However, this conception of God has been challenged, just as we have challenged an analogous conception of the values which form the target of the scientific naturalist's attack.

Levinas opposes this conception of God with the claim that we engage with Him personally by standing in moral relations to others. We are encouraged to suppose that this is the *only* way of doing so, and that anything more would compromise God's radical otherness, in which case the putative relationship would be broken. The further claim is that this moral mode of relating is just what it means for God to be a living presence amongst us. If this is right, then the expansive naturalist is already engaged with God, in spite of himself as it were. As I put it previously, he is a closet theist. It suggests also that he is already situated at the 'religious' level which, for Buckley, must be operative if we are to tackle the question of God aright—a level which is said to presuppose 'personal engagement as the permeating and fundamental relationship with God'.

Are we to conclude that the expansive naturalist is a closet *theologian*? That he is talking about God without realizing it? The claim sounds absurd, but one may wonder whether it is any more absurd than saying that the expansive scientific naturalist is a closet expansive naturalist—that he has 'humanized' social science and exceeded his preferred parameters in all but name. The expansive naturalist could protest that we have simply turned a terminological trick in the opposite direction, and that what we should really be saying is that theology is reducible to the philosophy of value. Furthermore, he would be quick to draw out the atheistic implications of this reduction given his reluctance to bring God into the equation. Levinas would applaud this reduction in one obvious respect, for he has doubts about the very idea of theology. However, these doubts are not motivated by any antipathy towards God. Rather, they stem from the worry that theology is bound to converge upon something unworthy of the name. The worry has a point as far as some brands of theology are concerned, but we have noted that Levinas is talking about God in one obvious sense, and that at least some of the things he says can be mapped onto the talk of the Christian theologian. To be sure, the focus is upon God's activity as it is revealed at the level of morality, the talk remains practically oriented, and theoretical conundrums are conspicuous by their absence. Furthermore, there are no arguments for God's existence, and we are encouraged to suppose that such an endeavour could only detract from the possibility of standing in a genuine relation to Him. After all, 'there can be no "knowledge" of God separated from the relationship with men'.[18]

This injunction does not rule out the kind of natural theology I have recommended we adopt. On the contrary, Levinas's position can help us to see how a focus upon our 'relationship with men' might yield 'knowledge' of God. It remains open then that the expansive naturalist is talking about God, and that this talk has something in common with that of the Christian theologian. It seems equally clear, however, that he is doing no such thing, and we know that Rahner would second this response on the ground that talk of God is irreducible to talk of value. He insists also that personal engagement with God is irreducible to moral relations with men.

According to one option then, talk of God is distinct from talk of value, and there is a doubt about whether we can talk properly about God. The expansive naturalist grants this distinction and would worry about the status of theology on the ground that God—if He exists at all—lies beyond the limits of nature. He describes this 'beyond' as the region of darkness, and finds an equal if not predictable difficulty in the idea that we could engage with God in any sense at all, at least *qua* natural beings. This conception of God has been challenged on expansive naturalist grounds, just as we have challenged an analogous conception of the values which are rejected by the scientific naturalist.

Levinas worries likewise about the status of theology, but he allows that we can relate to God in a moral context and must therefore deny that God is to be consigned to the region of darkness without remainder. On the contrary, there is the possibility of some light. If there were not, then Levinas's position would be excluded, we should be returned to secular expansive naturalism, and the question of value would lose any theistic significance. So Levinas concedes that we can talk about God to this degree at least, and there are grounds for allowing that the expansive naturalist is doing likewise. Rahner grants the possibility of theology, but denies that it is reducible to talk of value. This promises to vindicate the expansive naturalist's reluctance to describe his own theoretical endeavours in theistic terms, although it remains open that talk of value is *part* of what it means to talk about God. We then face the question of what more

[18] *Totality and Infinity*, trans. Alphonso Lingis (Pittsburgh: Duquesne University Press, 1969), p. 78.

can be said about God, and whether the envisaged addition remains compatible with His radical otherness—an otherness which motivates Levinas's resistance to theology and lends credence to the expansive naturalist's claim that
God belongs to the region of darkness.

The Christian theologian exceeds Levinas's parameters in one obvious
sense. However, I have argued that much of this talk can be mapped on to
what Levinas himself is saying. Theology in this sense involves reference to
God's divine action, and it raises questions about how the relevant concepts
are to be understood and whether they can be vindicated. Are we entitled to
tackle these theoretical issues? We are not if God remains irretrievably hidden, but this conception of God has been challenged. To be sure, we remain
confined to God as He is in relation to us, but this imposes a problematic
limitation only on the assumption that He lies beyond all possible relation,
and this assumption has likewise been questioned. What of the worries that
have been expressed about the very idea of taking a theoretical approach to
God? We have granted that there are misguided theoretical approaches, and
that some of the relevant difficulties stem from the imposition of questionable
assumptions. So, for example, we may be tempted to suppose that we have the
complete measure of God, and this can lead to the conclusion that atheism is
the only viable alternative. This temptation is not unique to the case of God,
and we have seen that there is an analogue of this atheistic response in the
philosophy of value.

I have suggested already that our theoretical endeavours must give due
weight to the nature of that we are seeking to comprehend. Again, the point
is not unique to theology. As far as theology is concerned, however, this
has gone hand in hand with the idea that it is—or at least ought to be—a
form of prayer. The question of what this means is itself a theoretical matter,
and I have suggested that one of the points of this description is to capture
the sense in which we must be open to God if we are to have a chance of
saying anything remotely appropriate in this context. I have granted that
the notion of openness in this context can be comprehended in Levinas's
preferred moral terms, and that it is broad enough to accommodate the
approach of one who is prepared to take such a position seriously. It is this
kind of open-mindedness which might lead one to countenance the possibility of being open to God in the narrower, more obviously prayerful, sense of
this term.

What of Kant's worry that a focus upon theory is a rather poor substitute for
genuine worship? The worry is comparable to Levinas's complaint that theory
can detract from our moral dealings with others, and there is an analogous
worry to be applied to the case of moral theory. We can agree that theory is
unimportant to the everyday believer, and that it is to be distinguished from
both worship and morality. We can allow also that it can become an end in

itself and that there will be contexts where its sole purpose is to undermine the credentials of its subject-matter. However, none of this suffices to show that theory must be rejected, nor that it precludes the possibility of relating to God in a non-theoretical sense. On the contrary, such an endeavour can help us to see what it could mean to stand in such a relation, and whether the idea withstands intellectual scrutiny. Again, the point is familiar from the case of value. All such endeavours remain provisional, and the atheist is free to undermine the relevant claims by imposing his own preferred faith. I hope that I have said enough to challenge the assumption that this alternative faith has the monopoly on the truth.

8.4 THEOLOGY, PHILOSOPHY, AND MYTH

The idea that the atheist has the monopoly on the truth goes hand in hand with the complaint that the theologian falsifies reality,[19] and one way of expressing this complaint is to say that he trades in myths and superstitions rather than with the facts. We are reminded of the so-called gods of pre-scientific superstition, and encouraged to suppose that theology is but a continuation of this primitive worldview. According to this way of thinking, myths/superstitions are falsifications of reality,[20] they are embraced by those who lack an eye for the truth, and stand to be exorcised by good philosophy and science. Modern science has indeed called into question the assumption that the workings of nature are the doings of magic-making gods, and it would be scientifically and philosophically naïve to resist this advance. So we must banish the gods from the ambit of scientific enquiry, and accept with McDowell that its subject-matter is to be duly disenchanted in this respect. We can allow also that it would be a falsification of reality to enchant nature in *this* sense, although it would be misguided to conclude that those who accepted such a worldview had no eye for the truth. After all, they were groping in the direction of science, albeit a form which is primitive by modern standards.

McDowell denies that nature itself is to be disenchanted, implying that we can banish the gods without succumbing to scientism, and grant a rightful place to our identity and nature as moral beings. The gods at issue were hardly moral, but their postulation exceeded the aforementioned quasi-scientific

---

[19] Compare my previous reference to Nietzsche: 'Whoever has theologians' blood in his veins, sees all things in a distorted and dishonest perspective to begin with' (*The Antichrist*, in *The Portable Nietzsche*, trans. Walter Kaufmann (New York: Viking Penguin Inc, 1959), s. 9).

[20] This conception of myth is criticized by Schubert Ogden in his 'Myth and Truth', in *The Reality of God and Other Essays* (Dallas: Southern Methodist University Press, 1963), p. 99.

terms, for they served also as expressions—no less primitive—of the human predicament, our place in nature, and the nature of the nature in which we are so placed. In particular, we are given a sense that we are not the measure of reality—contrast the ambitions of the hard-line scientific naturalist—and that this measure is itself to be understood in human terms, albeit terms we cannot fully meet and which fall short of capturing what it means to be *properly* human. As I put it previously, the gods lack a second nature, and are to be distinguished from us by virtue of their unsurpassed power to get what they want.

Should the gods be banished in this particular context? It is unclear that they can be rejected on scientific grounds, for their role here is irrelevant to the quest of comprehending the workings of nature. On the contrary, they serve more properly to give expression to a way of thinking about self and world which take us beyond the standpoint of science, although we can allow that the distinction between scientific and non-scientific forms of explanation was inadequately defined when they were originally put to use in this way. Nevertheless, we may well wish to banish them on *moral* grounds, for the picture with which we are presented leaves no room for a conception of humanity which exceeds the egoistic terms with which our protagonists take issue. Does this mean that we are entitled to populate the world with more properly moral gods? The answer *seems* to be an obvious 'no', but we must be clear about what such a position could really mean. First, it could be a matter of allowing that there are, in addition to human beings, other beings who are similarly moral, but who do not exist in quite the way that we do. The move seems superfluous, and it smacks of the kind of cosmic excess with which we are familiar. It is equally familiar that the notion of a cosmic excess is not philosophically innocent, and that such an accusation can betray a commitment to scientism. The scientific naturalist's response to the expansive naturalist's values provides an obvious case in point. This case is significant to the present line of thought, for according to a second interpretation, postulation of a realm of moral gods is really just a picturesque way of describing the values which make their demands upon us in a moral context. This move introduces a level of authority which takes us beyond the powers of the aforementioned gods, and it offers the prospects for lending superior expression to the intuition that we are not masters of the universe. It is *morally* superior, for there is no suggestion that we are to respond to this limitation by developing analogous mastering tendencies of our own, nor that we are doomed to be slaves. On the contrary, we are capable of acknowledging the relevant authorities, and it is by so doing that we become properly human. Is the picture not also *metaphysically* superior given that we have abandoned any reference to a realm of gods? Not from the scientific naturalist's point of view, for he sees an analogous metaphysical difficulty in the postulation of a realm of moral values; at least, in so far as these values exceed his own preferred scientific terms. From his perspective then, this move involves a falsification of reality, and, as such, is on the same level as that which is operative when the workings of nature are ascribed to the gods or when values are personified in their shape.

We have rejected the scientism which underlies this complaint, and granted that the relevant values are metaphysically innocent. So it is denied that their postulation falsifies reality—that it involves myth and superstition in *this* sense. We have allowed also, however, that these values have their source in God, that we relate to Him by virtue of being moral, and that nature is irreducibly open to His communicative action. Does this move involve myth and superstition? If myth and superstition amount to a falsification of reality, then it does from the point of view of our secular naturalist, but we have challenged this negative verdict. Should we accept that the notions of myth and superstition are to be comprehended in this pejorative sense? The fact that the role of the gods exceeded the quasi-scientific use to which they were put should not lead us to assume that the myth-maker is simply an aspiring scientist, and hence, that the relevant myths stand to be exorcised by modern science. On the contrary, they serve as primitive expressions of the human predicament, giving us a sense that we are beholden to something beyond ourselves. Indeed, the Latin etymology of the term 'superstition'—*super-stare*—serves to capture this sense, for it suggests a standing over, or, as the Latin dictionary definition puts it, a 'standing still over or by a thing; hence, amazement, wonder, dread, especially of the divine or supernatural'.[21] We are reminded of Mascall's 'intuition of God and finite being together'—an intuition which is said to involve an awareness 'of the creature as dependent upon its creator', and is 'closely linked with the capacity for contemplative wondering'.[22]

What of the element of story which seems fundamental to the notion of myth—an element which has been said to capture the original meaning of the term 'theology'?[23] According to this way of thinking, theology involves 'stories about divine beings and their happenings',[24] and it corresponds to the 'fabulous' or 'mythical' theology which is discussed by Augustine in his

---

[21] Charles T. Lewis, Charles Short, *A Latin Dictionary* (Oxford: Clarendon Press, 1890).

[22] *The Openness of Being*, p. 141.

[23] A. Durwood Foster Jr cites L. Ziehen's article in the Pauly-Wissowa Encyclopaedia (*Paulys Real-Encyclopädie der classischen Altertumswissenschaft*, 2te Reihe, 5te Band, Stuttgart: Metzler, 1934, pp. 2031–2033) in his 'Myth and Philosophy: Theology's Bipolar Essence', *Journal of Bible and Religion*, vol. 34, no. 4 (Oct. 1966), p. 316.

[24] See Durwood Foster's 'Myth and Philosophy', p. 317. Durwood Foster takes this expression from Gerhard Ebeling's 'Theologie: Begriffsgeschichtlich', in *Religion in Geschichte und Gegenwart*, 3te Auflage, 6te Band, Tübingen: J.C.B. Mohr, 1930, pp. 754–769. Durwood Foster relates this conception of theology to Tillich's definition of myth as a 'history of the gods' ('Mythus', *Religion in Geschichte und Gegenwart*, 2te Auflage, 4te Band, Tübingen: J.C.B. Mohr, 1930, pp. 363–370).

City of God.[25] Augustine tells us that theology in this sense is 'chiefly used by poets', 'best adapted to the theatre',[26] and that it 'contains a great deal of fiction'. He adds that it is important to 'separate divine matters from the follies and falsehoods of men',[27] suggesting that such theology counts as mythical in the aforementioned pejorative sense. That is to say that it involves a falsification of reality. The further implication is that it is not theology properly so called. At least, this follows if we grant the importance of separating divine matters from the follies and falsehoods of men and allow that such matters are the province of true theology.

Durwood Foster claims that the conception of theology as 'stories about divine beings and their happenings' is best comprehended as the 'coming to expression of *theos*, of the divine'. [28] The idea that it involves a coming to expression of the divine suggests that the expressions in question are more or less adequate, and this might lead us to categorize the 'follies and falsehoods' with which Augustine takes issue as less adequate expressions of the relevant divine matters. On this way of thinking, there are stories about divine beings and their happenings which contain a germ of the truth—compare those primitive forms of scientific thinking which can be read into such stories—but which require to be supplanted if we are to arrive at a more truthful vision of the divine. But what does this mean? Does it mean that the story element is to be transcended? Or is it, rather, that we are to transcend those stories which involve a falsification of reality? The first option suggests that theology should be purged of any reference to stories of divine beings and their happenings—a claim which is more or less compelling depending upon how we interpret the notion of story in this context. If a story is defined as a falsification of reality, then these two putative options merge into one, although it remains open that reference to divine beings and their happenings is perfectly in order. Alternatively, we can distinguish between stories that falsify and those that do not, and insist that theology remains confined to those of the latter category. This returns us to the second option which now becomes a terminological variant upon the claim that we are permitted to make reference to divine beings and their happenings.

For the Judaeo-Christian theologian this involves making reference to God's communicative action—'the recital of God's mighty acts in history' as G. Ernest Wright has put it.[29] This is the story of God, and it is to be distinguished from the stories of the pagan gods, which latter are on a level with

---

[25] Book VI, ch. 5. Augustine is reporting Marcus Terrentius Varro's division of theology into 'mythical', 'natural', and 'civil'.

[26] Book VI, ch. 5.

[27] Book VI, ch. 6.

[28] 'Myth and Philosophy', p. 317.

[29] *God Who Acts: Biblical Theology as Recital* (London: SCM Press, 1952), p. 11. Durwood Foster cites this claim in his 'Myth and Philosophy', p. 322.

the myths of pre-scientific superstition. Theology in this sense is revealed theology, it can be said to involve superstition in the sense that it carries an irreducibly supernatural dimension, and, in so far as it remains within 'the arena
of God's activity',[30] the happenings it describes involve a history which is shot
through with divine purpose. The atheist will complain that the use of the term
'history' in this context is a misnomer. After all, the story of God didn't really
happen, and it involves a falsification of reality to suppose otherwise. We can
agree that the story of God is inappropriately described as 'historical' if history
is taken to involve reference to a 'secular, naturalistic, cause and effect process
in which events are to explained solely by the interplay of environment and
geography on individual and social organisms'.[31] We may wish also to reject
the scientistic presuppositions of this particular definition so as to make room
for a conception of history which is more obviously appropriate to that of
human subjects.[32] Nevertheless, our expansive naturalist would be quick to
distinguish history in this broader, albeit naturalistic, sense from that which is
operative when we are concerned with 'the arena of God's activity'. He would
no doubt repeat the complaint that God's activity is not properly historical—
understandably so, given his assumption that the supernatural is permanently
sealed from the domain of nature and its happenings.

I have questioned this assumption, even whilst granting that the arena of God's
activity can be neither comprehended without remainder nor properly appreciated by one who lacks faith. Where does this leave the question of its history?
It would be inappropriate to comprehend its elements in the naturalistic/causal
terms with which Ernest Wright takes issue, although it is familiar enough that
these terms have been erroneously applied to the act of creation. Are we to conclude that God did not really create the world—that *this* did not really happen?
In one sense this is precisely what we must conclude, although it should be clear
that this is no concession to atheism. On the contrary, it is a matter of denying
that God is a part within a larger whole, and that the act of creation is just one
more historical event—the first—of a similar series to be dispensed with in the
light of modern science. We know also that the offending conception of God has
been operative in certain interpretations of the Incarnation. At the risk of over-
simplifying an understandably contentious issue, it doesn't seem outrageous to
suggest that the question of whether the Incarnation really happened demands

---

[30] *God Who Acts*, p. 38.

[31] See Wright, *God Who Acts*, p. 38.

[32] Schubert Ogden cites Rudolph Bultmann's (Heideggerian) conception of history as histo-
ricity (Geschichtlickeit). On this way of thinking, 'the "real subject" of history is the individual
person, existing in freedom over against the past which presents him with his limitations and
opportunities, and therefore also in responsibility in face of the future...Our relation to history is not to be viewed so much as a relation of subject to object, as it is as a relationship of
subject to subject...What we have to do with in history is ultimately ourselves' (*'The Debate on
"Demythologizing"'*, *Journal of Bible and Religion*, vol. 27, no. 1 (Jan. 1959), p. 17).

a similar response. That is to say that the answer is no if saying that it happened is taken to mean that it is just one more event within a historical sequence—one which is to be comprehended either in non-God-involving terms or in terms which turn God into a separable, causally efficacious part. Saying this much, however, is not a denial of the Incarnation. Rather, it is a matter of denying that it can be comprehended in the offending terms at issue. The further claim we made was that it is more properly interpreted as the supreme instantiation of God's omnipresence to the world—an omnipresence which is likewise expressed in creation and which, in this particular case, is inextricably tied to the redemptive purpose of God's communicative action. The implication again is that we are dealing with something rather more significant than a mere happening in the dim and distant past which stands to be rejected by those who have had the benefit of a good scientific education.

Durwood Foster argues that revealed theology—the recital of God's mighty acts in history—is to be distinguished from the more properly philosophical theology which involves the attempt to comprehend the content of revelation and submit its claims to rational scrutiny. He claims that these two poles of theology correspond to myth and philosophy respectively, and that we can abandon either one of them only at the cost of reverting to an impoverished and ultimately unsustainable conception of the theological task. The myth pole—'theology A'—prevents theology from dissolving into philosophy; the philosophy pole—'theology B'—prevents it from subsiding into myth.[33]

What would it be to eliminate all myth? If myths are taken to be falsifications of reality, then it is a matter of eliminating from the subject-matter of theology those aspects which involve falsification. The Judaeo-Christian theologian would eliminate the pagan myths on this ground; the atheist would extend the exercise to include any reference to divine action, concluding that the very subject-matter of theology—viz., God—stands to be exorcised. I have rejected this conclusion, and with it the assumption that the theologian is in the business of falsification. The elimination of myth in this latter sense involves the elimination of God, and if this is so, then we have a justification for insisting upon the aforementioned myth pole of theology. Could its content be 'demythologized' in a manner which does not lead to atheism? Perhaps this is Levinas's conception of his own preferred moral approach to God, although it would hardly be right to say that the picture is purged of any reference to God's communicative action. Nor, of course, is there any suggestion that theology be dissolved into philosophy. What of the idea that theology involves a pictorial element which stands to be eliminated? That we should be seeking to 'demythologize' its content in this sense?[34] If this means simply

---

[33] 'Myth and Philosophy', p. 325.

[34] Hegel is an obvious figure to mention in this context, for his position is often taken to be the prototype of a demythologizing approach to God, his aim being to transform Christian religion

that we must reject the conception of God as a man in the sky, then we can applaud such a move. We can agree also that we must resist thinking of God as a being who stands over and above the world in a realm which cannot be intelligibly related to it. However, it is unclear that we must forsake all reference to picture thinking provided that we are clear about its limitations. After all, the ordinary believer/worshipper needs some kind of handle upon God, and even philosophers can be excused for employing imagery in their attempts to give expression to His reality.

The myth pole gives theology its content, and philosophy can offer insight into its meaning and truth. However, there is another sense in which philosophy can be of service to theology, namely, by making it into something more than just the recital of God's acts. Philosophy can be instrumental in confining theology to this corner, when, for example, it insists upon viewing the theologian as the mere collator of philosophically insignificant sacred stories.[35] Furthermore, it is understandable that the theologian might respond to this conception of his activity by repudiating any reference to philosophy. In such a scenario, however, the philosophy which stands to be rejected is most likely to correspond to that which generates the offending conception of theology, and it is not ruled out that the theologian can continue to philosophize under another name.[36] The alternative is for him to remain at the level of recital and repetition, in which case the threat of fundamentalism looms large,[37] and the philosopher's negative judgement of his activity becomes compelling.

---

into his idealist metaphysics. Durwood Foster mentions Hegel in this context, claiming that he 'exemplifies "Pole B" work in relative remoteness from "Pole A"'. I reserve final judgement on the matter except to say that, on my reading of Hegel, he is doing exactly what Durwood Foster recommends, namely, ensuring that these two theological poles are maintained in polar tension.

[35] See 'Myth and Philosophy', p. 326.

[36] Durwood Foster mentions Schleiermacher, Ritchl, and Barth in this context. Of Barth he says: 'The *Kirchliche Dogmatik* has not been sufficiently appreciated as the monumental achievement in philosophical theology that it is. While Barth has rejected any second (apologetic) task alongside dogmatics, this has not meant for him a remission of the ontological exploration and articulation of Biblical faith. His thinking is saturated with kerygmatic content, but it is projected with a speculative vigour and thoroughness rarely if ever matched in Christian reflection' ('Myth and Philosophy', p. 327).

[37] Compare Lash: 'in the school of Christian Pedagogy, however, silence is interrupted by memory of a Word once spoken, a life once lived and death once undergone. Acknowledging that what was done and seen in him is of eternal and imperishable significance and validity, we could come up with a doctrine of the Word incarnate. It might even be a true doctrine, permitting us, once again, to worship. But, if we stopped there, we would be in danger of ascribing absolute significance to the past *as* past, in danger of idolatrously identifying the "nature" of God with given "form" and constituted meaning; in danger of divinising the language and particular institutions which mediate his memory (it is no accident that "fundamentalism" tends to be politically conservative). The pattern needs breaking up again, through acknowledgment that it is creativity and transformation, not in inherited stability, in new possibilities, not ancient meanings, that acquaintance with God is to be found' ('*Considering the Trinity*', *Modern Theology*, vol. 2, no. 3 (April 1986), pp. 192–193).

How does philosophical theology in this sense correspond to the two types of natural theology I have defined? Natural theology in the first sense operates in isolation from revelation. Its content is the natural world, and the world, thus understood, contains no trace of God. Theology in this sense leads to atheism and it is motivated by a philosophy which demands this result. I have argued that the methodological presuppositions of this philosophy can be questioned. Natural theology in the second sense is motivated by a philosophy which is shorn of the offending presuppositions, and it operates likewise in isolation from revelation. The difference, however, is that this philosophy's methodological presuppositions are amenable to a theistic framework. Philosophy, thus understood, is not bound to be concerned with sacred story, or indeed, with the stories of the pagan gods. However, its conception of nature is broad enough to accommodate such things, although they are repudiated by the secular exponent of such an approach. This repudiation can likewise be questioned, although we can agree that there are elements of the picture which require to be transcended. We can say, if you like, that McDowell's demythologizing project has a point, but that it remains compatible with the idea that nature is divinely enchanted. Once we reach this point, of course, we are in the business of raising philosophical questions about the content of nature thus conceived, and it is at this stage that we can aspire to do philosophical theology in the manner described by Durwood Foster.

8.5 EXPANSIVE NATURALISM RECONFIGURED

The position at which we have arrived involves a rejection of the claim that philosophy and theology are distinct disciplines with distinct subject-matters—that they add up to two in this sense. Likewise, we have rejected the idea that theology is to be dispensed with on scientific or philosophical grounds or because its subject-matter—God—resists all attempts to be comprehended. These contested claims rest upon the assumption that God and the world add up to two, leaving it open for the atheist to reject the first term of this distinction, and, with it, the discipline which takes this term as its subject-matter. God and world do not add up to two, but nor are they to be identified, for God is distinct from the world, albeit not as a distinct thing, and in such a way that He remains omnipresent to all things. So the world is irreducibly God-involving, but God is not reducible to the world. The idea that God is not reducible to the world suggests that we need to uphold a distinction between theology and philosophy, and it is no part of my position that the two disciplines are to be conflated. On the contrary, we can philosophize about things in the world without mentioning God, just as we can take as our focus God Himself. The conclusions we draw in this latter context will be confined to God as He is in relation to the world, for even if we endeavour to talk about God outside His relation to the world, such talk involves an implicit and irreducible reference to the one who is seeking to comprehend Him in this manner.[38] The mistake is to suppose that this imposes an irredeemable limitation.

The world returns us to the things we can consider in non-God-involving terms, when, for example, we strive to comprehend them scientifically. This level of comprehension is important, and we might even go so far as to say that there is a scientific explanation for everything. After all, this could simply mean that for any subject-matter we can raise explanatory questions that can be answered scientifically. However, it does not follow from this that, for everything, the *only* explanations are scientific explanations, and I have granted with the expansive naturalist that we must resist this implication so as to allow that there are other sorts of explanations which are consistent with scientific explanations but which make things intelligible in a different, non-scientific way. So philosophy raises doubts about whether the scientist has the monopoly on things, and it also grants us the right to allow that these things have theistic significance. The implication here is that there is an overlap between the respective subject-matters of science, philosophy, and theology.

What of the disciplines themselves? We have seen that the question of what counts as science is a matter of some dispute, and that Railton's 'humanized' social science has the potential to merge with the expansive naturalist's avowedly non-scientific standpoint. So we have an overlap of sorts, although there is no justification for insisting that the explanatory ground is to be covered without remainder in scientific terms, except in so far as science becomes equivalent to any approach which resists the temptations of cosmic excess. Likewise, we have seen that natural theology can merge with philosophy, that philosophy in this context can assume a scientistic guise, but that philosophy exposes this restriction as an ideological prejudice, granting us the right to allow that a move in the direction of God can be intellectually respectable. Subsequent talk of God overlaps with the expansive naturalist's talk of value, but it involves more besides, and I have argued that expansive naturalism can accommodate this additional dimension.

On this way of thinking, nature becomes the all-inclusive category, for God is no longer excluded from its ambit. Can we say also that naturalism has ceased to be a distinct 'ism'? The scientistic version of this claim has it that naturalism is to be comprehended in scientific terms, and that it has ceased to be a distinct 'ism' in the sense that we can explain everything in scientific terms. We have rejected this version on philosophical grounds, and philosophy has led us to a position which upholds a distinction between science, philosophy, and theology. Is this position a form of naturalism? It counts as such on at least some of

---

[38] This point is clearly made by Anselm K. Min in his '*Hegel's Absolute: Transcendent or Immanent*', *The Journal of Religion*, vol. 56, no. 1 (Jan. 1976), p. 85.

the criteria detailed in chapter 1. So, for example, it accommodates 'whatever man encounters in whatever way'—that 'mess of miscellaneous stuff' which, for Randall, comprises the natural.[39] It involves an 'examination of the status of these varieties of "stuff" in nature...and the discovery of their various relations to each other',[40] and rejects anything that is 'contradictory to scientific knowledge'.[41] It also involves an attempt to understand the world 'without appealing to anything that is entirely beyond the reach of empirical knowledge'.[42] Crucially, however, the relevant 'methods of empirical investigation' have been stretched beyond scientific parameters, and, to the extent that the relevant things are shown to be amenable to such methods, we can grant with Dupré that they no longer count as 'properly supernatural'—'supernatural' in this context being a placeholder for that to which we could never relate, and for whose existence there could be no evidence. Are we not committed to postulating special cognitive powers? Certainly we are if this means simply that we have gone beyond those which are operative at the level of scientific understanding. So the relevant powers count as 'special' in this sense, but they are not spookily special—except in so far as 'spooky' is just a needlessly pejorative way of describing whatever takes us beyond these parameters. Furthermore, they precisely *are* reconcilable with 'natural forms of understanding', provided of course that the term 'natural' is suitably and analogously expanded.

Naturalism in this sense accommodates phenomena which elude the grasp of the scientist, and we might even go so far as to say, in true Platonist spirit, that it can accommodate everything. In this respect then, it makes sense to suppose that naturalism is no longer a distinct 'ism'. However, the explanations it exploits do not conform to a single model, and it is therefore misguided to talk about *the* naturalistic method, nor can we say that the relevant methods can adequately explain everything. After all, God is part of the picture, and He cannot be comprehended without remainder. God is part of the picture, but because He is irreducible to anything within the world we must reject Randall's negative definition of naturalism as 'the refusal to take "nature" or "the natural" as a term of distinction'.[43]

Could a naturalist really accept that 'nature' is a term of distinction in this sense? Is it not fundamental to the position that there is *nothing* besides nature? The expansive naturalist rejects the scientific naturalist version of this

[39] 'Epilogue: The Nature of Naturalism', in *Naturalism and the Human Spirit*, ed. Yervant H. Krikorian (New York: Columbia University Press, 1944), p. 358.

[40] 'Epilogue: The Nature of Naturalism', p. 358.

[41] Mario De Caro and Alberto Voltolini, 'Is Liberal Naturalism Possible', in *Naturalism and Normativity*, ed. Mario De Caro and David Macarthur (New York: Columbia University Press, 2010), p. 74.

[42] John Dupré, *'How to be Naturalistic Without Being Simplistic in the Study of Human Nature'*, in *Naturalism and Normativity*, p. 290.

[43] 'Epilogue: The Nature of Naturalism', p. 357.

claim, for he allows that there is something besides nature as comprehended in exclusively scientific terms. We know also that, as far as the scientific naturalist is concerned, he precisely *is* postulating a further, problematic realm of being, and is committed hereby to the conclusion that 'nature' is a term of distinction. The expansive naturalist challenges this interpretation on the ground that the claim being advanced is that nature—all that there is—is to be comprehended in terms which exceed the parameters of the scientific naturalist, and that the supposition to the contrary is generated by an unwarranted commitment to scientism. Now we have rejected an analogous interpretation of the theistic naturalist's claim that 'nature' is a term of distinction. According to this interpretation, nature is to be set in opposition to God, and God is an unintelligible addition which can be rejected whilst leaving everything else in its place. Such a position invites the 'dualisms and gulfs' which remain anathema to the naturalist's standpoint. That is to say, it involves the postulation of a distinction whose terms are distinguished so as to make their relations to each other unintelligible.[44] The theistic naturalist has no truck with such dualisms, and challenges this interpretation of his position on the ground that nature is to be comprehended in terms which are already God-involving. So nature is no longer set in permanent opposition to God—it is open to His communicative action—but it is nonetheless to be distinguished from God because God is its source, and *qua* source, cannot be a part of it.

The idea that nature is God-involving has something in common with the expansive naturalist's claim that it is value-involving. Furthermore, the denial that God is a further, unintelligible, something else means that, at one level, the theistic naturalist is saying something similar to what the expansive naturalist is saying when he denies that value is to be opposed to nature. That is to say that, on both positions, the claim is that our conception of nature is to be suitably expanded, and it is denied that this expansion brings a problematic distinction. On the contrary, and here I borrow a metaphor from James Griffin, we can say that the relevant term of distinction is 'swallowed whole'[45]—the point of the metaphor being to capture the sense in which what goes into the swallowing mouth remains undiminished. Now this has important implications for the matter at hand, for there is a clear enough sense in which we must *deny* that nature is a term of distinction. We must do so in the sense

---

[44] I am exploiting here Robert Brandom's definition of a dualistic distinction: 'A distinction becomes a dualism when its components are distinguished in terms that make their characteristic relations to one another ultimately uninitelligible. (Descartes's dualism is, as always, the paradigm)' (*Making It Explicit* (Cambridge, Mass.: Harvard University Press, 1998), p. 615).

[45] Griffin works from within an expansive naturalist framework and tells us that '(v)alues are not reduced; they are swallowed whole' (*Value Judgement: Improving our Ethical Beliefs* (Oxford: Clarendon Press, 1996), p. 51). He insists also that they 'do not need any world except the ordinary world around us...An other-worldly realm of values just produces unnecessary problems about what it could possibly be and how we could learn about it' (pp. 43–44).

that it already involves the putatively distinct second term. Crucially, however, God is not reducible to nature, any more than value is reducible to nature as scientifically conceived. It follows from this that, in one important respect, we can agree that there is nothing besides nature, and we can agree also that nature thus conceived—i.e. God-involving nature—can be comprehended in naturalistic terms. After all, we have rejected the offending dualisms and gulfs, and have granted nothing which is entirely beyond the reach of empirical knowledge. In another equally important respect, however, we precisely have introduced a term of distinction, for God-involving nature has its source in God—how could it not? To be sure, there are aspects of this source which remain unknowable—in this respect the relation between God and nature is not wholly intelligible. Nor, however, is it wholly unintelligible, for we are open to God, and this gives us some kind of purchase—however faltering—upon the nature of the relation, and, indeed, the distinction, between God and nature.

Where does this leave our initial question of whether philosophers should be naturalists? The answer is no if naturalism is understood in exclusively scientific terms, for there are no good philosophical or scientific reasons for accepting this restriction. Should philosophers be expansive naturalists? If this amounts to asking whether they should accept everything that is said by the typical expansive naturalist, then the answer must likewise be no, for the matters at issue are hardly closed, and this is so even before we come to consider the theistic ingredients which remain anathema to such figures. Our expansive naturalist is committed to applauding this negative response in one obvious sense, for it is fundamental to his approach that we remain alert to the imposition of distortive metaphysical frameworks. I have argued that this spirit of open-mindedness involves a preparedness to question the secular parameters which have defined the programme of expansive naturalism as currently practised. I have claimed also that this attitude must go hand in hand with an equal willingness to engage with the question of God on its own terms rather than those which happen to conduce to one's own preferred way of thinking. The idea that 'everybody would agree' that theism is a non-starter, or, worse, that 'most philosophers for at least one hundred years'[46] have done so is no justification for refusing this possibility.

Our expansive naturalist remains unimpressed by the claims of theology, and he would deny that philosophy becomes impoverished in its absence. Nevertheless, he works with versions of all of the claims which would be exploited by the theologian in the context of defending his own preferred stance. His fundamental aim is to lead us away from an impoverished conception of philosophy—the kind of philosophy which is forced upon us if we commit to scientific naturalism—and he holds that this reductive impulse leads to

---

[46] Barry Stroud, 'The Charm of Naturalism', in *Naturalism in Question*, ed. Mario De Caro and David Macarthur (Cambridge, Mass.: Harvard University Press, 2004), p. 23.

an impoverishment of self and world. As he sees it then, we are required by philosophy to expand its limits, and this will bring a corresponding expansion of the limits of nature. He allows that such a move will be challenged by one who remains locked within the disputed framework, and that it can appear to be an invitation for courting bad philosophy. His response to this complaint is twofold. First, he points out that it stems from a commitment to a contestable framework—one which leads us to suppose that philosophy is respectable only if it is reducible to science, and that self and world must be understood accordingly. Second, he demonstrates that his own preferred standpoint is rationally defensible. It is rationally defensible not simply because it offers a corrective to the impoverished worldview of the scientific naturalist, but because it can subject itself to critical scrutiny, albeit a scrutiny which involves and applies to a range of concepts which exceed these reductive limits. (Again, we have a sense in which the philosopher must work 'from within', albeit with no implication that this imposes any kind of limitation. After all, how else could we proceed?)

Our theologian agrees that there are impoverished conceptions of philosophy, and that such conceptions lead to an impoverishment of self and world. He believes, however, that philosophy is enriched by theology, and that our being is enriched to the extent that we are inwardly transformed by God. The expansive naturalist rejects the idea that philosophy is enriched by theology, doing so on the ground that philosophy has the resources to enrich itself. It does so by exposing the errors of scientific naturalism and broadening its scope accordingly. Likewise, he would deny that God's action is required to remedy any deficiencies in our being. All that is required is that we move beyond the parameters dictated by science so as to allow that we are capable of participating in evaluative life and thought. As McDowell puts it, 'our eyes are opened to the very existence of this tract of the space of reasons'.[47] This openness is no 'occult power, something extra to our being the kind of animals we are, which is our situation in nature'.[48] On the contrary, it is something of which we are capable by virtue of being the natural beings we are, and the dimension of reality to which we become receptive is 'essentially within reach of human beings'.[49]

It should be clear from all that has been said that, for McDowell, the theologian's conception of the supernatural precisely does involve some 'occult power' which is isolated from man's natural being, and out of reach of human beings. The offending conception abounds, but we have seen that it is not mandatory, and that it is fundamental to good theology that the supernatural is a dimension of nature which serves to enrich our natural being and that of the nature we inhabit. Indeed, it is tempting to turn the tables at this point and throw at the expansive naturalist a version of the argument *he* uses to

---

[47] *Mind and World* (Cambridge, Mass.: Harvard University Press, 1994), p. 82.
[48] *Mind and World*, p. 82. [49] *Mind and World*, p. 84.

undermine the position of the scientific naturalist. That is to say, we can point out that the expansive naturalist is operating with a framework which leads to the conclusion that philosophy is respectable only if it remains untainted by theology—a framework which implies that theology can only ever amount to idle superstition, and that its subject-matter has no bearing upon the lives of natural beings. However, this framework is not mandatory, and its imposition risks leaving us with an impoverished conception of philosophy, self, and world. These deficiencies can be overcome if we allow that theology can enrich philosophy, and that God's action can enrich nature. This can look like an invitation to bad philosophy, and there are versions of this move which warrant such a complaint. However, the theologian under present consideration is critically astute, and believes that there are good reasons for taking seriously his position. Yes, he is introducing a range of concepts which will strike the expansive naturalist as problematic, just as the expansive naturalist introduces a range of concepts which are problematic to the scientific naturalist. However, he believes that they admit of rational defence, albeit a defence which will be difficult to appreciate by one who is closed to this way of thinking and being.

It will be *difficult* to appreciate, and perhaps impossible for the kind of philosopher who remains locked within the parameters of scientific naturalism. However, the expansive naturalist has escaped these parameters, and, to the extent that he shares at least some of the aspirations of the theologian, he may come to see that the theologian's reasoning makes some kind of sense, and that there is significant common ground to their respective endeavours. At this point, and in the spirit of his expansive naturalist approach, he may be persuaded to enter into dialogue with the theologian. If my conclusions are justified then he can forsake such a task only at the risk of compromising his insights and robbing theology of a fundamental philosophical resource. After all, he offers the prospects for demonstrating that belief in God is intellectually respectable, and that this conclusion can be appreciated by those who have taken on board the lessons of the best naturalistic philosophy of our time. It is at this point, I would contend, that we truly combine the wisdom of Plato and the sanity of Aristotle.

Bibliography

Anselm of Canterbury, *Cur Deus Homo*, translated by Sidney Norton Deane (Texas: RDMc Publishing, 2005).

Atterton, Peter, 'Face-to-Face with the Other Animal?' In *Levinas and Buber: Dialogue and Difference*, edited by Peter Atterton, Matthew Calarco, and Maurice Friedman (Pittsburgh, Pennsylvania: Duquesne University Press, 2004).

Augustine of Hippo, *City of God*, translated by Henry Bettenson (London: Penguin Classics, 2003).

Augustine of Hippo, *The Trinity*, translated by E. Hill (New York: New York City Press, 1990).

Benedict XVI, *Deus Caritas Est* <http://www.vatican.va/holy_father/benedict_xvi/ encyclicals/documents/hf_ben-xvi_enc_20051225_deus-caritas-est_en.html>

Bernstein, Richard, '*Whatever Happened to Naturalism?*' *Proceedings and Addresses of the American Philosophical Association*, vol. 69, no. 2 (November 1995), pp. 57–76.

Bilgrami, Akeel, 'The Wider Significance of Naturalism: A Genealogical Essay'. In *Naturalism and Normativity*, edited by Mario De Caro and David Macarthur (New York: Columbia University Press, 2010).

Brandom, Robert, *Making It Explicit* (Cambridge, Mass.: Harvard University Press, 1998).

Brennan, J.G., 'On Nagel's Reconsideration of Naturalism'. *Journal of Philosophy*, vol. 53, no. 14 (1956), pp. 443–448.

Buckley, Michael J., *At the Origins of Modern Atheism* (Yale: Yale University Press, 1987).

Coakley, Sarah, 'Kenōsis and Subversion'. In *Powers and Submissions: Spirituality, Philosophy and Gender* (Oxford: Blackwell, 2002).

Coakley, Sarah, '"Persons" in the "Social" Doctrine of the Trinity'. In *Powers and Submissions: Spirituality, Philosophy and Gender* (Oxford: Blackwell, 2002).

Copan, Paul, 'The Moral Argument'. In *The Rationality of Theism*, edited by Paul Copan and Paul K. Moser (London: Routledge, 2003).

Corrington, Robert S., 'An Introduction to Ecstatic Naturalism: Interview with Robert S. Corrington', *Kinesis*, vol. 36, no. 1 (2009), pp. 1–29.

Corrington, Robert S., *Nature and Spirit: An Essay in Ecstatic Naturalism* (New York: Fordham University Press, 1992).

Costello, Harry Todd, 'The Naturalism of Frederick Woodbridge'. In *Naturalism and the Human Spirit*, edited by Yervant H. Krikorian (New York: Columbia University Press, 1944).

Cottingham, John, 'Sceptical Detachment or Loving Submission to the Good? Reason, Faith, and the Passions in Descartes'. *Faith and Philosophy*, vol. 28, no. 1, (January 2011), pp. 44–53.

Cottingham, John, *Why Believe?* (London: Continuum, 2009).

Craig, William Lane, *Reasonable Faith* (Wheaton, IL: Crossway Books, 1994).

Craig, William Lane and Walter Sinnott-Armstrong, *God? A Debate Between a Christian and an Atheist* (Oxford: Oxford University Press, 2004).

Davies, Brian, 'The Doctrine of Divine Simplicity'. In *Language, Meaning and God: Essays in Honour of Herbert McCabe OP*, edited by Brian Davies (Eugene, Oregon: Wipf and Stock, 2010).

Davies, Brian, 'Miracles'. *New Blackfriars*, vol. 73, issue 857 (2007), pp. 102–120.

Dawkins, Richard, *The God Delusion* (London: Bantam Press, 2006).

De Caro, Mario and Macarthur, David, 'Introduction: The Nature of Naturalism'. In *Naturalism in Question*, edited by Mario De Caro and David Macarthur (Cambridge, Mass.: Harvard University Press, 2004).

De Caro, Mario and Voltolini, Alberto, 'Is Liberal Naturalism Possible'. In *Naturalism and Normativity*, edited by Mario De Caro and David Macarthur (New York: Columbia University Press, 2010).

De Lubac, Henri, *Catholicism: Christ and the Common Destiny of Man* (London: Burns and Oates, 1950).

Dewey, John, 'Antinaturalism in Extremis', in *Naturalism and the Human Spirit*, edited by Yervant H. Krikorian (New York: Columbia University Press, 1944).

Dunn, James, *Jesus and the Spirit* (London: SCM, 1975).

Dupré, John, 'How to be Naturalistic Without Being Simplistic in the Study of Human Nature'. In *Naturalism and Normativity*, edited by Mario De Caro and David Macarthur (New York: Columbia University Press, 2010).

Dupré, John, 'The Miracle of Monism'. In *Naturalism in Question*, edited by Mario de Caro and David Macarthur (Cambridge, Mass.: Harvard University Press, 2004).

Durwood Foster, A., 'Myth and Philosophy: Theology's Bipolar Essence'. *Journal of Bible and Religion*, vol. 34, no. 4 (October 1966), pp. 316–328.

Ebeling, Gerhard, 'Theologie: Begriffsgeschichtlich'. In *Religion in Geschichte und Gegenwart*, 3te Auflage, 6te Band (Tübingen: J.C.B. Mohr, 1930).

Feuerbach, Ludwig, *The Essence of Christianity*, translated by George Eliot (New York: Dover Publications, 2008).

Foot, Philippa, 'Morality as a System of Hypothetical Imperatives'. *The Philosophical Review*, vol. 81, no. 3 (July 1972), pp. 305–316.

Gallagher, Michael Paul, 'Show Atheists the Trinity'. *The Tablet* (January 1998), p. 104.

Gilson, Étienne, *Elements of Christian Philosophy* (New York: Doubleday, 1960).

Gregory, Brad S., 'No Room for God? History, Science, Metaphysics, and the Study of Religion'. *History and Theory*, vol. 47 (December 2008), pp. 495–519.

Gregory, Brad S., *The Unintended Reformation: How a Religious Revolution Secularized Society* (Cambridge, Mass.: Harvard University Press, 2012).

Griffin, James, *Value Judgement: Improving our Ethical Beliefs* (Oxford: Clarendon Press, 1996).

Hadot, Pierre, *The Veil of Isis: An Essay on the History of the Idea of Nature*, translated by Michael Chase (Cambridge, Mass.: The Belknap Press of Harvard University Press, 2006).

Hampton, Jean, 'Hobbes and Ethical Naturalism'. *Philosophical Perspectives*, vol. 6, Ethics (1992), pp. 333–353.

Hampton, Jean, 'Rethinking Reason'. *American Philosophical Quarterly*, vol. 29, no. 3 (July 1992), pp. 219–236.

Hegel, G.W.F., *Lectures on the Philosophy of Religion, I: Introduction and Conception of Religion*, edited by Peter C. Hodgson (Berkeley: University of California Press, 1984).

Heidegger, Martin, 'The Age of the World Picture', in *The Question Concerning Technology and Other Essays*, translated by William Lovitt (New York: Harper and Row, 1977).

Heidegger, Martin, *Identity and Difference*, translated by Joan Stambaugh (Chicago: HarperCollins Inc., 1969).

Heidegger, Martin, 'Letter on Humanism', translated by F.A. Capuzzi. In *Basic Writings*, edited by D.F. Krell (London: Routledge Press, 1978).

Heidegger, Martin, 'The Question Concerning Technology', in *The Question Concerning Technology and Other Essays*, translated by William Lovitt (New York: Harper and Row, 1977).

Hobbes, Thomas, *Leviathan* (London: Dent, 1914).

Hume, David, *A Treatise of Human Nature* (Oxford: Oxford University Press, 1978).

Hutchison, John, '*The Uses of Natural Theology: An Essay in Redefinition*'. *The Journal of Philosophy*, vol. 55, no. 22 (23 October 1958), pp. 936–944.

Jeanrond, Werner G., *A Theology of Love* (London: T&T Clark, 2010).

Jenkins, David, 'Concerning Theism'. In *The Honest to God Debate*, edited by John A.T. Robinson and David L. Edwards (London: SCM Press, 1963).

Jollimore, Troy, *Love's Vision* (Princeton: Princeton University Press, 2011).

Kant, Immanuel, *Conflict of the Faculties*. In *Religion and Rational Theology*, translated by Allen W. Wood and George di Giovanni, The Cambridge Edition of the Works of Immanuel Kant (Cambridge: Cambridge University Press, 1996).

Kant, Immanuel, *Foundations of the Metaphysic of Morals*, translated by L.J. Beck (Indianapolis: Liberal Arts Press/Bobs Merrill, 1959).

Kant, Immanuel, *Metaphysics of Morals*, translated by Mary Gregor (Cambridge: Cambridge University Press, 1996).

Kasper, Walter, *The God of Jesus Christ* (London: Continuum, 2012).

Kerr, Fergus, *After Aquinas: Versions of Thomism* (Oxford: Blackwell, 2002).

Kerr, Fergus, *Immortal Longings: Versions of Transcending Humanity* (London: SPCK, 1997).

Korsgaard, Christine M., *Creating the Kingdom of Ends* (Cambridge: Cambridge University Press, 1996).

Korsgaard, Christine M., *The Sources of Normativity* (Cambridge: Cambridge University Press, 1996).

Lash, Nicholas, 'Considering the Trinity'. *Modern Theology*, vol. 2, no. 3 (April 1986), pp. 183–196.

Lash, Nicholas, 'The Impossibility of Atheism'. In *Theology for Pilgrims* (London: Darton, Longman and Todd, 2008).

Lash, Nicholas, 'Thinking, Attending, Praying'. In *Philosophers and God: At the Frontiers of Faith and Reason*, edited by John Cornwell and Michael McGhee (London: Continuum, 2009).

Lauer, Quentin, *Hegel's Concept of God*, (Albany: State University of New York Press, 1982).

Levinas, Emmanuel, 'Education and Prayer'. In *Difficult Freedom: Essays on Judaism*, translated by Seán Hand (Baltimore: Johns Hopkins University Press, 1990).

Levinas, Emmanuel, *Ethics and Infinity: Conversations with Philippe Nemo*, translated by R.A. Cohen (Pittsburgh: Duquesne University Press, 1985).

Levinas, Emmanuel, 'God and Philosophy'. In *Of God Who Comes to Mind*, translated by Bettina Bergo (Stanford: Stanford University Press, 1998).

Levinas, Emmanuel, 'The I and the Totality'. In *Entre Nous*, translated by Michael B. Smith and Barbara Harshav (London: Continuum Press, 2006).

Levinas, Emmanuel, 'Loving the Torah More Than God'. In *Difficult Freedom: Essays on Judaism*, translated by Seán Hand (Baltimore: Johns Hopkins University Press, 1990).

Levinas, Emmanuel, 'A Man-God?' In *Entre Nous*, translated by Michael B. Smith and Barbara Harshav (London: Continuum Press, 2006).

Levinas, Emmanuel, 'Meaning and Sense'. In *Basic Philosophical Writings*, edited by Adriaan T. Peperzak, Simon Critchley, and Robert Bernasconi (Bloomington: Indiana University Press, 1996).

Levinas, Emmanuel, *Of God Who Comes to Mind*, translated by Bettina Bergo (Stanford: Stanford University Press, 1998).

Levinas, Emmanuel, *Otherwise Than Being or Beyond Essence*, translated by Alphonso Lingis (Dordecht: Kluwer, 1991).

Levinas, Emmanuel, 'Philosophy and the Idea of the Infinite'. In *To the Other: An Introduction to the Philosophy of Emmanuel Levinas* (West Lafayette: Purdue University Press, 1993).

Levinas, Emmanuel, 'A Religion for Adults'. In *Difficult Freedom: Essays on Judaism*, translated by Seán Hand (Baltimore: Johns Hopkins University Press, 1990).

Levinas, Emmanuel, *Time and the Other*, translated by Richard A. Cohen (Pittsburgh, Pennsylvania: Duquesne University Press, 1987).

Levinas, Emmanuel, *Totality and Infinity*, translated by Alphonso Lingis (Pittsburgh: Duquesne University Press, 1969).

Lewis, Charles T., and Charles Short, *A Latin Dictionary* (Oxford: Clarendon Press, 1890).

Lewis, C.S., 'Some Reviews'. In *The Honest to God Debate*, edited by John A.T. Robinson and David L. Edwards (London: SCM Press, 1963).

MacArthur, David, 'Naturalizing the Human or Humanizing Nature: Science, Nature and the Supernatural'. *Erkenntnis*, vol. 61, no. 1 (July 2004), pp. 29–51.

McCabe, Herbert, 'Creation', in *God Matters* (London: Continuum Press, 1987).

McCabe, Herbert, 'The God of Truth'. In *God Still Matters* (London: Continuum, 2002).

McDade, John, 'Creation and Salvation' (unpublished).

McDade, John, 'Creation and Salvation: Green Faith and Christian Themes'. *The Month* (November 1990).

McDade, John, 'Some Thoughts on "Miracles"' (unpublished).

McDowell, John, 'Aesthetic Value, Objectivity, and the Fabric of the World'. In *Mind, Value, and Reality* (Cambridge, Mass.: Harvard University Press, 1998).

McDowell, John, 'Are Moral Requirements Hypothetical Imperatives?' In *Mind, Value, and Reality* (Cambridge, Mass.: Harvard University Press, 1998).

McDowell, John, 'Might There Be External Reasons?' In *Mind, Value, and Reality* (Cambridge, Mass.: Harvard University Press, 1998).

McDowell, John, *Mind and World* (Cambridge, Mass.: Harvard University Press, 1994).

McDowell, John, 'Naturalism in the Philosophy of Mind'. In *Naturalism in Question*, edited by Mario de Caro and David Macarthur (Cambridge, Mass.: Harvard University Press, 2004).

McDowell, John, 'Projection and Truth in Ethics'. In *Mind, Value, and Reality* (Cambridge, Mass.: Harvard University Press, 1998).

McDowell, John, 'Reply to Charles Larmore'. In *Reading McDowell on Mind and World*, edited by Nicholas H. Smith (London: Routledge, 2002).

McDowell, John, 'Reply to Fink'. In *John McDowell: Experience, Norm, and Nature*, edited by Jakob Lindgaard (Oxford: Blackwell, 2008).

McDowell, John, 'Reply to J.M. Bernstein'. In *Reading McDowell on Mind and World*, edited by Nicholas H. Smith (London: Routledge, 2002).

McDowell, John, 'Response to Axel Honneth'. In *Reading McDowell on Mind and World*, edited by Nicholas H. Smith (London: Routledge, 2002).

McDowell, John, 'Response to Charles Lamore'. In *Reading McDowell on Mind and World*, edited by Nicholas H. Smith (London: Routledge, 2002).

McDowell, John, 'Response to Christoph Halbig'. In *John McDowell: Experience, Norm, and Nature*, edited by Jakob Lindgaard (Oxford: Blackwell, 2008).

McDowell, John, 'Response to Robert B. Pippin'. In *Reading McDowell on Mind and World*, edited by Nicholas H. Smith (London: Routledge, 2002).

McDowell, John, 'Two Sorts of Naturalism'. In *Mind, Value, and Reality* (Cambridge, Mass.: Harvard University Press, 1998).

McDowell, John, 'Values and Secondary Qualities'. In *Mind, Value, and Reality* (Cambridge, Mass.: Harvard University Press, 1998).

MacIntyre, Alasdair, *After Virtue* (London: Duckworth, 1981).

MacIntyre, Alasdair, 'God and the Theologians'. In *The Honest to God Debate*, edited by John A.T. Robinson and David L. Edwards (London: SCM Press, 1963).

Mackey, James P., *The Christian Experience of God as Trinity* (London: SCM Press, 1983).

Mackie, J.L., *Ethics: Inventing Right and Wrong* (Harmondsworth: Penguin, 1977).

Marion, Jean-Luc, 'Thomas Aquinas and Onto-theo-logy'. In *Mystics: Presence and Aporia*, edited by Michael Kessler and Christian Sheppard (Chicago: University of Chicago Press, 2003).

Mascall, E.L., 'Some Reviews'. In *The Honest to God Debate*, edited by John A.T. Robinson and David L. Edwards (London: SCM Press, 1963).

Mascall, E.L., *The Openness of Being: Natural Theology Today* (London: Darton, Longman, and Todd, 1971).

Mascall, E.L., *Via Media: An Essay in Theological Synthesis* (London: Longmans, Green and Co., 1956).

Meynell, Hugo, *The New Theology and Modern Theologians* (London: Sheed and Ward, 1967).

Miller, Kenneth, *Finding Darwin's God: A Scientist's Search for Common Ground between God and Evolution* (New York: HarperCollins, 1999).

Min, Anselm K., 'Hegel's Absolute: Transcendent or Immanent?' *The Journal of Religion*, vol. 56, no. 1 (January 1976), pp. 61–87.

Min, Anselm K., 'The Trinity and the Incarnation: Hegel and Classical Approaches', *The Journal of Religion*, vol. 66, no. 2 (April 1986), pp. 173–193.

Morgan, Michael, *Discovering Levinas* (Cambridge: Cambridge University Press, 2007).

Moser, Paul, *The Elusive God* (Cambridge: Cambridge University Press, 2008).

Nagel, Ernest, 'Naturalism Reconsidered'. *Proceedings and Addresses of the American Philosophical Association*, vol. 28 (October 1955), pp. 5–17.

Nichols, Terence, *The Sacred Cosmos: Christian Faith and the Challenge of Naturalism* (Oregon: Brazos Press, 2003).

Nietzsche, Friedrich, *The Antichrist*. In *The Portable Nietzsche*, translated by Walter Kaufmann (New York: Viking Penguin Inc, 1959).

Norton, David Fate, 'Hume and the Foundations of Morality'. In *The Cambridge Companion to Hume*, edited by David Fate Norton (Cambridge: Cambridge University Press, 1993).

O'Collins, Gerald, 'The Holy Trinity: The State of the Questions'. In *The Trinity*, edited by Stephen T. Davies, Daniel Kendall, and Gerald O'Collins (Oxford: Oxford University Press, 1999).

Ogden, Schubert, *'The Debate on "Demythologizing"'*. *Journal of Bible and Religion*, vol. 27, no. 1 (January 1959), pp. 17–27.

Ogden, Schubert, 'Myth and Truth'. In *The Reality of God and Other Essays* (Dallas: Southern Methodist University Press, 1963).

Paulys Real-Encyclopädie der Classischen Altertumswissenschaft, 2te Reihe, 5te Band, (Stuttgart: Metzler, 1934).

Peirce, C.S., *Collected Papers* (Cambridge, Mass.: Harvard University Press, 1932).

Peperzak, Adriaan, 'Beyond Being'. In *To the Other: An Introduction to the Philosophy of Emmanuel Levinas* (West Lafayette: Purdue University Press, 1993).

Peperzak, Adriaan, 'A Commentary on "Philosophy and the Idea of the Infinite"'. In *To the Other: An Introduction to the Philosophy of Emmanuel Levinas* (West Lafayette: Purdue University Press, 1993).

Peperzak, Adriaan, 'A Key to Totality and Infinity'. In *To the Other: An Introduction to the Philosophy of Emmanuel Levinas* (West Lafayette: Purdue University Press, 1993).

Plantinga, Alvin, *Where the Conflict Really Lies: Science, Religion, and Naturalism* (Oxford: Oxford University Press, 2011).

Purcell, Michael, *Levinas and Theology* (Cambridge: Cambridge University Press, 2006).

Putnam, Hilary, *The Collapse of the Fact/Value Dichotomy* (Cambridge, Mass.: Harvard University Press, 2002).

Putnam, Hilary, *Jewish Philosophy as a Guide to Life: Rosenzweig, Buber, Levinas, Wittgenstein* (Bloomington: Indiana University Press, 2008).

Putnam, Hilary, 'Levinas and Judaism', *The Cambridge Companion to Levinas*, edited by Simon Critchley and Robert Bernasconi (Cambridge: Cambridge University Press, 2002).

Rahner, Karl, *Foundations of Christian Faith: An Introduction to the Idea of Christianity*, translated by William V. Dych, (London: Darton, Longman and Todd, 1978).

Railton, Peter, 'Alienation, Consequentialism, and the Demands of Morality'. *Philosophy and Public Affairs*, vol. 13, no. 2 (Spring 1984).134-171

Railton, Peter, 'Moral Realism'. *The Philosophical Review*, vol. 95, no. 2 (April 1986), pp. 163–207.

Railton, Peter, 'Naturalism and Prescriptivity'. *Social Philosophy and Policy*, vol. 7, no. 1 (1989), pp. 151–174.

Railton, Peter, 'Précis of Facts, Values, and Norms'. *Philosophical Studies*, vol. 126 (2005), pp. 429–432.

Railton, Peter, 'Reply to David Wiggins'. In *Reality, Representation, and Projection*, edited by John Haldane and Crispin Wright (Oxford: Oxford University Press, 1993).

Railton, Peter, 'What the Non-Cognitivist Helps Us to See the Naturalist Must Help Us to Explain'. In *Reality, Representation, and Projection*, edited by John Haldane and Crispin Wright (Oxford: Oxford University Press, 1993).

Randall Jr, John Herman, 'Epilogue: The Nature of Naturalism'. In *Naturalism and the Human Spirit*, edited by Yervant H. Krikorian (New York: Columbia University Press, 1944).

Rein'l, Robert, *'Naturalism and Supernaturalism in East and West'. Philosophy East and West*, vol. 6, no. 1 (April 1956), pp. 49–67.

Robbins, Jill, 'Tracing Responsibility in Levinas's Ethical Thought'. In *Ethics as First Philosophy: The Significance of Emmanuel Levinas for Philosophy, Literature and Religion*, edited by Adriaan Peperzak (London: Routledge, 1995).

Robinson, John, *Exploration into God* (London: SCM Press, 1967).

Robinson, John, *Honest to God* (London: SCM Press, 1963).

Sartre, Jean-Paul, *Being and Nothingness: An Essay on Phenomenological Ontology*, translated by Hazel Barnes (London: Routledge, 1958).

Scheler, Max, *Ressentiment*, translated by Lewis B. Coser and William W. Holdheim (Wisconsin: Marquette University Press, 2003).

Sellars, Wilfrid, *Science, Perception and Reality* (London: Routledge, 1963).

Smith, John E., *'The Present Status of Natural Theology'. The Journal of Philosophy*, vol. 55, no. 22 (October 1958), pp. 925–936.

Smith, Michael, 'Moral Realism'. In *The Blackwell Guide to Ethical Theory*, edited by Hugh LaFollette (Malden, MA: Blackwell Publishers, 2000).

Sokolowski, Robert, *The God of Faith and Reason: Foundations of Christian Theology* (Washington, DC: The Catholic University of America Press, 1982).

Soskice, Janet, 'Philosophical Theology'. In *God's Advocates: Christian Thinkers in Conversation*, Rupert Shortt (London: Darton, Longman, and Todd, 2005).

Spiegelberg, Herbert, *'Supernaturalism or Naturalism: A Study in Meaning and Verifiability'. Philosophy of Science*, vol. 18, no. 4 (October 1951), pp. 339–368.

Stroud, Barry, 'The Charm of Naturalism'. In *Naturalism in Question*, edited by Mario De Caro and David Macarthur (Cambridge, Mass.: Harvard University Press, 2004).

Tanner, Kathryn, *God and Creation in Christian Theology* (Oxford: Blackwell Press, 1988).

Taylor, Charles, 'Responsibility for Self'. In *The Identities of Persons*, edited by Amélie Oksenberg Rorty (Berkeley and Los Angeles, California: University of California Press, 1976).

Tennant, F.R., *Philosophical Theology*, vol. II (Cambridge: Cambridge University Press, 1930).

Tillich, Paul, 'Mythus'. In *Religion in Geschichte und Gegenwart*, 2te Auflage, 4te Band (Tübingen: J.C.B. Mohr, 1930).

Tillich, Paul, *Systematic Theology: Existence and the Christ*, vol. II (Chicago: University of Chicago Press, 1975).

Tillich, Paul, *'The Two Types of the Philosophy of Religion'. Union Seminary Quarterly Review*, vol. 1, no. 4 (May 1946), pp. 3–17.

Tugwell, Simon, 'Prayer, Humpty Dumpty and Thomas Aquinas'. In *Language, Meaning and God: Essays in Honour of Herbert McCabe OP*, edited by Brian Davies OP (Eugene, Oregon: WIPF & Stock, 2010).

Van Beeck, Frans Jozef, 'God's Love and God's Law: The Incompleteness of Salvation'. In *Loving the Torah More Than God?* (Chicago: Loyola University Press, 1989).

Van Beeck, Frans Jozef, 'Trinitarian Theology as Participation'. In *The Trinity*, edited by Stephen T. Davies, Daniel Kendall, and Gerald O'Collins (Oxford: Oxford University Press, 1999).

Weber, Max, 'Science as a Vocation'. In *The Vocation Lectures*, edited by David Owen and Tracy B. Strong, translated by Rodney Livingstone (Indianapolis: Hackett, 2004).

Westphal, Merold, 'Aquinas and Onto-theology'. *American Catholic Philosophical Quarterly*, vol. 80, no. 2 (2006), pp. 73–91.

Westphal, Merold, 'Divine Excess: The God Who Comes After'. In *Overcoming Onto-theology: Toward a Postmodern Christian Faith* (New York: Fordham University Press, 2001).

Westphal, Merold, 'Overcoming Onto-theology'. In *Overcoming Onto-theology: Toward a Post-Modern Christian Faith* (New York: Fordham University Press, 2001).

Wielenberg, Erik J., 'In Defense of Non-Natural, Non-Theistic Moral Realism'. *Faith and Philosophy*, vol. 26, no. 1 (January 2009), pp. 23–41.

Wiggins, David, 'Categorical Requirements: Kant and Hume on the Idea of Duty'. In *Virtues and Reasons: Philippa Foot and Moral Theory*, edited by Rosalind Hursthouse, Gavin Lawrence, and Warren Quinn (Oxford: Clarendon Press 1995).

Wiggins, David, 'Cognitivism, Naturalism, and Normativity: A Reply to Peter Railton'. In *Reality, Representation, and Projection*, edited by John Haldane and Crispin Wright (Oxford: Oxford University Press, 1993).

Wiggins, David, *Ethics: Twelve Lectures on the Philosophy of Morality* (London: Penguin, 2006).

Wiggins, David, 'Moral Cognitivism, Moral Relativism, and Motivating Moral Beliefs'. *Proceedings of the Aristotelian Society*, New Series, vol. 91 (1990–91), pp. 61–85.

Wiggins, David, *Needs, Values, Truth: Essays in the Philosophy of Value* (Oxford: Oxford University Press, 1991).

Wiggins, David, 'A Neglected Position?' In *Reality, Representation, and Projection*, edited by John Haldane and Crispin Wright (Oxford: Oxford University Press, 1993).

Wiggins, David, 'Reply to Roger Crisp'. In *Identity, Truth, and Value: Essays for David Wiggins*, edited by Sabina Lovibond and S.G. Williams (Oxford: Blackwell Publishers Ltd, 1996).

Wiggins, David, 'Truth, Invention, and the Meaning of Life'. In *Needs, Values, Truth: Essays in the Philosophy of Value* (Oxford: Oxford University Press, 1991).

Williams, A.N., *The Ground of Union: Deification in Aquinas and Palamas* (Oxford: Oxford University Press, 1999).

Williams, Bernard, *Ethics and the Limits of Philosophy* (Cambridge, Mass.: Harvard University Press, 1985).

Williams, Bernard, 'Internal and External Reasons'. In *Moral Luck* (Cambridge: Cambridge University Press, 1981).

Williams, Bernard, *Morality: An Introduction to Ethics* (Cambridge: Cambridge University Press, 1972).

Williams, Bernard, and J.J.C. Smart, *Utilitarianism: For and Against* (Cambridge: Cambridge University Press, 1973).

Williams, Rowan, 'Belief and Theology: Some Basic Questions'. In *God's Advocates: Christian Thinkers in Conversation*, edited by Rupert Shortt (London: Darton, Longman and Todd Ltd, 2005).

Williams, Rowan, 'The Deflections of Desire: Negative Theology in Trinitarian Discourse'. In *Silence and the Word: Negative Theology and Incarnation*, edited by Oliver Davies and Denys Turner (Cambridge: Cambridge University Press, 2002).

Wren-Lewis, John, 'Modern Philosophy and the Doctrine of the Trinity'. *The Philosophical Quarterly*, vol. 5, no. 20 (July 1955), pp. 214–224.

Wright, G. Ernest, *God Who Acts: Biblical Theology as Recital* (London: SCM Press, 1952).

Index